CHRIST IN RUSSIA

Is not all of Russia in her Church? Outside her walls what would remain? — V. ROZANOV

HELENE ISWOLSKY

Christ in Russia

The History, Tradition, and Life of the Russian Church

THE BRUCE PUBLISHING COMPANY
MILWAUKEE

NIHIL OBSTAT:

John A. Schulien, S.T.D.
Censor librorum

IMPRIMATUR:

✠ William E. Cousins
Archbishop of Milwaukee
April 8, 1960

IN LOVING MEMORY OF
SISTER THOMAS AQUINAS, O.P.,
WHO LOVED THE RUSSIAN PEOPLE

Library of Congress Catalog Card Number: 60–12648

© 1960 THE BRUCE PUBLISHING COMPANY
MADE IN THE UNITED STATES OF AMERICA

Introduction

THE perspectives opened by the convocation of the Ecumenical Council raise many problems referring to the Russian Church and have stimulated a new interest in this field. But even before His Holiness Pope John XXIII made known his great decision, a number of distinguished scholars, historians, and theologians, Catholic and Russian-Orthodox, had considerably widened the scope and tenor of ecumenical studies.

We do not pretend, nor would we dare, to compete with these men of profound learning and great ecumenical experience. Our work has a different task to fulfill: to offer a panorama, a "birds-eye" view of the Russian Church as she appears in history, tradition, and life. By this we mean the life of a nation, as well as the everyday life of the people. For we feel that Church and people are so closely linked together, that it is impossible to speak of the one without the other. This is why we have chosen as our book's epigraph, the words of the great Russian essayist, Vassily Rozanov: "Is not all of Russia in her Church? Outside her walls what would remain?" Since Rozanov died in the early days of the communist rule, he saw Russian spiritual culture reeling under the impact of the godless. Had he lived, however, he would have seen that after forty years and more of anti-religious persecution, the walls of the Russian Church have not crumbled, that the Russian people are still seeking refuge within these walls, outside of which little remains that can be considered spiritually and culturally creative.

To explain how all this happened and why Christ protected the Russian people is the aim of our work. It will bring out certain historic landmarks and characteristic traits, some of which need definition and clarification for the Western reader. Neither the textbooks nor the many volumes of scholarly research, nor even the journies to Moscow undertaken in our days by so many eager voyagers, can offer the key to the hidden chambers of the Russian soul. This is a small key, but it may fit the lock. It is the key of love and of simplicity, the way of true *familiarity*, which does not "breed contempt," but opens, on the contrary, a short cut to understanding and from understanding to respect. This is the key we want to offer to our readers, putting aside the heavy controversial material, the conflicting political theories and statements, the intricate commentaries which too often lead to a dead end.

This does not mean, of course, that we have neglected the solid foundations which our theologians and ecclesiologists have built for us and which we studied first of all. In each chapter we give the indispensable analysis, as well as reference to the great works which have inspired it. But we have set aside the useless trimmings, to avoid things too often said in haste, then repeated by others, and finally growing into a misunderstanding which blocks the way to that Unity to which the Holy Father calls us.

Being Russian-born, and coming from a Russian-Orthodox family which combined a deeply religious attitude toward life with national and European culture, we may, as we have said, speak familiarly of these things. They have been for us objects not only of academic study but of a personal experience, a source of gladness or pain — sometimes of both. We are still deeply attached to them. Having become a member of the Universal Church, we have been freed from the tenets of a narrow and wistful national pride. We have realized through many years of prayer and study, under great Catholic teachers, that Russia *does not necessarily* need to be an "outsider." All that is good and creative, all that is truly still alive today in the Russian Church, may share, and actually does share providentially, the common Christian heritage.

Our story is not an *apologia*. We have simply tried to point out certain essential and positive values in the life of the Russian Church; values which are not sufficiently known nor clearly understood, obscured as they sometimes are by lack of charity and generosity. This does not concern history or ecclesiology alone. The simplest manifestations, the candid expression of a people's faith, often have deep roots, and acquire a profound meaning, if one is willing to probe to their sources. Age-old struggles; defeats and victories; sorrows and joys deeply hidden in the Russian heart — all these make the story of the Russian Church and her people.

In order to bring these things closer to our reader's attention, we have studied all the works of Catholic authors versed in these questions; we have also consulted our Russian-Orthodox friends, many of them experts in this field; we have had access to works in Russian, as yet untranslated, attended lectures and seminars in Russian, at which the most recent theological and historical research is analyzed, often by Russian-Orthodox and Catholics together. Finally we have turned, as we have said, to our own experience, in spiritual life, in liturgy and art, to tell of what we love so deeply in our separated brethren. We shall enfold scrolls written by famous monks, describe Russia's favorite devotions, tell of the lives of her saints and of the people's customs. And above all we shall try to show how the Russian people pray, in great cathedrals and before humble icons, in the peasant's hut and the monk's underground cell. For all this is Russia, and all of it is *inside* the walls of her Church — ripening for the great day when the harvest will come, in peace and unity.

HELENE ISWOLSKY

Acknowledgments

My sincere gratitude is due for permission to quote from:

G. Fedotov, *Treasury of Russian Spirituality*, Sheed & Ward.

Hapgood, tr., *Service Book of the Holy Orth. Cath. Apost. Church*, Y.M.C.A. Association Press.

Rev. J. Raya and Baron J. de Vinck, *Byzantine Missal*, St. George's R. C. Byzantine Church.

Rev. Alexander Schmemann, *Istorichesky Putj Pravoslavya*, Chekhov Publishing House.

A. Pushkin, *Boris Godunov*, tr. Alfred Hayes, E. P. Dutton and Co., Inc.

Thanks are also due to *Jubilee* for permission to reproduce two of my articles . . .

and I gratefully acknowledge the help rendered by Father Paul Mailleux, S.J., and Father Nicholas Bock, S.J., in research and illustrations from the Library of the Fordham Russian Center.

Contents

PART ONE
The Russian Church in History

PART TWO
The Russian Church in Tradition and Life

PART ONE

The Russian Church in History

CHAPTER ONE

In St. Andrew's Footsteps

THE historic birth year of the Russian Church is 988. In that year the Russian prince Vladimir brought Christianity to his people from Byzantium, and had them baptized in the river Dnieper, at the foot of the hills of Kiev, his capital. The christening of the Russian people is described in Russia's earliest historic document: this is the "primary chronicle," also known as the *Povyest Vremennikh Lyet* (The Tale of Years of Time). The *Povyest* has been analyzed and scrutinized by many scholars; it is still considered the initial source of Russian history. While many events pictured by the ancient chroniclers can be historically confirmed, others belong to legendary times. However, the more this research advances, the closer we can follow the main trends which prepared and announced the beginnings of the Russian Church long before the official date of her birth.

Most outstanding among these legends is the story of St. Andrew the Apostle visiting in the first century A.D. the regions where two famous Russian towns, Kiev and Novgorod, were to be founded hundreds of years later. According to tradition, St. Andrew preached on the shore of the Black Sea, in the cities of Synope and Korsun (Chersonese), in what is now known as the Sevastopol area; it was from this shore that he is said to have journeyed to Russia. This is how the apostle's voyage is related by the chronicler:

> When Andrew preached in Synope and in Korsun, he learned that not far from there was the mouth of the river Dniepr; he wanted to go to Rome, reached the mouth of the Dniepr and sailed up the river. And it came to pass that he stopped at the foot of

some hills. In the morning he arose and said to the disciples who
accompanied him: "See ye these hills?; on them will shine the
Grace of God, and there will arise a great city, and God will erect
many churches within its walls." And he ascended these hills, and
planted a cross and prayed on the site where now stands the city
of Kiev, and descending, went up the Dniepr. And he came to the
region where now stands the city of Novgorod.

St. Andrew's voyage to Scythia (i.e., Russia) was first mentioned
by Eusebius, bishop of Caesarea, the first historian of the Church,
in the third century A.D. As to the apostle's further journey up
the Dnieper and to the Novgorod region — this still belongs to the
realm of legend. The route to the Baltic sea seems, according to
the chronicler, to have been chosen by St. Andrew, because he
intended to sail from there to Western Europe and Italy. He
visited his brother Peter in Rome, later returned to Synope, then
came to Patras in Greece where he was martyred on the X-shaped
cross which bears his name.

St. Andrew's journey to the Dnieper and to the regions of
Novgorod and the Baltic was considered in Russia as the symbol
of her great religious vocation. Russians were indeed very proud
that the "first called of the apostles," as he is known in the Eastern
Church (*Protoclete* in Greek),[1] should have visited their land at
the very dawn of the Christian era. Was not his prophecy fulfilled
on the hills above the Dnieper river, where not only the great
city of Kiev was built, but also a great monastery, the cradle of
Russian monasticism — the Kievo-Prtcherrsky Laura? And is not
St. Andrew's memory also preserved in the Russian North, near
Novgorod, where another famous monastery was built on the
apostle's itinerary: the Valaamo hermitage on Lake Ladoga?

For many centuries, St. Andrew's cross was specially venerated
in Russia; it became the emblem of the Russian navy, and its
name was given to the highest order conferred by the tsars on
princes and the most distinguished statesmen. Whether fact or
legend,[2] St. Andrew's journey to Russia offers us the key to

---

[1] St. Andrew was the first to follow Christ (Jn. 1:35–51). Later St. Andrew
was *called* with his brother, Simon Peter (Mt. 4:18–22).

[2] For F. Dvornik's extensive work on St. Andrew, *see* Bibliography.

Russian church history as well as to Russian spirituality. In the light of the Protoclete's Apostolate we can behold Christianity in Russia not as something alien, imported from without, but deeply rooted in a people's memory. Indeed, if we examine the early maps of the Russian land, we discover that this was not a closed world, withdrawn into itself, but on the contrary, linked by many waterways and seaways with other lands: as the chronicle of the *Povyest* tells us, there was even in those early days, a communication line from the Greeks to the Dnieper, and from the Dnieper to Lake Ilmen, and from Lake Ilmen to the Varangian (Baltic) sea, and from that sea to Rome. It was to Rome that St. Andrew finally made his way, at a time when this was the most logical journey's end, since Peter still lived there and would soon be martyred. There was in those days but one Church, which knew no divisions, and was still listening to the voice of Christ's own disciples.

Another great saint and martyr of these early times is linked to the birth of Christianity in Russia. He is St. Clement, third successor of St. Peter, first of the Apostolic Fathers. According to St. Irenaeus, St. Clement knew the blessed apostles and conversed with them. We also know that he preached on the Black Sea shore, in the area known as the Crimea. He too came to Korsun, where he was martyred by the pagans. His body was hurled into the sea and was later discovered in an underwater chapel, miraculously erected. St. Clement's relics were preserved in the Crimea and were brought in the tenth century to Kiev as a gift of the Byzantine emperor to the newly founded Russian Church.

St. Andrew and St. Clement can thus be said to have presided over the Christianizing of Russia.

*   *   *

But at the time of St. Andrew and St. Clement, Russia herself was not yet born; in fact, the religious and cultural future which awaited her could be seen only dimly, even by prophetic eyes.

The land to which St. Andrew carried his mission was at that time inhabited by the Scythians, an Iranian people who had settled in the basins of the Don and the Dnieper and whom

Herodotus described in the fifth century B.C.; in the days of Herodotus the Scythians were a nomadic and barbaric people, but as centuries passed they developed a way of life which was no longer primitive. Contemporary archaeologists tend to prove that there existed in the beginning of our era a Scythian civilization of considerable interest, as shown by the excavation of tombs in the Crimean region. At that period the Scythians were trading with their neighbors, the highly civilized Greek colonies on the Black Sea shore. Under these colonists' influence, they developed a peculiar form of Greco-Scythian art and craftsmanship: arms, ceramics, tools, silver and gold jewelry, some specimens of which are preserved in the museum of the Hermitage in Leningrad. The more the Greco-Scythian period of Russian pre-history is explored, the more the story of St. Andrew and St. Clement comes to light. These Southeastern European plains, so near to the Black Sea and the Mediterranean, were not a "wasteland." They were mission territory of great interest and value, and continued to be so in the days of St. Jerome, who prophetically wrote that the "Frozen climes of Scythia were aflame with faith."

However, the time of the flowering of this faith was still far ahead. The great Scythian empire was soon to vanish under the impacts of new migrations and conquests; as early as the fourth century B.C. the power of the Scythians had been disputed by another Iranian people, the Sarmatians, who also occupied the shores of the Black Sea. They, too, evolved an industry and civilization of their own, and were skilled in armory and jewelry. The Sarmatians were divided in a number of tribes, one of which, the Alans, can be considered as the direct forefathers of the Slavs. An Alan clan was called Rukhs-As; it may have been the original tribe of Ross or Russ — which later formed the nucleus of the Russian people.[3]

---

[3] This is the opinion of the Russian historian G. Vernadsky of Yale University (*see* Bibliography). However, another theory points to the Scandinavian origin of the word *Russ* or *Ross;* both spellings are used by Vernadsky and other authors. The *Povyest* and other ancient documents speak of the Russian land and its people as *Russ.* Later, the land was described as *Russkaya Zemlya,* and the people as *Russky narod.* In the eighteenth century we find the word *Rossiya*

As centuries rolled by the picture changed again and again. The Sarmatians and Scythians were defeated by Goth-Germanic and Hun Turco-Mongol invaders. They were pushed back even further or conquered by the Khazars, a people of mixed origin, half Turk, half North Caucasian, with Hun and Bulgar strains. The Khazars who settled in the land of Tmutarakan, between the Black Sea and the Caspian, founded a powerful kingdom, which was to defy the other peoples of that region, and even Byzantium itself, for many centuries. Though not belonging to the Semitic race, the Khazars had embraced Judaism, while their neighbors, the Bulgars, of Turkish origin, professed the heathen faith. These latter also formed a powerful empire, extending over the Balkan peninsula. Here they mingled with Slav tribes who were likewise seeking refuge from the Khazars. These were the groups later known as Western and Southern Slavs. As to the Eastern Slavs, successors to the Sarmatians, Scythians, and Alans, they became for a time the vassals of the Khazar Kaganate,[4] but later gained their independence and formed the so-called Kaganate of Eastern Slavs. This principality was formed on the banks of the river Dnieper, which St. Andrew the Apostle had blessed as the future cradle of the Russian Church.

How the Eastern Slavs were related to their Scythian and Sarmatian ancestors, is hard to say. They certainly retained from the peoples of Scythia certain traditions — the warrior-like breeding of many generations exposed to continuous attacks by enemy hordes. There was a constant fear and awareness of danger in the vast steppes and wastelands of Tmutarakan and the Khazar Kaganate. This was to stimulate the military virtues of the Eastern Slavs, and at the same time draw them farther and farther away from the scene of battle.

---

used to denote the Russian empire. In our first chapters, dealing with medieval Russia we shall use the word *Russ*, both for land and people.

[4] The Khazar word *kaganate* (principality) was adopted by the Kiev rulers and retained for a time in medieval Russian terminology. *Kaganate* meant a territory or state subject to a *kagan* or prince. Later *kagan* was transformed into its slavonic contraction *knyaz*, as the Russian princes called themselves up to the sixteenth century, when the prince of Moscow adopted the title of Tsar/Caesar. *See* Chapter Four.

The Russ gradually moved to more peaceful lands up the Dnieper to the fields where the sword could be turned into a plow; to the forests where one could hide from the enemy or build wooden fortresses and log cabins. On the whole, if undisturbed, the Eastern Slavs became a peaceful nation, or rather a confederation of tribes, known as the *Polyane* and *Drevlyane* (field and forest peoples). At first they led a nomadic life, mostly fishing and hunting; later they settled down in primitive villages under a tribal, patriarchal system. These were mainly agricultural communities, but little by little agriculture led to an exchange of goods with neighboring tribes and then with other countries.

The Greek colonies of the Black Sea shore and especially the great Eastern Empire's capital Byzantium, became the main markets of export for the Slavic people. The waterways, which St. Andrew is said to have followed many centuries ago, now became essential routes. These routes led from the Bosphorus to the Dnieper, from the Dnieper to the Northern lakes and rivers — and to the Baltic or Varangian Sea, so called because of the Varangians (Norsemen) who lived on its Northwestern shores. Of course, these rivers were not all connected, as our modern seaways; part of the route had to be covered by "portage," just as in primitive North America. But there existed a lifeline — commercial, political, and cultural — of primary importance. It was known as the *Great Way, from the Varangians to the Greeks,* for it was between these two geographic areas that early Russian history began to develop.

The Varangians, Norsemen or Vikings, as they are often called, inhabited the Scandinavian lands today known as Sweden, Norway, and Denmark. This was a dynamic people of mariners, tradesmen, and explorers, who came in the sixth century to the Eastern shores of the Baltic and moved on to the upper Volga region. We find them often co-operating with the Slavs, sharing their commercial interests — and at times controlling them. The Vikings made armor, shields, and swords of fine steel which they used for their conquests and also sold to their customers. The

Slavs traded in costly furs, wax, and timber. The Vikings had a fleet of ships to carry the various merchandise down the waterways. These ships were manned by well-armed soldiers who could protect the floating caravans against the attacks of pirates, the nomadic tribes of the steppes who posed a continuous threat to both Slavs and Norsemen. At the end of the long voyage lay Constantinople, the capital of the Eastern empire, the great center of Byzantine political and ecclesiastical power, of culture, art, philosophy, and belles lettres.

From the sixth to the eighth and ninth centuries, relations between the people of Russ, their Varangian escorts, and Byzantium were constant; they led to the development of the Russian State.

The story of the birth of this state is well known, as described by the *Povyest*: the Slavs first welcomed the Varangians' help and protection, but later resented their control. They refused to pay the usual tribute due to the Vikings for their military and commercial services and pushed them back to Scandinavia. But without the Norsemen's protection the trade routes were no longer safe; they were threatened by pirates and nomad warriors, and by the aggressive Khazars. Moreover, the Slavs themselves were divided by internal feuds and outside competition; and so, finally, the *Povyest* tells us, the people of Russ called a meeting of all the tribes and clans, who decided as follows: "Let us look for a prince who will rule us and judge us according to the right law." The Russ ambassadors "crossed the sea" and presented their petition to the Varangian warriors, saying: "Our land is great and rich, but there is no order in it; come and govern us."

The call was answered by the Varangian prince Ryurik and his two brothers, Sinius and Truver, who spread their rule over the Eastern Slavs. Ryurik founded his capital in Novgorod while his two brothers divided the other East-Slav lands between them. From overseas came also two other Varangian princes, Askold and Dir, who established their rule in Kiev. This city, built according to St. Andrew's prophecy, was to become one of Russia's most famous historic and cultural landmarks. Meanwhile, however, Ryurik of Novgorod was the supreme ruler. After his brothers' death, their lands were placed under Ryurik's leadership. Thus was founded the dynasty of the *Ryurikovichy,* who reigned in Russia from 862 to 1598. Ryurik's direct descendants became princes and tsars; some of them remained at the princes' court as boyars, i.e., members of an influential aristocracy, who played an important role in Russian history.

The *Povyest* chronicle further tells us how Russian society was formed in Novgorod (and this may apply also to other Russian cities and regions). The Varangians were the *nakhodniki,* i.e., recent settlers — while the local population was Slav or Finnish. Here we have a process, starting from the very birth of the Russian State, a "melting pot," where Slavs and Scandinavians and other Baltic tribes were constantly mingling. The Scandinavian element, which came with Ryurik, formed the ruling class; but it was a minority, some 100,000, which was soon absorbed by the Slav aborigines, adopting their language and customs. As to the Baltic tribes, the Finns, the Letts, and the Ests, they came into the orbit of the newly formed Russ state, preserving their distinct racial and linguistic traits, which still persist in our times.

*   *   *

Slavs, Scandinavians, and Baltic clans all were pagans, at least in the early days of Viking rule. The Norsemen had their own mythology, the gods and heroes of the Scandinavian Saga. The Slavs had their pantheon too — symbolizing for the most part the forces of Nature: Perun, the mighty god of thunder; Dazhdbog, the sun-god, protector of the harvest; Veless, presiding over fields and cattle; Stribog, the god of winds, and others. The statues of these gods carved in wood, gilded and richly decorated, stood on the hills of Kiev and Novgorod, and were publicly worshiped. Beside these major divinities, the Slavs had many minor gods, or rather spirits, haunting the world with fantastic and weird manifestations. The goblins of the woods, the kings of the lakes and the nymphs of the rivers, all figure in old Russian folklore; so do the wicked witches and magicians, and the spirits of the home, the *Domovoy* — mostly friendly to its inhabitants if treated with respect, but dangerous if despised or molested. To an even more primitive cycle belong the gods of fertility, known under the names of *Rod* and *Rozhenitzy,* and the god of music and song, *Lad,* whose name is still used in the Russian language to denote harmony.

The Slavs also worshiped trees, especially the birch, which grows in Northern and Central Russia and was as sacred as the Roman olive and the Gaelic oak. Many folk songs still sung today in Russia refer to the pagan gods; thus, for instance, the birch tree is featured in the "Volga Boatmen," though its pagan meaning has long been forgotten. Russian folk dances, especially the *chorovod* or peasant round dance, with choral accompaniment[5] are obviously the remnants of a pagan ritual; so are the *podblyudny pesny,* the songs and pantomimes which symbolize the exchange of wedding rings in magic terms. These choral performances are very ancient, and their exact meaning has been almost entirely lost.[6] Russian composers have revived for the modern public much of the archaic art, which still exercises its fascination through the media of song, orchestra, and ballet.[7]

To be sure, the study of Russian folklore presents a fascinating field in itself. But this study is also necessary for an understanding of the Russian religious mind. The Slav gods and the rituals linked to their worship were not as clear cut as those of Greece or Rome or the Germanic world; there was no Olympus and no Valhalla in ancient Russia. However, there was a magic world of mysterious forces, of primeval elements, of good and evil influences, which could be set loose or held under control. So powerful was the pagan world that it continued to live long after Christianity came to Russia. This created, as we shall see, an ambivalence of Christian-pagan elements. It is part of con-

---

[5] As presented by Moyseyeff, Berezka companies and the Piatnitzsky chorus and dancers who toured the U. S. A. in 1958–59.

[6] L. Findeisen, in his *History of Russian Music,* relates the Russian choral performances to the Greek tragic chorus. *See* Bibliography.

[7] Musorgski's "Night on the Bald Mountain"; Stravinsky's "Sacre du Printemps" and "Wedding," Rimski-Korsakov's "Snow Maiden," etc.

temporary research to fix the frontiers of this ambivalent world, but as yet its task is far from completed.

*   *   *

In order to understand the Russian mind, another brief survey is necessary; this has to do with the Russian *habitat*, the life conditions, climate, and geographical location of the Russian people at the time of the formation of their first political nucleus. For this we shall turn to the Russian historian V. Klyuchevsky. At the opening of his course at Moscow University,[8] Professor Klyuchevsky stressed that three main elements shaped the Russian national character. These were the woods, the steppe, and the rivers.

The woods, Professor Klyuchevsky tells us, were the typical habitat of the Russian people. Their towns and villages were set up in clearings opened among the protecting thickets. Indeed, these forest strongholds were the Russian's "castle" against the invaders always threatening him from the open steppes. Even today, something of this setting is to be found in the typical landscape of central Russia, as described by Klyuchevsky: "a more or less vast horizon, limited by a blue wooded skyline."

The woods offered the Russian people various economic advantages. They provided this people with pine and oak for their log cabins, birch and poplar for their fuel. They provided tapers for light, and material for primitive cooking utensils. The skins and furs of wild animals could be used for warm winter clothing and could be traded at local posts or even at distant markets.

And yet, Professor Klyuchevsky goes on to say, "the woods weighed heavily on the soul of the Russian people." They were hard to clear and their sprawling overgrowth barred the roads. Their fierce inhabitants, wolf and bear, attacked the flocks. There were robbers, too, in the woods, armed for murder and plunder. And "the deep, dreamy silence" of the forest "seemed to convey

---

[8] Professor Klyuchevsky, one of Russia's greatest historians of the nineteenth and early twentieth centuries, taught at Moscow University. Born in 1842, he died in 1911, seven years before the Revolution. Klyuchevsky's course on Russian History at the Moscow University was recorded with the help of stenography in five volumes.

a secret threat" . . . "the eery atmosphere put the woodman's nerves on edge," as if haunted by monsters and goblins.

After the woods, Klyuchevsky takes us to the steppes. These, he tells us, had a beneficent influence on the Russian mind. They offered fertile, easily cultivated plowland and immense pastures. Moreover, the steppes, stretching southward, were the road to the Black Sea. This was the gateway through which medieval Russia was in touch with the culture of Byzantium and of Southern Europe.

But, as Klyuchevsky points out, there is something more about the steppe than a historic setting. It is a limitless horizon. The steppe is a *psychological factor;* it conveys that peculiar feeling of infinite space and freedom which the Russians call *prostor*. This word means both physical space and a spiritual breadth of vision. It is the boundless and it is the absolute. But Klyuchevsky reminds us that the steppe also carried its threat: it was the hunting ground of fierce nomadic tribes ceaselessly attacking the Russian populations. This struggle forms the "darkest, most terrifying memory of the Russian people." Indeed the struggle lasted throughout centuries of wars and devastations.

Thus woods and steppes presented conflicting elements of good and evil. But the Russian river did not create such conflicts. On the contrary, the Russian people felt *at home* on their great waterways. These routes were friendly and peaceful, leading settlers and pioneers to new lands. Klyuchevsky gives a fine description of the tremendous river network of ancient Russ:

> New villages were built on river's banks, it floated boats and timber in summer; when it froze in winter, it served as the smoothest and surest of high-ways for sleigh and horses. The river fed the village people with its many kinds of fish. And the river also served as educator, teaching the people the principles of ethics and social order. Its freezing in the fall and the breaking up of its ice in the spring occur with strict regularity. Its basin with its many affluents irrigates good land for cultivation, encourages shipbuilding and commerce. Its banks, thickly populated, promote good-neighbor relations and community life. At the same time, these men, established on the Russian rivers, kept alive the pioneering spirit. They were

used to travel, to visit many far-away towns and settlements, to meet new people in a new setting. And so these river-populations were aware of the existence of other men; they did not look upon them as outsiders. Since they lived on the banks of the same river, upstream or downstream, even the most distant of these men were still neighbors. Goods could be exchanged with them, business pursued on friendly terms, and services mutually rendered. Yes, men who lived along the rivers observed other people's customs, understood other people's interests, sought cooperation and unity.

As we see the Russian *habitat* presented and still presents a great variety of scene and *mores*. It is against this background that we will enfold the panorama of the Russian Church in history and life.

CHAPTER TWO

Dawn of Christianity in Russia

AS WE have seen, the great route from the "Varangians to the Greeks" connected the cities of Novgorod in the North and of Kiev in the South with the Byzantine Empire. Though most of the Varangians were pagan, there were among them also Christians, whose role in early history is of considerable importance. One of these Christian vikings was Askold, a distant relative of Ryurik, who became the ruler of Kiev. Askold's story is paradoxical. This Scandinavian prince had a mighty army which he led first against the Khazar Kaganate of Tmutarakan, and then against Constantinople, with which he had a political and economic conflict. Askold commanded a formidable fleet which (circa 860) reached the waters of the Bosphorus, threatening the Byzantine capital with almost immediate disaster.

The *Povyest* describes Askold's expedition to Constantinople. This campaign started in the fourteenth year of the reign of the Byzantine emperor Michael; the Russ entered the city and murdered many Christians, while their two hundred ships laid siege on its harbor. The emperor and the patriarch prayed all night in the Church of Our Lady of Blakherna. They carried the icon of the Blessed Virgin in procession to the seashore and immersed it in the water. "At that time," the *Povyest* goes on to say, "all was quiet and the sea was smooth; then, suddenly a storm arose and mighty waves tossed the ships of the pagan Russ; they were driven to the shore and broken up, so that only a few of the crew escaped and returned to the homeland."

Our Lady's miraculous intervention not only saved Constantinople but also deeply impressed Askold and his warriors. They

retreated, ceased their attacks on Byzantium, and brought back
to Kiev the wondrous tale of our Lady's protection. According to
the legend, the Blakherna icon's gilded cover or robe was immersed in the sea; it spread a veil over the city threatened by
Askold. This event was therefore called the Feast of Our Lady
of the Veil, or of Protection. Askold told the story of the miracle
to the people of Kiev. From that time on, the Christian faith
began to spread among the Varangian rulers (the *nakhodniky*)
as well as among the Kiev population. Our Lady of Protection
became one of the most famous icons venerated in ancient Russ
and then in Russia up to our times. As to prince Askold — he
was baptized about 867, i.e., not long after his attack on Constantinople and our Lady's miracle. In baptism, Askold received
the name of Nicholas, probably because his conversion took place
under the pontificate of Pope Nicholas I. After Askold's death,
one of the first Kiev churches, St. Nicholas, was built on the
hill where his body was laid to rest. "Askold's grave" is still one
of the landmarks of Kiev antiquities.

Askold's defeat, due to the Blakherna miracle, and his conversion, furnish sufficient evidence of Christian influences among
the ancient Russ. There is further evidence concerning the "infiltration" of Christianity in Russia. The peaceful trade along the
"great waterway from the Varangians to the Greeks" established
contacts with the Black Sea shore Christian Greek colonies —
Korsun and Synope, which preserved the memories of St. Andrew
and St. Clement. The Christianization[1] of these southern regions
is attested by the appointment of a bishop in the Black Sea region
in 867; this diocese was established in the area of Tmutarakan,
which had been formerly subject to Khazar rule, but was occupied in the ninth century by Slavo-Varangian forces. The founding of this diocese was solemnly announced in an encyclical letter
of Patriarch Photius stating that the Russ who had besieged Constantinople no longer manifested "a cruel or warlike spirit," that
they lived in peace with the empire (i.e., Byzantium) and had

---

[1] For details of this process of Christianization, *see* F. Dvornik and M. de
Taube (Bibliography).

even accepted a bishop appointed by the patriarch.[2]

This statement of the patriarch of Constantinople had led a number of Russian scholars to date Russia's early conversion to the establishment of the Tmutarakan diocese. The historian G. Vernadsky[3] calls this diocese "the nucleus of the Russian Church." Indeed the Black Sea region was the normal channel for bringing Christianity to Russia. This process of Christianization was confirmed by the exchange of diplomatic missions between Kiev and Constantinople and the signing of a peace treaty between Russ and Byzantium. Pacification on the political level was closely followed by a partial conversion of the Russ population on the Dnieper, probably in Kiev, brought about by a prelate sent by the patriarch of Constantinople, about 877. According to historic material of that time,[4] this conversion was due to a miracle. The pagans listening to the prelate's sermons were still dubious and undecided. They were not convinced of the truth of the miracles described in the Bible until the preacher threw his gospel book into a fire. The book remained intact, and a mass baptism followed.

*   *   *

The events leading to the first conversions to Christianity in the land of Russ were determined, as we have seen, by the patriarch of Constantinople — Photius. It must be recalled here that this famous prelate was at that time involved in a conflict with Rome, which brought about the first serious dissensions between Byzantium and the Holy See. For many centuries following these events, the quarrel of 867 between Pope Nicholas I and Photius was considered as the actual date of the final schism between East and West. However, recent historic research has disproved this theory. The break between Rome and Byzantium came only in 1054, and even so, as we shall see, it was not final.

As to the conflict between Photius and Pope Nicholas, it was mainly due, on one hand, to the rise of Constantinople to great

---

[2] Migne, *Patr. Gr.* 102, col. 735 s.s., quoted by Michel de Taube.
[3] G. Vernadsky, *Ancient Russia.*
[4] As described in Theophorus, cont.

temporal and religious power; Byzantium had thus become an extremely important factor in both political and ecclesiastical affairs.

On the other hand, the dissension was due to the crowning of Charlemagne as emperor of the West. The coronation, performed in 800 in Rome by Pope Leo III, defied the prerogatives which Byzantium had so proudly assumed.[5] Constantinople could not accept this transference of power from its highly developed and culturally refined empire to the domain of Charlemagne, the "barbaric" Frankish chieftain. Hence Photius' critical attitude toward Rome, complicated by his difficulty — or reluctance — to establish regular communications with the Holy See.

To these factors we must add the tension existing within Constantinople itself. Two politico-religious camps, the Intransigeants and the Liberals, divided the Byzantine Church at that time, seeking to seize power. The leader of the Intransigeants was patriarch Ignatius who resigned under the opposition's pressure and was replaced by Photius. A representative of the Intransigeants set out to present his protest to Rome. This emissary reached the Holy See in time to win the favor of Pope Nicholas by falsely denouncing Photius. On this presumption, Photius was excommunicated in 863 by the Pope, but was later rehabilitated and placed once more on the patriarchal throne. In Pope Nicholas' own words, "he was a man of great virtue and world wide knowledge."[6] During the interim, the patriarchal see of Constantinople was given to Ignatius, the leader of the Intransigeants. To be sure, Photius did start the controversy of the *Filioque,* i.e., the dispute concerning the procession of the Holy Ghost: while Rome had adopted in the Creed the words: "who proceedeth from the Father and the Son" (*Filioque procedit*) — the Byzantine theologians insisted upon the version of the Nicean Creed: "and in the Holy Ghost, the life-giver, who proceeds from the Father." This controversy, however, did not at that time raise an unsurmountable barrier between Rome and Byzantium; it reappeared in further

[5] Donald Attwater, *The Dissident Eastern Churches,* pp. 7–8.
[6] *Ibid.*

discussions leading to the final eleventh century break.[7] Meanwhile, as we have pointed out, recent research has come to the following conclusions, as stated in the scholarly works of F. Dvornik:

> There is no truth in the assertion that Photius was hostile to the Holy See and that he endeavored to win the Pope's favors by false pretenses. Neither is it true that Photius attacked the Western Church as such at the 867 Synod and that he denied the papacy its prominent position in the Church.

Dvornik very clearly states that, despite these controversies, Photius at the time of his death was in communion with Rome.[8]

Thanks to this new, authentic interpretation of the conflict between Photius and Pope Nicholas I, we are able to realize more fully the situation existing after 860 — i.e., at the time when the land of Russ was being slowly drawn into the Christian orbit — into the One Catholic Apostolic Church.

*   *   *

The second part of the ninth century was an important period of apostolate in many Slav lands. In 868 the Greek monk Cyril-Constantine and his brother Methodius were sent from Byzantium to the Carpathian area, inhabited by the Southern slavs. Here the two brothers were to accomplish their great missionary work. Cyril-Constantine and Methodius were both highly educated men, members of Constantinople's cultural elite. Born in Salonica, where a considerable number of Slav natives had mingled with the Greek population, the brothers spoke the Slavonic tongue as fluently as their own and were naturally inclined toward a Slav apostolate. Hence they readily answered the call of the Moravian prince Rostislav, who had asked Byzantium for Christian missionaries. The brothers were the first to spread directly the Christian teaching among these people. But their most remarkable achievement was that they brought this teaching not in Greek, but in the people's *own vernacular*. Indeed, a deep understanding of

---

[7] This controversial point has been recently closely examined by both Catholic and Greek-Orthodox theologians, and the solution of this problem seems near at hand.

[8] *Third Hour,* issue III, 1947, "Patriarch Photius in the Tradition of the Western Church."

the spirit of their primitive flocks (for whom the official languages of the Church, either Greek or Latin, remained incomprehensible) moved the brothers to undertake a tremendous task: the translating of the liturgy, Scripture, and other Church books into the Slavonic tongue. But in order to do this, first an alphabet was needed. The Slavs used only a few crude phonetic signs, called *glagolitzo,* which were sufficient to note the main sounds of their language, but could not be used for any cultural purpose. So the two learned men set to work; taking the original *glagolitzo* they put it into shape by adding signs borrowed from the Greek and Latin but considerably simplified. They also reshaped the Slav language itself; they created theological and scriptural terms accessible to an uncouth congregation, at the same time tending to raise the standard of the Slavonic vocabulary. This was indeed a gigantic task. The ancient Russian chronicles of the *Povyest* recording this feat, tells us that Methodius translated "all the books" in six months, with the help of only two "able speed-writers."[9] By "all the books," the chronicler probably means the scriptural and liturgical texts used in the churches as well as instructions and homilies from the Greek Fathers; these are still the main books of the Byzantine and Slavonic rites.

Beside their immediate practical value, these early translations were of great beauty, reflecting both the true spirit of the Greek original and the spontaneous colorful savor of the Slavonic native idiom.

This remarkable work was encouraged both by Byzantium, which had initiated it, and by Rome, which was soon informed of its success. Cyril-Constantine and Methodius visited the Eternal City and received the blessing of Pope Hadrian II. The Slavonic Gospel was placed on the altar of the Church of Santa Maria, and the Slavonic liturgy was celebrated in many Roman churches.[10]

Cyril was consecrated bishop but died in Rome before returning to the land of the Slavs. His brother Methodius, who was also elevated to the episcopate, was assigned the See of Sirmium which had jurisdiction over Moravia and Pannonia — comprising

---

[9] *Povyest* I (p. 22).
[10] A. Schmemann, *The History of Russian Orthodoxy,* p. 303 (Bibliography).

the territories later known as Croatia, Czechoslovakia, Dalmatia, and Hungary. The missionary work of Methodius, as initiated by his brother, seemed most promising. Unfortunately it encountered the opposition of other bishops, whom the Franks had installed in the adjoining areas. The Frankish empire founded by Charlemagne comprised at that time not only France, Spain, Northern Italy, and Germany, but also part of the Slav lands. The Franks brought with them the bishops of Salzburg, Passau, and Ratisbon, who claimed jurisdiction in the regions where Methodius pursued his own apostolic task. A long and tragic conflict began to develop.

The German prelates disagreed with Methodius on the subject of the vernacular. They admitted the Latin tongue only for the liturgy and Scripture. Methodius was denounced as breaking canon law, and was tried in the German city of Ratisbon which had obtained jurisdiction over Moravia. His desperate appeals to Rome were intercepted and he was not only deposed but imprisoned for two and a half years.

Methodius, finally freed and rehabilitated by Pope John VIII, was appointed by him once more Archbishop of Moravia. But his enemies renewed their attacks again and again, trying in every way to hinder his apostolate and to impair his reputation in the eyes of Rome. The persecution suffered by Methodius from the German episcopate is recorded by the *Povyest,* which also stresses Rome's strong support of the vernacular. The chronicler tells us that this persecution had started even before the death of Cyril who had already been condemned by the Western bishops on the basis of a decision of a local council that only three languages were permitted for the liturgy: Latin, Greek, and Hebrew — i.e., the three languages in which Christ's name was inscribed on the cross. Hearing of the German prelates' opposition, the Pope strongly protested, saying: "may the words of the scriptures be fulfilled: let all tongues praise God" and "let all tongues praise the Majesty of God, as the Holy Spirit inspires them." The *Povyest* adds that the Pope threatened to excommunicate those who condemned the Slavonic books.[11]

---

[11] *Ibid.*

Despite these decisive measures, the struggle went on, and the German episcopate would not surrender. After Methodius' death in 885, Moravia was latinized against the wish of the people, who clung to the Slavonic liturgy. The Church of Dalmatia alone retained the Eastern rite and transmitted it to another Slavonic nation, which had precisely during that period acquired considerable political and cultural importance. This was Bulgaria, the kingdom ruled by the dynamic and enterprising Tsar Boris.

Bulgaria was the first powerful Slav state developed according to the pattern of the Byzantine empire. It was also from Constantinople that Boris brought Christianity to his people. In fact the Christian faith had been imposed on him by Emperor Michael III who defeated him in battle in 869. Bulgaria accepted Christianity but at the same time sought independence from victorious Byzantium.

Boris turned to his Dalmatian brother-Slavs and to their liturgy and books in the vernacular. The heritage of Cyril and Methodius, which had almost perished in Moravia, was now brought to Bulgaria, where its true flowering began. The Slavonic alphabet created by the two learned brothers, the many volumes of their translations, the very tongue which they had fashioned out of the raw material of primitive sounds — all these instruments of missionary work were now promoted on a high cultural level.

This development was continued after the death of Boris by his successor Simeon. He founded schools and libraries, and contributed to the training of priests and scholars; they in turn perfected and enriched the vocabulary of their native tongue, which closely followed the pattern of Greek writings, at the same time preserving the forms of original Slavonic. Thus was born the tongue known as Church-Slavonic, which later, as we shall soon see, came to Russia.

After many centuries and a number of complex metamorphoses, this language finally emerged as what is now known as modern Russian.

*   *   *

Dramatic tensions between East and West often darkened the

Christian horizon in the ninth and tenth centuries; — however, a peaceful and even cordial intercourse between Roman and Slav promoters of the Christian faith was far from uncommon. We have already shown the Pope's interest in the Slavonic apostolate of Cyril and Methodius. As to the Slavs themselves, they recognized the authority of both Byzantium and Rome. Simeon of Bulgaria had his rights to kingship confirmed by the Pope and also obtained from him the approval for the establishment of a Bulgarian patriarchate.[12]

As to the Western Apostolates, there seems to exist some evidence of Scandinavian missionaries visiting Kiev in the time of Askold. One of them may have been the Danish prelate Rimbertus, bishop of Sweden and disciple of St. Ansharus, the Apostle of the North. These missionaries from Scandinavia belonged to the Roman (Latin) Church. A German prelate, Adalbertus, was even appointed bishop of Kiev in the second part of the tenth century, but was fiercely opposed by the population of Kiev, at that time mostly pagan.[13] We have further evidence that St. Bruno, on his way to evangelize the nomad tribes of the steppes, was a guest of prince Vladimir of Kiev.[14] For a long time there were no decisive conflicts between the Byzantines, the Slavs, and Rome. Even at the time of Photius, whose dissensions with Pope Nicholas brought about the first rift in the ninth century, there was, as we have seen, no definite break, no dark shadow cast as yet upon the Holy See and the Church Universal. To be sure it is heartening to realize, as contemporary research is making more and more clear, that in those days there still was an *Una Sancta* without any flaw of human error and hostility. And it was this *Una Sancta* which presided over the Christianization of Russia.

We must not be misled, however, historically speaking, by too hastily devised and sketchy perspectives. Though cordial relations existed between Rome, Scandinavia, and Germany, the entire orientation of ancient Russ was not toward the West, but toward the East. Kiev and Novgorod, the first two powerful Russian cities,

[12] A. Schmemann, *ibid.*, 310.
[13] Taube, pp. 48 and 99.
[14] Pierling, *La Russie et le Saint Siege*, Vol. I, p. x f.

were, first of all, economically and politically linked with Byzantium. Constantinople dictated war and peace to the Russ, or vice versa. Culturally, and spiritually too, the Russian people were influenced by Byzantine patterns. They admired the splendor of the *Basileus* (the emperor), the beauty of Constantinople, of its palaces and churches; they also admired Byzantine scholars and philosophers, who had inherited the wisdom of Athens and had adapted it to Christian thought. All this the Russian people wanted to acquire and were soon to receive through the media of the young Bulgarian culture; for this culture had already absorbed the Byzantine spirit and had created a language to convey it to the Russian neighbors.

*   *   *

When Askold and his retinue, and probably a number of his subjects, were christened in Kiev — the prince of Novgorod, Ryurik, and his successors remained pagan. Now it was the Ryurik dynasty which became the central power in Russ, and Kiev did not remain an independent territory. Ryurik's son, Oleg, attacked his Kiev rivals. Askold and his brother Dir were murdered by the Novgorod forces, and Oleg transferred his capital to Kiev. As we have said, a church, St. Nicholas, was built on Askold's tomb and became one of the oldest shrines of Kiev. Oleg had no inclination toward the Christian faith. The newly founded Russian State was threatened by the nomad tribe of Petchenegs, but was defended by Oleg who became the supreme ruler of the Russ land. He is also noted for having conducted a campaign against Byzantium. According to contemporary records, Oleg hung his shield on the gates of Constantinople. He could not, however, pursue his victory and returned to Kiev, his new capital.

The *Povyest* illustrates Oleg's pagan background by the colorful description of his end. At the height of his victories, Oleg met a soothsayer or witch doctor, who told him that he would meet his death from his horse. Oleg was filled with fear and decided to give up the faithful steed on which he so often rode to battle. A few years later he visited the place where the skeleton of his horse was buried. As he stood near the bones, a snake emerged from the dead horse's skull and bit prince Oleg, causing his death.[15] The "tale of Oleg" inspired the famous ballad written by the great poet Pushkin. It is one of the last episodes of the pagan tradition of ancient Russ.

*   *   *

Oleg's successor, prince Igor, wanted to renew the campaigns against Byzantium, but was prevented from further attacks by a delegation sent by Constantinople to seek an agreement. Oleg's peace treaty was renewed. Its statements follow the original pattern; we find here certain details of procedure concerning the oath demanded from Igor's representatives which indicate that only some of the Russians were pagans, while others were Christians. Those who were Christians pronounced their oath in the Church of St. Elijah before the Cross; the "non-baptized Russians," as the document defines them, laid down their swords, shields, and other arms as a symbol of their peaceful intentions.[16]

The various historical material we have cited brings out quite definitely that in the land of Russ there were already many Christian elements. However, it was only after Igor's death that his widow Olga embraced Christianity. Here again we must turn to the *Povyest*,[17] which tells of Olga's conversion.

Prince Igor was murdered by the Petchenegs, and since his son Svyatoslav was too young to rule the people of Kiev, his mother Olga became regent. She was the first Russian ruler to be officially baptized. We do not know the motives of Olga's conversion; all the *Povyest* tells us is that she visited Constantinople in 954 with the intention of receiving baptism. The Russian princess was welcomed with great solemnity by the emperor, Constantine Porphyrogenetus, who admired both her beauty and her wisdom. Moreover, he had designs on Olga as the heir of the Ryurik dynasty. Constantine therefore offered her marriage, with the intention of adding Kiev and its people to his empire. Olga, aware of his designs, wisely postponed her answer. She merely told the

---

[15] *Povyest*, p. 226.
[16] *Povyest*, p. 38. There must have been at that time a Church of St. Elijah in Kiev. But no trace of it has been so far discovered.
[17] *Povyest*, p. 45.

Basileus: "I am a pagan. If you want to baptize me, then do so yourself, otherwise I will not be baptized." The emperor readily agreed to be Olga's godfather. She was baptized by the patriarch and received the name of Helen, in memory of the Saint, finder of the Cross. After her baptism, the emperor renewed his offer of marriage. But Olga reminded him that, according to canon law, a godfather could not marry his godchild. And so, the shrewd princess defeated the emperor's designs, returned to Kiev and remained regent until her son Svyatoslav's majority.

Princess Olga of Kiev was later canonized by the Russian Church. Since her conversion took place before the schism, she is also a saint of the Universal Church. The Russian-Orthodox call her: "equal to the Apostles," a title given in Russia only to saints who contributed to the evangelization of their country. The chronicle tells us that "as the dawn of morning which announces the sun and as the moon shining at night, she [Olga] shone among the unbelievers." The *troparion*[18] on the feast of St. Olga thus sums up her mission: "Having covered herself with the wings of prudence, she flew above the visible creatures; having sought God and the Creator and having found him, she was reborn by Baptism. Having tasted of the tree of Life, she is forever incorruptible. Olga — to be praised for all eternity!"

The dawn was, however, slow to rise above Russia. Olga's son Svyatoslav was not to follow his mother's footsteps. When he attained his majority, he became the ruling prince of Kiev; to his mother's repeated requests to receive Baptism, he answered: "How shall I alone adopt another faith. My retinue will make fun of me."

*   *   *

Olga died without seeing Russia brought into the fold. It was her grandson, Vladimir, who baptized his people in 988 — which, as we have said, is the official date of Russia's Christianization.

Vladimir is a historic and at the same time, a semilegendary

---

[18] The *troparion* is a prayer dedicated to each saint of the Eastern Calendar, lauding his particular virtues and merits.

figure. Before embracing Christianity, he was a typically pagan ruler, whose court in Kiev was known for its splendor and revelry. But Prince Vladimir, was not satisfied with his pagan environment. Following Olga's example he wanted to bring to Kiev higher religious and moral principles. Unlike Olga, however, Vladimir was still hesitant as to what faith he should adopt. He had, as the *Povyest* tells us, three choices: Christianity, Islamism, and Judaism. Christianity already had its representatives in Kiev. The Jewish faith was probably promoted by the Khazars. As to the Moslems, their faith was spreading among the peoples of Asia Minor and other areas close to Russia. Once more we must refer to the *Povyest* describing prince Vladimir's conferences with the representatives of the three faiths. It seems that the Kiev ruler was interested in all three of them; he argued with Moslem, Jew, and Christian, manifesting considerable prudence, as well as an open and inquisitive mind. He soon reached a decision. The chronicle candidly states that Vladimir rejected the Moslems because their religion forbade wine which the Kiev prince declared was a beverage indispensable to Russia. As to the Jews, Vladimir hesitated to adopt the religion of a people which had been dispersed and was therefore homeless. Finally, the prince received the envoy of the Byzantine Church: he was a "philosopher" who presented a complete picture of salvation as founded on Christian dogma, Scripture, and tradition. This explanation covers more than 12 pages of the ancient chronicle. We cannot vouch how far Vladimir, the pagan prince, could assimilate the entire doctrinal message. But "the philosopher" had certainly a decisive influence on his choice. Soon after these consultations, Vladimir decided to adopt the Christian faith; however, he still hesitated whether to turn to Eastern or Western Christianity. Once again, the *Povyest* gives us a colorful account of his decision. The Kiev prince, the chronicle tells us, sent embassies to cities where the Roman and the Byzantine rites were observed. The Roman rite did not impress the ambassadors but the Byzantine churches filled them with wonder and admiration; this is how the chronicle records their report:

We came to the land of the Greeks and we were led to the place where they serve their God, and we knew not whether we were in heaven or in earth.

And so prince Vladimir reached his final decision; to be baptized by the Byzantine Church. This story, vivid, as are most records preserved by the *Povyest,* is often quoted and sometimes misquoted by historians. In St. Vladimir's last choice, the ambassadors to Constantinople, no doubt, did play a decisive role: they were impressed, as we have seen, by the Byzantine liturgy. There was the aesthetic element; it was obvious enough, if we recall that the ambassadors attended the liturgy at Sancta Sophia, the magnificent shrine of Eastern Christianity, the monument *par excellence* of Byzantine architecture, iconography, and mosaics. The liturgy itself, performed by the patriarch and his assistant clergy fully vested in their shining robes, must have surpassed all that Vladimir's uncouth emissaries had ever seen.[19] The large choir singing the responses, the hymns, and the antiphons, filled the dome with mighty and perfectly attuned voices. And this was not all. There is in the Eastern liturgy a symbolism, a liturgical action, which can be easily followed and understood by the primitive mind. Thus, for instance, the two processions (or entrances) with the celebrants carrying first the Gospel and then the Gifts to be consecrated, bring the holy sacrifice of the Mass, so to say, *into the very midst of the congregation.* And the clouds of incense, enveloping both the faithful and Sancta Sophia's beautiful mosaics, may have been indeed for the Russian visitors, like a foretaste of heaven.

No wonder that the splendors of this liturgy were immediately grasped by Vladimir's ambassadors. Moreover, previous relations with Constantinople and with the diocese of Tmutarakan had paved the way for a deeper understanding of the Byzantine Mass. No doubt that the translations of Greek texts into the Slavonic vernacular as used in Bulgaria were also known to the ambassadors. Thus their choice was predetermined; it was the only one which could

---

[19] The *Povyest* tells us that the patriarch commanded a most solemn service with elaborate preparations: choir, vestments, etc., p. 273.

appeal directly to themselves and to their prince in Kiev.

However, as we must stress once more, Vladimir's final decision in no way implied hostility to Rome. There could be no break on his part with the Western Church for the simple reason that such a break *did not as yet exist in Byzantium.* The story of Vladimir's conversion is often misinterpreted in so far as it is presented as a deliberate choice between two enemy churches — Rome and Byzantium. Such an interpretation, as presented in certain outdated textbooks, is not only untrue — it is dangerous, since it deepens the rift between the Russian Church and Rome. At the time of Vladimir's conversion there still was only one Church Universal. As the great Russian religious thinker, Solovyev writes:

> There was a glorious time, when on Christian soil and under the banner of the universal Church, the two Romes, that of the West and that of the East, were joined in the name of one common aim; the Establishment of Christian truth. In those days, their peculiarities, the peculiarities of the Eastern and of the Western character, did not exclude but completed each other.[20]

And so we come to prince Vladimir's baptism in 988. It took place probably at Khorsun (Chersonese)[21] and was immediately followed by Vladimir's marriage with princess Anne, sister of the emperors Basile and Constantine, at that time the co-rulers of Byzantium. Vladimir and his bride returned to Kiev bringing with them the priests who were to evangelize the Russian people. They also brought the liturgical books in Church Slavonic, the holy vessels, the vestments, and the icons. The *Povyest* tells us that Vladimir received a precious gift from the emperors: the skull of St. Clement, who was, as may be recalled, martyred at Korsun. The relic was taken by Vladimir to Kiev, where he immediately proceeded to the evangelization of his people. The Kiev citizens were christened collectively in the river Dnieper, by immersion, according to the Eastern rite, the priest reading the baptismal prayers over them. Vladimir destroyed the pagan idols and threw

---

[20] *Russia and the Universal Church.*

[21] A few ancient texts place this event not in Korsun, but in Kiev, but this is a controversial and uncertain point, irrelevant to our brief survey.

them into the Dnieper. The wooden statue of Perun with silver head and golden beard floated down the river without arousing protest or regret. The "god of thunder" was later found amid driftwood washed on a sandy beach which was named after him: "Perun's landing." Other idols followed his wake. One of these pagan divinities met with a less tragic fate: Veles, god of cattle, protector of the rural population, was so popular that the Christian missionaries did not want to create ill feeling. So they renamed, or one might say, "baptized" Veles: he was assimilated to St. Vlassy (St. Blaise), whose name suggests that of Veles, and so Veles-Vlassy became the patron saint of the Russian peasant. His name is very popular in Russia's rural districts.

Here is a typical example of paganism gradually yielding to Christianity in Kiev: not by force but by a wise and patient process of integration. This was due in part to the spirit of the age — the first years of medieval Christian Russia. The process of Christianization was also determined by prince Vladimir's personality. He was a man at the same time dynamic and prudent; he weighed the "pros" and "cons" of Christianization most carefully and, when his decision was reached, acted without fear or hesitation. Prince Vladimir is not only featured in historic records; he is also a hero of Russian folklore, in which he is called "Vladimir — the bright sun." He is the Russian "King Arthur," whose knights, as soon as they were christened, fought against "the infidels," i.e., the nomads of the steppes and the highway robbers. The cycle of ancient Russian epics tells the story of Vladimir and his knights, of their banquets in the Kiev palace, and of their faraway campaigns. These stories are colorful, gay, dramatic — profoundly human, and also profoundly Christian. We feel that with Vladimir and his retinue, the Church had come to stay in Russia.

CHAPTER THREE

The Golden Age

SOON after his conversion and the baptism of his people, prince
Vladimir built the first stone church in Kiev. The church was
dedicated to the Assumption of Our Lady; it was called the
"*Dessyatinnaya*" (i.e., Church of the Tithe) because Vladimir
endowed it with one tenth of his riches. In order to build this
shrine, the prince called an architect from Constantinople — a
master of stone and masonry crafts. Kiev was at that time a small
city, and its structures were built of wood. The Dessyatinnaya
church was built of stone and marble and its design was inspired
by the most elaborate Byzantine architecture. Nothing remains,
alas! of this ancient shrine, which was partly destroyed by fire
and later reduced to rubble during the wars which devastated
Russia in the twelfth and thirteenth centuries. However, the main
features of the Church are known from ancient documents,
sketches, and descriptions, as well as from excavations pursued by
Russian archaeologists: the Dessyatinnaya was a fair-sized, three-
nave basilica with a main cupola and four minor ones; the fragments of the inside walls discovered during the excavations retain
the traces of rich ornaments and frescoes; the marble floor, of
which only a few slabs remain, was inlaid with mosaics of the
finest multicolored pattern. Thanks to these few but impressive
vestiges, we can see how rapid was the advancement of religious
art and architecture in a city where but a few years earlier the
uncouth, wooden shrine of St. Elijah had been the only Christian
place of worship.

Kiev with its splendid basilica became the seat of a Greek
hierarchy and Greek missionaries were sent to other areas of

Vladimir's domain. However, the liturgy and religious instruction were conducted in Slavonic, the use of the vernacular considerably hastening the task of evangelization. Beside the Dessyatinnaya, Vladimir promoted the building of other churches in the main cities which had sprung up around Kiev. Moreover, he opened schools and enrolled his retinue's children in order to give them a Christian education. These were the first schools ever established in Russia; they caused surprise and even a certain commotion. The Chronicle candidly relates that mothers wept seeing their children go to school, "as if they were dead."[1]

Despite these emotional reactions, the spread of Christianity met little opposition among the people of Russia. True, the Christian faith came to them within the severe framework of Byzantine tradition — but it was gradually integrated according to the Russian national character. The strict and formal Byzantine patterns were *mellowed* and humanized by a people naturally inclined to love Christ and His mother more in their merciful and humble aspect than in their triumphant splendor. Thus, for instance, one of the primitive Russians' favorite legends was the "Holy Virgin's descent into Hell" — the Greek Apocrypha (translated into Church Slavonic in the twelfth century). In this legend, our Lady visits hell, where she sees the sinners undergoing punishment. Moved by their sufferings, Mary implores her Son to take pity on them. She obtains from Christ a temporary release from suffering for all inmates of hell: from Holy Thursday to Pentecost.[2]

The pagan elements which persisted, especially among the rural population, were gradually absorbed, although some of their elements did survive in folklore, in fairy tales, and in song, but so transformed and "toned down" as to meet halfway a new saga — the golden legend. Very early, Russian oral tradition replaced pagan tales by lives of saints which became the Russian children's bedside stories. Prince Vladimir saw the beginning of this gradual transformation and rejoiced in it; but being, as it seems, the least doctrinaire of men, he let the Church do its work without inter-

---

[1] *Povyest*, p. 81.

[2] This legend is included in the *Soviet Anthology of Ancient Slavonic Texts*, edited by Gudzy, 1952.

ference, gave his tithe to the Dessyatinnaya Basilica, and distributed alms to the poor. He told all beggars to come to his palace for food and money and sent cartloads of meat and fish to the sick and aged. For the rest he feasted with his knights and made merry with them every Sunday. But he also consulted them on State affairs, holding counsel with them as well as with the most prominent Kiev citizens. This was a democratic age, and it was soon to develop into what is known as "the Golden Age" of ancient Russia.

Vladimir died in 1015, and was buried in the Dessyatinnaya Basilica. He was canonized some two hundred years later, and since he lived and evangelized Russia before the schism of 1054, he like his grandmother Olga, is recognized by Rome as a saint of the Universal Church.

Vladimir's death led to tragic events. His sons rose against one another to seize his crown; one of them, Svyatopolk, occupied Kiev by force, but the bitter dispute went on. During this feud only two of Svyatopolk's brothers, Boris and Gleb, did not challenge his rights. The Kiev people who were devoted to Boris offered him soldiers and arms to depose Svyatopolk, but he declared: "I shall not raise my hand against my elder brother." Not satisfied with such obedience, Svyatopolk sent assassins to murder Boris as he was singing matins. Boris offered no resistance and died asking God to forgive his brother. The same fate awaited Gleb, who was killed a few days later, while praying and mourning for Boris. The two youths were buried side by side in the Church of St. Basile in the city of Vyshgerod. Relating their tragic death, the Chronicle calls the two brothers "*Strastoterpzy,*" "*passion bearers.*"[3] This is the first time the expression "passion bearers" was used in a historic document. It has since then become the *keynote* of Russian sanctity and its highest ideal: not active heroism, not feats of valor, but nonresistance, in the image of Christ — "obedient unto death."

The story of Boris and Gleb as told in the *Povyest* is one of

[3] *Povyest,* pp. 91–93.

the masterpieces of early Russian literature.[4] As such it is a "must" for every student of medieval writings; even the communist godless have to read it if they want an academic degree in Russian antiquities. Both for believers and unbelievers this story has a strong appeal, and hundreds of years later we find its echo in Tolstoy's doctrine of "non-resistance to evil."

Boris and Gleb were canonized before their father, Vladimir, and their great-grandmother, Olga. They are the first Russian saints whom the *Povyest* eloquently describes as the two "morning stars of Russia." However, the procedure of their canonization raised certain difficulties. This procedure was still under Byzantine law which found no precedents for the case of Svyatopolk's two victims. They had not died confessing their faith and therefore could not be considered martyrs. They had performed no miracles during their lives or after death, neither had they been hermits nor missionaries. Their act of self-sacrifice, however sublime, could not fit into the framework of "heroic virtues." And yet, the people of Russia, who had known the two brothers and had witnessed their death, insisted that they *were* worthy of the Crown. And so after prolonged debates and hesitations, the Greek hierarchy gave in — the two brothers were canonized as *"Strastoterpzy."*

The names of Boris and Gleb (the latter scarcely known in the West) are very popular in Russia. Though representing two different personalities in life, they have become inseparable in suffering and death. Russian icons always represent the two brothers together, and churches are always dedicated to them both, as is the town which still bears their twin names: Borissoglebsk.

The murder of the two saintly brothers did not ensure for long Svyatopolk's rule in Kiev. Though he threatened to exterminate all his surviving brothers, he was defeated by one of them, Prince Yaroslav, who in 1019 became the legitimate prince of Kiev and one of the most remarkable rulers of his time.

Known in Russian history as Yaroslav the Wise, this prince was a worthy successor to Vladimir. His was the mind presiding

---

[4] The death and burial of Boris and Gleb are also represented most strikingly in ancient Russian miniatures (Radziville documents).

over Kiev's future development which was indeed the "Golden Age" of both religious and secular culture.

Yaroslav ended, for a time at least, the fatal feuds which had torn the realm of Kiev. He defeated not only Svyatopolk and his allies, but also the Petchenegs, the tireless nomadic tribe of the steppes, which constantly attacked Kiev and the adjoining territories. But Yaroslav is especially known for his peaceful political and civic activities. He initiated the codification of Russian law, which had been evolved by Varangian and Slavonic tradition. The new code, known as "Russian Truth"[5] limited the custom of blood vengeance, which still prevailed at that time, replacing the expiation of a crime by a fine or penalty. He also promoted the translation of Eastern canon law (*nomokanon*) to regulate ecclesiastical matters of the Kiev diocese.

Yaroslav continued his father's project — the embellishment of Kiev, by building a new basilica, St. Sophia. Like his father, Vladimir, he called Byzantine architects to his capital. The foundation stone was laid in 1036, but this famous shrine was completed only after Yaroslav's death. After the original structure was erected, St. Sophia was several times rebuilt and restored — from the strict Byzantine style of the eleventh century to the seventeenth century Ukrainian baroque. The original, central part and ground plan, however, remained almost intact until the second world war when it was heavily bombed.

As originally planned, St. Sophia had thirteen cupolas symbolizing Christ and His twelve Apostles. This is a most unusual arrangement, which, as Samuel Hazard Cross, expert on Eastern religious architecture points out, "has no Byzantine or Oriental parallel. . . ." "In its architectural silhouette," Mr. Cross goes on to say, "St. Sophia stands as an independent Russian artistic creation."[6]

Pursuing his cultural work, Yaroslav collected a great number of religious and learned books, thus founding the first Russian library. He opened schools and enrolled many students; mothers

---

[5] This body of laws was completed by Yaroslav's successors.
[6] Samuel Hazard Cross, *Medieval Russian Churches*, p. 12.

finally became accustomed to these educational improvements and no longer "mourned" for their children. Under Yaroslav's rule, the Kiev Church gained its independence from Byzantium. True, the Russian hierarchy was still subject to the Patriarch of Constantinople, but a Russian prelate, Hilarion, was appointed Metropolitan of Kiev in 1051.[7] The choice was a most fortunate one, for Hilarion was a highly cultured and spiritually gifted prelate. In his early monastic days he had lived as a hermit in a cave near Kiev. This was one of the caves which formed the initial hermitage, later destined to become the famous Kievo-Pechersk Laura. Hilarion combined excellently the contemplative and the active life: he was a man of deep spirituality, an able ecclesiastical leader, and an exceptionally gifted preacher and public speaker. In fact, his address on "Law and Grace," which is a theological sermon and a panegyric of St. Vladimir, is considered as the first example of Russian oratory. Another famous orator of that time was bishop Cyril of Turov, whose sermon "on the first week of Easter" dramatically exemplifies the joy of the Resurrection.

In Yaroslav's time also the first Russian monastery was founded in the caves of the Kiev hills. Eremitical life had been brought to this underground world by the monk Anthony, who followed the ascetic rule of the fathers of the desert. To Anthony came a youth, Theodosius by name, who became his disciple undergoing extreme mortification. We shall describe him later in greater detail.[8] For the present, it is enough that Theodosius can be considered as the founder of the great monastery, known up to this day as the Kiev-Pechersk Laura.[9] For it was Theodosius who continued Anthony's task after the latter's death; but he led the hermits out of the underground. He established his community *above* the original caves, and built under the open sky a church and the brethren's quarters; now they could be seen by everybody and could be visited by the faithful.

---

[7] The Metropolitan is the highest ranking hierarch after the Patriarch; his jurisdiction may extend to several dioceses, to a province, or even to an entire land.

[8] See Chapter Thirteen.

[9] *Laura* or *Lavra* is a community of cenobitic monks of strict observance but no longer living in seclusion, like the primitive hermits.

The new foundation drew the monks out of their solitude in order to make them aware of the tribulations and suffering of the outside world. Having become abbot of the new Pechersk Laura, Theodosius set a pattern according to the Greek *studite* monastic rule which was later followed by all Russian religious communities. The monastery observed contemplative life, prayer, manual labor, and strict fasting; at the same time Theodosius helped the poor, fed the hungry, and took care of the sick. Hundreds of beggars came to the monastery; on the other hand, wealthy men and women prayed at the shrines, attended mass and vespers, and brought generous donations of food and money.

Theodosius also received the visits of men in power, and of the ruling princes themselves. He often admonished them, reminding them of their religious and moral duties. This became necessary after the death of Yaroslav the Wise when his heritage was once more disputed as Vladimir's had been. One of Yaroslav's heirs, Izyaslav, turned against his brother in a relentless feud. Theodosius boldly rebuked him and was threatened with imprisonment and exile by the enraged prince; Izyaslav was, however, powerless against the good abbot's inflexible will to see that justice should be done.

The Pechersk Laura became a center of learning and scholarly works. One of Theodosius' contemporaries, the monk Nestor, together with a group of expert writers, began to keep the historical records of his time. These writings covering year by year the events of early Russian history, form the original Chronicle or *Povyest,* from which we have so often quoted.

The Pechersky Chronicle offers, indeed, considerable source material, which must, however, be carefully sifted, as many historians have done, and are still doing. Though the subtitle of the *Povyest* is: "Where the Russian land comes from," it actually begins with biblical times, i.e., with Noah's sons, the Russians having sprung, the Chronicle tells us, from the seed of Japheth. There follow the semilegendary records, as St. Andrew's voyage up the Dnieper and Oleg's death from his horse; then as we move from one century to the other, we have Vladimir's conversion, the baptism of his people, Yaroslav's reign, and the rest.

The *Povyest* brings us through the eleventh century, then other chronicles took over. There are several collections of Russian historical records done by monks of different monasteries and probably many times recopied. The Pechersky original version set the general rules for all similar records; it presents the following main features: first, a careful and attentive listing of events, as well as of "facts and figures," according to historical standards of that time; second, a broad and often colorful "coverage" of these events, combined with what, in terms of modern journalism, we might call the "human element"; third, a clear political approach, which stresses Russia as an entity held together by national consciousness. Last, but not least, the *Povyest* has a strong religious and moral undercurrent: political, national, and human interests are in the chronicler's mind subjected to God's will. It is *Providence* and not man which guides the course of history. Man, as a private individual and as a member of society, must obey the moral law and this law binds every citizen, as well as the ruler of the city.

We have seen Theodosius boldly condemning the feuds of Russian princes. The *Povyest* relates this episode, putting special stress on it; moreover, we find in the Chronicle a number of references to the religious and moral obligations of a Christian ruler. The Russian-Orthodox Church has often been said to be "passive" and "subservient" under the ferule of the State. The *Povyest* shows us that this was not always so: the medieval Russian Church was strongly opposed to injustice, tyranny, and bloodshed. However strong headed was Izyaslav, he had to bow to a monk, a man of prayer and contemplation. Another episode shows us the almighty prince knocking at the gate of the monastery and begging admittance, whereas Theodosius never closed the doors to the poor and the sick who could always be certain of his welcome. Thus the Chronicle reflects, as we see, a strong religious and moral factor in the building-up of Kiev, center of the Russian land.

But even apart from the ethical and spiritual angle, the *Povyest* has also a quite unique literary value. Just as the "orations" of

Hilarion and Cyril of Turov, the Pechersk story reveals excellent writing. Less than a century after the introduction of Church-Slavonic to Kiev, we have a literary monument of primary importance. Most outstanding among the pages of the *Povyest* are the two fragments attributed to Nestor: the life of St. Theodosius,[10] and the story of Saints Boris and Gleb.

*   *   *

Izyaslav, who defied Theodosius and was so severely rebuked by him, lost his throne to his brothers, who continued to fight among themselves. Some of them found allies in foreign lands — Hungary and Poland,[11] as well as in the camps of the Cuman, or Polovtzian nomad tribes, as powerful and deadly as the Petchenegs. This was indeed a tragic feud.[12] It was temporarily stemmed by Yaroslav's grandson, Vladimir Monomakh,[13] who called for a general alliance of all Russian princes, and was recognized as the legitimate heir of the throne of Kiev.[14] In spite of his being the one and supreme ruler of Russia, Vladimir Monomakh was no dictator. On the contrary, he was, perhaps, the last to symbolize the "golden age" of Kiev's Christian democracy. He also represented the ideal of the prince as promoted by the *Povyest*: a just and prudent ruler, mindful of moral principles and of the commandments of love and charity. We know a great deal about Vladimir Monomakh's exceptional Christian virtues from a historical document, the *Pouchenye*, or "Instructions" — a spiritual testament this prince left to his sons.[15] In the *Pouchenye*, Vladimir

---

[10] Theodosius was canonized soon after his death. Since he lived before the schism, he is recognized by Rome as a Saint of the Universal Church.

[11] Vernadsky, *History*, p. 37.

[12] After the death of Yaroslav, Russia was divided into so-called "principalities," governed by his sons and grandsons. This was not, however, a permanent distribution of land and power. The princes moved from one principality to another, according to the rule of seniority; their chief goal was the central capital, Kiev (Vernadsky, *ibid.*).

[13] *Monomakhos*, in Greek, means the *one* ruler. Vladimir's mother was a Byzantine princess.

[14] His crown, the "Monomakh hat," is still preserved in the Kremlin museum.

[15] "The Instructions" of Vladimir Monomakh are included in the *Povyest* under the year 1096; it has been conclusively proved, however, that this document was not composed by the monks of the Pechersky Laura, but is the original writing of Vladimir Monomakh.

Monomakh offers his sons not so much practical advice as a religious and moral code of Christian behavior. In these precepts, directly inspired by Scripture, Monomakh tells his heirs to "feed the destitute, to make gifts to the orphans, to defend the widows, and not to let the strong oppress the people, etc." The *Pouchenye* condemns violence whether exercised justly or unjustly: "do not kill the righteous nor the unrighteous," says Monomakh, "neither shall ye order the murderer to be slain. . . . When travelling through your lands, do not permit your servants or some other man's retinue to ravage the villages and fields, lest ye be cursed." And the *Pouchenye* further advises the princes to be ambassadors of good will: "Wherever ye stop on your way, bring the poor food and drink. Above all, respect the stranger, no matter whence he comes, whether common man, nobleman, or envoy. For wherever the traveller goes, he will speak of ye, either kindly or unkindly. Visit the sick, attend funerals, for we are all mortal. Do not pass a man without saying to him a kind word. Cherish your wives but let them not rule you." The last item of the *Pouchenye* may well make us smile, but it has an interesting angle. Monomakh's warning proves that in his time the Russian woman played an important role in her household. Whereas, later, in the fifteenth to the seventeenth centuries, Russian women were confined to the gyneceum.

Monomakh's instructions were addressed collectively to all his sons, since all of them were princes in their own right, and each was destined to rule a principality. Unfortunately, Monomakh's successors did not honor his Christian precepts. After his death, his crown (the bejeweled, fur-trimmed headgear exhibited today in the Kremlin museum) was disputed by Vladimir's numerous children, uncles, cousins, and nephews. These bitter feuds arose out of the so-called "law of seniority" which at that time prevailed in Russia. This law did not respect the primogeniture of the Grand Prince's direct descendants. It was the senior member of the Ryurikovich family in toto who was lawful heir to the throne of Kiev. The principle was not clearly defined, nor could seniority always be proved, still less defended, even by armed force. This led to continuous strife and bloodshed. Even when a senior mounted the Kiev throne, his rights continued to be disputed. The princes kept shifting from one principality to the other, forming alliances and often inviting their Western neighbors (Hungarians, Poles, and Lithuanians) or the nomadic tribes of the Steppes (the Cumens and the Petchenegs) to fight on their side. Some of these princes or princelets were powerless in this intensive competition. They lost their thrones, and were called *Izgoi*, i.e., "expellees," driven out of their own lands. This was a bitter humiliation which led to more hatred and foreign interventions. Several powerful centers were formed, now threatening Kiev, now joining the Grand Prince in his struggle against the *Izgoi*; the main centers were Novgorod in the North, the Galician principality in the West, and the cities of Vladimir in the Northeast.

Moscow was founded in 1156 by Monomakh's son, Yury Dolgoruky, Grand Prince of Kiev. For a long period of time, the small town on the river Moskva, from which it took its name, was used as a citadel against nomad incursions or *Izgoi* attacks. Not until two hundred years later did it become the capital of Russia, as Kiev had previously been. But long before the rise of Moscow, Kiev had ceased to be the seat of the Grand Prince. Its power had gradually waned because of the constant disputes around the throne. These disputes were excessively bitter and marked by extreme cruelty. Thus for instance, Vladimir Monomakh's grandson, Andrei Bogolyubsky, who was the rightful heir to the Kiev crown, had to wrest it from his uncle. He laid siege to the city, and having succeeded in capturing it, burned and plundered his own capital. In 1175, he transferred his seat to Vladimir, where he and his successors reigned. Andrei Bogolyubsky was himself savagely murdered in another feud. But before he died, he had consolidated and centralized the power of the Grand Prince, and even established a right of primogeniture. It was his lineage which became for more than three centuries the reigning branch of the Ryurikovichi.

This unifying process, often described by historians as the prologue of Russian absolutism, was actually an attempt to stem disintegration caused by the feuds. Other factors also worked for unity. One of them was the common language (vernacular and Church Slavonic) which was spoken in all the various areas of this as yet loosely knit nation. The other and, no doubt, the most important factor was the common faith shared by the people and their rulers. Even when the latter were at war with each other, the Church in Russia remained unshaken, and often intervened in order to reconcile the parties and to condemn their excesses. The Church herself was considerably strengthened; gaining her independence from Byzantium, electing her own hierarchy, and building her own cathedrals and monasteries. Neither must we forget that after the sack of Constantinople by the crusaders in 1204, Byzantium's wealth and influence began to decline. Political and economic ties on the "Great Waterway" were loosened, and Russia was, as we have seen, developing her own secular and religious culture.

*   *   *

The structure of the Byzantine world and of its diaspora, however, had been so solidly built in the preceding ages, that the Russian Church inevitably followed this declining world's destinies. Greek theology formed the Russian hierarchy's magister. The great Monastery of Mount Athos and its teaching[16] was the predominant factor in the shaping of Russian monastic life. The Basilian (Studite rule) was observed in all Russian religious communities, and is still followed in our days by monasteries in the Soviet Union as well as outside the U.S.S.R. All this means, on the one hand, that tradition was not broken: the Russian hierarchy received intact the doctrinal teaching of the first seven ecumenical councils. But, on the other hand, it means that the Russian Church sided, almost blindly, with the Greek hierarchy in the latter's quarrel with Rome.

Before Vladimir was baptized, Patriarch Photius had been in conflict with the Pope. Though a break was avoided at that time, the conflict marked the beginning of a dissent which lasted almost two hundred years, creating an ever growing bitterness on both

---

16 This teaching was essentially ascetic and mystic.

sides. The final separation took place in 1054, when the Pope's legates placed on the altar of Sancta Sophia the bull excommunicating Patriarch Michael Caerularius.

Briefly recalled, the reasons for this tragic event were as follows: Caerularius stirred anti-Western feelings; in his hostility to the Pope, he had the latter's name omitted from the Mass, and closed the Latin Churches of Constantinople. His antagonism led him to revive the main points of controversy already raised by Photius: the question of the procession of the Holy Ghost from the Father and from the Son (*Filioque*) as said in the Latin creed. This in Caerularius' as in Photius' opinion was an addition to the original Nicene Creed. Besides this dogmatic objection, there were others, particularly stressed by Caerularius: the usage of *azyme* (unleavened bread) in the Latin Mass; the omission of the word *Theotokos* (Mother of God) replaced in Latin prayers by "Holy Mary," and the forced celibacy of Latin priests. To these major criticisms, Caerularius added a number of minor ones, concerning vestments, liturgical colors, and many other usages adopted by Rome and contrary to Eastern tradition. Among the objections raised by the Byzantine Patriarch, some related to circumstances which had arisen at that time. Thus for instance, it was important to preserve the term Theotokos, because it was rejected by the Nestorian heresy.[17] Many minor complaints raised by Caerularius are long ago forgotten, but here again it is necessary to discover what lay beyond the letter of the dispute and formed its very core: this was the traditional symbolic meaning attached by the Eastern Church not only to the liturgy and to every word of the *Opus Dei,* but to the least of the customs and even to protocol, which accompanies it. The liturgy was not only an exalted form of worship, it was also a medium to illustrate dogma, to teach theology and catechism. This is why the Byzantine hierarchy was concerned as much with worship and custom as with dogma; in fact, as contemporary church-historians (Catholic, Greek, and Russian-Orthodox) point out, Caerularius did not actually raise

---

[17] The Nestorians asserted that Mary had given birth only to Christ the Man. Therefore the word "Mother of god" was essential in the eyes of Caerularius.

the question of the Pope's primacy and authority so much as that
of the Pope's liturgy.

No doubt, Caerularius' opposition to Rome bore an extreme
character and grew out of his misinterpretation of spiritual values
which the Western and the Eastern liturgies expressed in different
ways, but both faithfully preserved. Speaking of the bull of ex-
communication issued against Caerularius, the Catholic scholar,
Clement Englert writes:

> Historians question the prudence of Papal legates who should
> have remembered that the excesses of one poorly informed patriarch
> did not necessarily represent the thinking of the whole East. More-
> over, on July 16, 1054, Pope Leo IX, whom the legates represented,
> was already dead. Could they then still act in his name?[18]

Englert further points out that the legates did not excommunicate
the entire Greek Church, but only the patriarch, a Bulgarian
bishop, and Caerularius' chancellor who had gone so far as to
trample the Host because it was made of unleavened bread. But
the bull did mark a tragic rift, far wider and deeper than those
which had previously occurred. And yet, Clement Englert tells us
that the schism was actually completed only in the fifteenth century. Until then, "the Pope often received letters from Eastern
bishops asking him to decide points for them."

As to Russia, which had entered the Church scarcely more than
fifty years before the schism, she took Caerularius' decision for
granted without participating directly in his controversies. No
formal act of separation was issued by the Russian Church.

Let us here recall that the final rift between Rome and Byzantium took place when Russia had entered her own Golden Age.
Relations with the Holy See must have gone on for a certain
period of time, and remained undefined. This fact is recognized
both by Catholic and Orthodox historians. The daughter of Yaroslav the Wise, Princess Ann, married a Catholic King, Henry I
of France; she was crowned at Rheims; and the Slavonic gospel
which she brought with her is preserved among the treasures of

---

[18] Clement C. Englert, C.Ss.R., "Will Catholic and Orthodox Unite?" *The
Sign*, May, 1959.

Rheims Cathedral. Princess Euphrosinia, another Russian princess, lived in Rome and was canonized by Pope Gregory X, though there is no record of her adopting the Roman faith.

Despite these and quite a number of similar examples preserved by tradition, we should not underestimate the rift between the two churches, a rift which became wider and deeper from year to year, owing both to dogmatic and to psychological reasons. Russia was deeply smitten by disunion just as her Mother Church had been. And the responsibility for this disunion did not entirely rest with the East. There were misunderstandings and psychological mistakes on the side of the West as well. One of the most unfortunate occasions was the sack of Constantinople in 1204, by Western warriors during the Fourth Crusade. This act of vandalism including the destruction of many Greek-Orthodox shrines and the establishment of a Latin empire in the East, deeply shocked and revolted the Greek people. "From that day on," writes Father Alexander Schmemann, the well-known Russian-Orthodox historian and liturgist, "the separation of the Church ceased to be a quarrel of hierarchies and a theological quarrel — it entered for ever the flesh and blood of the Church's people and became the constant effect of the Churches' consciousness; 'Latinism' in the East, 'the Greeks' in the West became the synonyms of evil, heresy, hostility — they grew to be words of insult."[19]

But even this tragic development did not definitely destroy the lifeline binding the two *ecclesias*. Though separated from Rome, the Eastern Churches retained all the sacraments, Apostolic succession, and the Nicene Creed; so that her foundations were, and are to this day, considered valid by the Holy See. The great Russian religious thinker of the nineteenth century, Vladimir Solovyev, who became a Catholic, could therefore write about the Russian-Orthodox Church in which he was baptized.

Our religion is completely Catholic inasmuch as it is manifested in the faith of our people and in the liturgy. Insofar as the Russian Church preserves the true faith, the continuity of Apostolic succes-

---

[19] A. Schmemann, *The Historic Way of Orthodoxy.*

sion and the reality of the sacraments, she participates essentially
in the Unity of the Universal Church, founded by Christ.[20]

We shall have further opportunity to speak of this sacramental
survival, which Solovyev called the "hidden condition of unity."
To be sure, none regretted more than Solovyev that this hidden
unity had not become visible at the time when he lived. None
more than he wanted this continuity to be openly reasserted and
he worked for it with a prophetic intuition. For Solovyev knew
not only how deep was the wound of division, but also how strong
were Russia's religious roots — roots which had begun to sprout
almost as soon as the people were baptized. This is why Solovyev
put such an emphasis on popular faith. Without this fertile soil,
both Yaroslav's wisdom and Monomakh's ethics would not have
survived the bitter feuds of princes and the ravages of nomad
incursions. Soon a far greater ordeal was to test the strength of
the land of Russia and its spiritual reserves.

---

[20] Vladimir Solovyev, *The Russian Idea.*

CHAPTER FOUR

From the Mongol Yoke to the Rise of Moscow

IN 1223, the first encounter with the Russian princes and the Mongol forces of Ghengis Khan took place in the Steppes of the Don region. But the great wave of the Mongol invasion led by Khan Batu swept Russia seventeen years later in full force. Its terrible impact was felt throughout the entire land; cities were sacked, their people massacred, and their rulers killed in battle or forced to abandon their seats. Soon Vladimir, capital of the Grand Prince, fell to the invaders; its cathedral was burned down and its metropolitan[1] ruthlessly murdered.

This conquest which brought terror and devastation in its wake was long remembered by the Russians; it inflicted a deep wound to their national consciousness. After those tragic years, Russia lived in fear of invasion; and she was to relive this tragedy again and again, from the capture of Moscow by the Poles in the seventeenth century to Napoleon's campaign in the nineteenth, and two world wars in the twentieth.

As the Mongols advanced, the villages were burned and abandoned; palaces and shrines plundered; men, women, and children were destroyed en masse, except those who had fled in time. The people, as Klyuchevsky tells us, sought refuge in the woods — a fortified castle offered by nature. And to the woods they brought with them the only treasures which could be rescued and increased, their faith and their religious way of life, which they kept alive in their hearts. Dostoyevsky portrays this truly providen-

---

[1] The Metropolitan of Vladimir was *de facto* the head of the entire Russian Church.

tial survival, by saying that the Russian people's "main school of Christianity was the ages of endless suffering he endured in the course of history when . . . he remained alone with Christ the Comforter, whom he received then in his soul and who saved him from despair."[2] From that time on and for a period of nearly two hundred years the land of Russia was subjected to the severe hardships of the yoke of the Mongols, or Tatars, as they were called and as their descendants are still called in Russia.

These were, indeed, the most fateful years of Russian medieval history, for while invaded and conquered by the Mongols from the East, the country was also threatened by her Western neighbors. In 1240 (the very year of Batu's march on Russia) the Swedes attacked the city of Novgorod, which at that time was part of the domains of the Grand Prince of Vladimir. The Swedish army was met and defeated on the banks of the river Neva by young Prince Alexander who, because of that victory, was called Nevsky. Alexander Nevsky later became Grand Prince of Vladimir and once again defended the Russian land against Western enemies, this time, the Teutonic knights, a Germanic order of crusaders who together with another order of knights, the Livonian Sword Bearers, had conquered the pagan Lithuanian and Lett tribes of the Baltic.

The Teutonic and the Livonian knights were both filials of the Templars; they wore the emblem of the cross on their armor and shields, and were considered as missionaries come from the Holy Land to Christianize the Baltic regions. Actually these shores had already been peacefully evangelized, at least in part. The city of Riga, built by German tradesmen at the mouth of the river Dvina, was a prosperous port, a member of the Hanseatic league. But the crusading knights were eager to push forward. Though not supported by the Holy See, they had been called to the Baltic by Bishop Albert and claimed to bring Christianity to the pagans by "sword and fire." After completing the conquest of the seashore, they marched on the land of Russ ignoring the fact that its people had been Christian for more than one hundred fifty years, and regard-

---

[2] *Writer's Diary* (*see* Bibliography).

ing them as merely "schismatics." They surmised that the Russians, weakened by the Mongol invasion, would soon surrender. And so, once more Alexander Nevsky summoned his forces. It must have seemed that the odds were all against him. Not only was he under the impact of Mongol assaults, but his military equipment was inferior to that of the Teutons. The Knights wore heavy armor and formidable weapons, whereas Alexander's men had fragile coats of mail and primitive arms. But two powerful factors were on their side: national pride which survived the recent defeats inflicted by the Mongols, and the conviction of defending their faith against the pseudo missionaries. The decisive battle was fought on Lake Peipus which during this winter season was completely frozen and covered with deep snow. These conditions were favorable to the Russians and disastrous to the enemy. The steel clad knights and their armored steeds were bogged down or lost balance on the slippery terrain, or else crashed through the ice into the freezing waters. There is a strange analogy between these medieval "armored" troops and Hitler's panzer divisions stalled by the less heavily equipped Red army. The defeat of the Teutonic Knights on Lake Peipus has come down in history as the "ice slaughter." It has often been described or pictured by the Russians, from the first reports of "eyewitnesses," to the Soviet movie "Alexander Nevsky" directed by Eisenstein with a musical score by Sergei Prokofiev. For this battle has become the symbol of Russian defense and patriotic valor. It has also, unfortunately, become the symbol of the Russian-Orthodox versus the Catholic, attempting to proselytize their people with armed force. As to the communist antireligious propaganda machine, it saw an opportunity to mock the Catholic Church: the Soviet movie could portray and ridicule the Teutonic and Livonian Knights presented as covetous conquistadors. Research, however, has long ago toned down this crude picture. It is a matter of common knowledge that no Crusade was preached against Russia. The Knights acted on their own initiative. They held the Baltic shores and founded a powerful stronghold in East Prussia. But their march on Russia was more or less incidental. Moreover, not only Catholic scholars, but even a well-informed Russian historian[3] has pointed out that at the time of the "ice slaughter," it was not so much dogmatic conflicts, as the differences of rite and liturgical customs which the Russians and the Germans held against each other.

The fact remains, however, that this Western military expedition left a deep scar in Russia's national and religious consciousness. The earliest Russian records of the Swedes' assault against Alexander describe these invaders not as Swedish warriors, but as "Romans of the Midnight (Northern) lands." This implies that, like the Teutonic Knights, the Swedes were also of the Roman faith, and for that reason enemies of the Orthodox Russians.

Because of his heroic valor, exemplary life, and devotion to his faith, Alexander Nevsky was canonized by the Russian Church. Thus providentially the victor of Lake Peipus figures both in history textbooks of the official Soviet brand and in the Russian-Orthodox calendar.

*   *   *

On the banks of the Neva and of the icebound Lake Peipus, Alexander proved his strength to the West. But in the East, i.e., in his relations with the Mongols, he had to proceed with the greatest caution. After his military victories over the Swedes and the Germans he had to win a diplomatic victory over the khans. At that time, the wave of terror and plunder had receded in Russia. The Mongols had turned their attention elsewhere; they overran Poland and Hungary. Later they returned and made their headquarters at Sarai, on the estuary of the Volga and the Caspian sea. Sarai was not a city but a huge armed camp, for despite their victories, the Mongols were still nomads. In this camp, the khan held his court amid great pomp and magnificence, as described by the Franciscan monk Piano Carpini. In his zeal to convert the Mongols this intrepid voyager came all the way from Italy, crossing the Russian steppes till he reached Sarai soon after it had been founded. Carpini, who actually retraced St. Andrew's footsteps,

---

[3] D. Tolstoy (*see* Bibliography).

was unsuccessful in his mission of evangelization, but brought back invaluable information about the lords of Sarai.[4]

The Mongols, who worshiped idols and later became Moslems, were indifferent to the religion of the peoples they conquered. The devastation and burning of churches and shrines were not prompted by antireligious motives; they were designed to subdue the population by terror and to loot the treasures. Once their conquest was accomplished, they left the inhabitants alone, provided they paid tribute. The princes were made responsible for this heavy tribute. One by one they were summoned to Sarai to pay homage to the khan. Those who refused to submit were killed or enslaved. Alexander's own father had been poisoned. Now his turn had come to bow before the conqueror.

The victor over the Swedes and Teutons realized that he was no match for the powerful Mongol lords. He lay down his arms and began to negotiate. So did a number of other Russian princes. Through their obedience, more pretended than real, they saved Russia from further devastations. They gradually gained the khan's confidence and were even appointed tax collectors in their respective principalities. This afforded a considerable alleviation of the people's suffering, for until then the heavy dues were extorted from rich and poor by the *baskaks,* the dreaded Mongol officials reputed for their cruelty.

Meanwhile, other promising signs appeared in the devastated land. What remained of order and authority was gradually drawn to a new center. A city arose in the heart of the woods. Or more correctly speaking this city had stood there for a century or so without making itself conspicuous. Neither did its rulers, of the junior Monomakh lineage, join in the competitions and feuds of their senior cousins. This city, Moscow, now became the refuge and the undisputed seat of the surviving Russian elite and of the Grand Prince himself.

---

[4] Piano or Plano di Carpini was the first West European to visit the Mongols. While journeying through Russia he was well received and honored by the grand prince of Kiev. Carpini recorded his travels in his famous *Liber Tartarorum* (see Bibliography).

At the time of the Mongol invasion, Moscow was a cluster of wooden houses on the banks of two rivers; it took its name from the main of these two rivers, Moskva, or Moscow as we call it in English. As we have said, this small town in the heart of a dense forest had been founded in 1247, by Monomakh's son Yury Dolgoruky[5] as an outpost to defend the Suzdal-Vladimir territory from enemy incursions. Several times it was captured and devastated, but each time it was rebuilt and more strongly fortified. As the Mongols extended their sway over Russia, it was to this stronghold that political and military power, or what remained of it in Russian hands, began to move. The Russian hierarchy also moved to Moscow, though for a time the head of the Church still called himself metropolitan of Kiev and Vladimir. This shows the fluidity of Church and State after the triumph of the Mongol hordes; at the same time this very fluidity was the token of continuity and of an eventual concentration in a new environment.

Metropolitan Peter was first to establish his see in Moscow. He had known the horrors of the invasion and the gradual pacification which followed. Like Alexander Nevsky, he visited Sarai, opening negotiations with the khan and obtaining certain privileges for the church. Because of his many years of devoted service in the midst of calamity, he was called the "Sufferer for the Russian land." The Metropolitan prophesied that if a Church were built in Moscow in honor of our Lady, Moscow would become a great and powerful city. He was buried in this Church, and was canonized together with his successor, Metropolitan Alexis, whose relics are preserved until this day in the church of Epiphany. In June, 1949, the Moscow patriarch, also Alexis by name, celebrated Mass at the foot of these relics, as we see from a photograph published in the U.S.S.R.[6]

*   *   *

Alexander Nevsky's descendants consolidated the Russian State

---

[5] Or, as some historians assert, by his son Andrei Bogolyubsky. Yury Dolgoruky is, however, officially considered the founder of Moscow. His equestrian statue was erected in Moscow under the tsars and has been preserved by the Soviet Government (as shown in the Moscow guidebooks).

[6] Orthodox Calendar of Moscow Patriarchate (*see* Bibliography).

and continued his task of easing Mongol pressure. In the mid-fourteenth century, Grand Prince Ivan, firmly established Moscow's primacy over the other principalities. The Khan not only respected this primacy but entrusted Ivan with the direction of considerable financial affairs. The Moscow ruler was now to collect all tribute and hand it over to Sarai headquarters. Ivan, whose nickname *Kalita* meant "money pouch" in Greek, drew his own profit from these collections, part of which filled his coffers. With the money he began buying up land from his neighbors, the heads of smaller principalities. These lands passed under the sway of Moscow, together with their rulers. Other adjacent areas were conquered by Kalita, whose men at arms had grown in number, and had borrowed the methods of the Mongol army, based on a well-trained force of horsemen and archers. Even the weapons of the Moscow warriors[7] were copied from the Mongol arsenal. At the end of Kalita's reign, Moscow had increased her territories seven-fold. This gradual acquisition of land and merging of "lots," lent Russia a special character which marked her for many centuries — the character of a landed estate rather than that of a State. Kalita was not so much the ruler as the *landowner;* he was both master and manager of the estate. Hence a peculiar political and economic setup; the Moscow territory belonged to the prince alone; he had a title of ownership, given to him by God. "The land is God's," the "land is the prince's," such were the two principles on which primitive Russian economics were founded. The prince gave the land to whom he chose and could take it back as he chose. This is why, no doubt, as many sociologists point out, the Russian people did not have the strong and clearly defined sense of private property which we find in the West. This is not to say that no private ownership existed in medieval Russia. The petty rulers whose territories had been "integrated" into the Moscow principality retained some of their lands. Instead of reigning princes, they became "boyars," both wealthy and influential. They also retained the serfs who worked in their fields. But they had to be at the prince's beck and call, serve at his court, fight in his campaigns,

---

[7] Some of these weapons are still preserved in the Kremlin arsenal.

and furnish both men (serfs) and weapons to the prince's army.

The State also owned serfs, who were part of State economy, and worked in vast agricultural areas subject to the crown. These serfs had to fight, of course, in their prince's army, but their status differed in many ways from that of the slaves of the boyars.

In the days of Kalita, the Church too acquired land and other property which she received either from the Crown or through the donations of the faithful. And a special category of serfs worked on these ecclesiastical domains. Unlike the boyars, the Church had no obligations toward the State; though she gave away generously both money and food, these were voluntary contributions, distributed through the monasteries as alms to the needy and to the pilgrims. The time was near when the growing prosperity of the Church was to arouse the State's displeasure and jealousy.

Meanwhile, however, Church and State co-operated closely in the strengthening of Moscow and defiance of the Mongol lords. Moscow's political and military center was already in these days the Kremlin. Kalita rebuilt it as a fortified palace, using huge logs and beams of solid oak, surrounded with a stockade which later became a wall; the logs were firmly held together with clay, insulated with moss, and the inner chambers of the palace were heated with brick stoves. But while Kalita used wood for his palace, he built two Cathedrals in stone. The metropolitan's house was also built in stone. This shows us the high esteem accorded the Church in these days, even higher perhaps, than in the time of Kiev. It also disproves the theory, maintained by some historians, that the Russian Church was always "subservient" to the secular power. There were periods in Russia's history when the Church dominated the secular scene; it made an equal or even greater contribution to the formation and defense of civilized society.

After Kalita's death, his grandson Dimitry became the ruling prince. He continued the work of consolidation symbolized by his rebuilding of the entire Kremlin in stone quarried in the immediate vicinity of Moscow. These quarries offered for many centuries the gleaming white limestone from which so many houses, churches, and fortifying walls were built or rebuilt in the city. This is why it is so often called in Russian folk song and poetry, "Moscow of the white stones." Tall, gleaming white towers pierced with embrasures rose above the crenelated white Kremlin walls. Though later destroyed, these watchtowers were reconstructed and still stand where Prince Dimitry placed them. They remain the typical features of Moscow's fortified palace, as do the strong iron gates protecting every entrance. These gates, the ramparts, and the deep moat surrounding the prince's abode were set up to protect him from the Mongol attack which still threatened him if he failed to pay sufficient tribute.

In this fourteenth century stronghold, Russia's twentieth century dictator, Stalin lived, continuously afraid of assault and treachery. He spent the many years of his reign literally entrenched and strictly guarded.

To Dimitry's new buildings another church, St. Lazarus, was added. Though most of the constructions put up by him have long since crumbled and were replaced by others, St. Lazarus remained hidden beneath the ruins, to be discovered and excavated from the rubble some five hundred years later. This church is considered as the Kremlin's oldest monument.

Prince Dimitry was no less shrewd than his grandfather, but he presents to the historian's scrutiny a far nobler and more refined nature. Deeply devoted to his country as well as to his Mother Church he often sought the advice of Metropolitan Alexis. Together they examined every angle of the problem which was the main object of their preoccupation: the liberation of Russia from the Mongol yoke. Dimitry also often consulted a man who lived in the woods some thirty miles from the capital, near the town of Radonezh. His name was Sergius and he was a monk residing with a few brethren in a small hermitage built by their own hands. This man became one of Russia's greatest saints.

A new type of monasticism had appeared in Russia. After the terrible devastations caused by the Mongols, the Russian people, as we have seen, had fled to the woods. With them came also the "holy men," the hermits. They were not seeking safety, neither did they wish to build new cities; they were called "seekers of

silence," and they settled far away from the other refugees, in
their *pustyny* or deserts. The Russian monk gave this name to
the thick of the woods, the wilderness, where he led a life of
solitude, mortification, and prayer like the *desert fathers* of Egypt
or Palestine. St. Sergius was one of the first to seek out such a
"desert" where he spent many years alone before founding a
monastic community, the Abbey of the Holy Trinity.

The life of St. Sergius has been related by one of his contemporaries, Epiphanius the Wise. We have, therefore, a vivid picture of this holy man, who possessed to the highest degree the
heroic virtues. He was born in Rostov of noble parentage and
was given the name of Bartholomew. Under the impact of the
Mongol invasion he fled with his parents to the Moscow region
and grew up in the town of Radonezh. Wandering one day in the
nearby woods he met an old man wearing the black robe of a
monk who offered him a piece of consecrated bread and predicted
that he would one day serve the Holy Trinity. Then he vanished
filling the young boy with wonder. This scene in the deep Russian
forest, full of beauty and mystery was depicted in the nineteenth
century by the famous painter Nesterev in his picture: "The
vision of the youth Bartholomew."[8] From that day on the boy
began to lead a life of deep devotion and soon joined his brother,
a monk, in one of the neighboring monasteries. But this too easy
and secure community life did not satisfy him for long. He per-
suaded his brother to retire with him to the wilderness of Radonezh
where they could pray in silence and severe mortification. So the
two brothers left the monastery and found a secluded place in
the deep woods. This was to be their "desert." They built for
themselves two cells or log cabins, and a chapel which the local
bishop consecrated in the name of the Holy Trinity. Bartholomew's
brother, however, unable to endure the hardships of the "desert,"
soon returned to his monastery.

Bartholomew was now completely alone, but he did not waver.
He remained in his cell, praying and fasting, living on a few

---

[8] Though essentially a painter of religious pictures, Nesterev is held in high
esteem in the U.S.S.R.

vegetables he cultivated on the arid soil, and the crusts of bread which pious peasants brought him from time to time. He was visited by some troublesome guests: a robber tried to steal his belongings but found that it was scarcely worth his while to take away from the hermit the little he possessed. A hungry bear prowled around the cell, the hermit shared his breakfast with the wild beast and soon tamed it. Far more terrifying were the assaults of the devil who tried to invade the hermitage, but was each time repulsed. After a long period of probation, Bartholomew at last felt ready to take vows. He made his monastic profession in the presence of an abbot, and was given the name of Sergius. Later he was ordained a priest but continued for a long time to live in his former solitude. Little by little, however, some other hermits joined him in his "desert," where they formed the small community of Radonezh in order to lead a life of prayer, contemplation, poverty, and labor. Sergius was elected abbot but insisted on following as formerly the way of humility and self-abasement. He was so poorly clad that the pilgrims who began to flock to the monastery mistook him for a beggar. He built his brethren's cells, cutting down the trees and carrying heavy logs on his shoulders; he was continually giving an example of *ora et labora,* plowing, sowing, digging, threshing the grain, and doing many other chores which the brethren were often reluctant to perform. Because of his great meekness, he was called "the abbot without authority." But in reality he not only led his community toward the highest goals but he also formed them admirably. Despite the manual labor which was so often exhausting, he devoted considerable time to study; he was a scholar and theologian, and above all a great spiritual director. Sergius prepared *an entire monastic generation,* which not only continued his work at Holy Trinity, but also went out to other "deserts" to found new communities. Thus, the Russian pioneer monks of the fourteenth century spread Christian culture and civilization to faraway regions and to the very shores of the White Sea. These pioneers were often followed by laymen, who established their own agricultural settlements around the monasteries. This started the migration of many thousands of men and women — a peaceful colonization, which was at the same time a great missionary enterprise. For as the spiritual sons of St. Sergius pushed onward, they found the pagan tribes of the Arctic land. The monks brought to these primitive people not "the fire and Sword," but the word of God. One of the greatest missionaries of the Russian North was St. Stephen of Perm, a contemporary of St. Sergius, who evangelized one of these Northern tribes, the Zyranye, and composed an alphabet for them.

*   *   *

As we have said, Dimitry, Grand Prince of Moscow, frequently visited St. Sergius and sat at his table in consultation. It was on the abbot's advice that he undertook one of his most urgent tasks, the pacification of the princes who had been expropriated or dominated by Ivan Kalita, and who after his death resumed their fierce quarrels for the throne. Dimitry ably negotiated with his cousins, and still retained the right of primogeniture, which was now firmly established in the line of the Moscow rulers. Common interests had finally brought the enemy princes together under Dimitry's leadership. This meant the stiffening of Russian resistance to the Mongols. Should this resistance grow into open attack? This was the gist of the problem discussed by Dimitry and Sergius. For a long time the abbot of the Holy Trinity preached caution, insisting that the time had not come to act, instructing Dimitry to be patient. Meanwhile the prestige of the holy man grew from day to day. When metropolitan Alexis died, Sergius was offered his place. He refused to accept it, but agreed to come to Moscow for a consultation with the grand prince concerning his plans against Sarai. And so, after many years of seclusion, the holy abbot left his monastery for a while to answer Dimitry's call. He went on foot, leaning on his staff, clothed in his tattered black robe, like the begging monks he met on his way. After his visit to the princely court, Sergius returned to Holy Trinity observing the rules of poverty and humility. Not only did he refuse all gifts and honors, he would not even receive the blessing of the

Patriarch of Constantinople, saying that he was unworthy of so great a favor.

In 1380, the abbot of Holy Trinity made a decision which was to have great importance both for Russian history, and for the history of the Russian Church. Khan Mamai, who reigned at that time in Sarai, exacted a heavy tribute which the Russian princes refused to pay. The Mongols mustered a great force to punish their disobedient vassals. But thanks to their reconciliation, the princes were now ready to prove their solidarity. Once more Dimitry asked Sergius to bless an armed attack; this time the holy man granted his blessing, predicting a hard won victory. The battle was fought on September 8 on the field of Kulikovo.[9] Mamai was defeated, and for the first time the Russians had the upper hand in their struggle against the khans. Meanwhile, as his biographer tells us, Sergius had assembled his brethren in the monastery hall, miles away from Kulikovo. As the battle was fought, the saint named one by one the warriors who had fallen on Dimitry's side and prayed for the souls of the departed. Sergius' life story tells of other episodes showing that he had the supernatural power to be informed of things at a distance. Thus for instance, one day, as he sat with his monks in the refectory he greeted St. Stephen of Perm, the missionary of the North, who was passing by but had no time to stop at the monastery. Sergius was granted visions of the Holy Virgin, and one day a beam of light fell on the chalice from which he took communion. Some of the brethren knew this or had even seen it with their own eyes, but he forbade them to speak of it to anyone.

At the end of Sergius' life, the monastery had grown in size and the number of monks increased from year to year. Holy Trinity became the center of many pilgrimages. After his death the holy abbot's relics were placed in the church, and it was for this sacred shrine that the great artist Rublev painted the famous icon of the Holy Trinity, a masterpiece of Russian medieval art.[10]

---

[9] Kulikovo was in the Don area. Dimitry was therefore called Donskoy.
[10] Today the icon is in the Trediakovsky Gallery in Moscow.

Sergius of Radonezh was canonized by the Russian Church; by a special decision of the Holy See he has also been recognized as a saint of the Universal Church. Not only is he especially venerated by the faithful, but he is also, like St. Alexander Nevsky an outstanding figure of Russian history. It is impossible to speak of the victory at Kulikovo without recalling the important part played by the abbot of Holy Trinity in the decision taken at that time by Grand Prince Dimitry.

This is one of the reasons why the Abbey of the Holy Trinity near Zagorsk has been permitted by the Soviet Government to reopen its doors. Thousands of pilgrims visit once more the shrine of St. Sergius and tourists are encouraged to make a trip to the Abbey; in fact, it is almost a "must" on the intourist program.

*   *   *

After the battle of Kulikovo, the Mongols still retained their sway for a hundred years, but the entire atmosphere of Moscow gradually changed. Dimitry's successors consolidated their estate, centralizing power more and more in their hands. At the same time they were drawing nearer to the forms of an autocratic government.

The nature of the Moscow State has often been discussed. Some historians and political writers see in the Moscow pattern the characteristic features of the *Mongol governmental system:*[11] a strongly unified military and bureaucratic machine under an omnipotent kahn. Others contend that Moscow had become even in the early days a replica of Byzantium — i.e., Church and State almost blended together.

We can but briefly examine these two schools of historic analysis. There is no doubt that Mongol influence molded in part Moscow's government institutions. Modern research has discovered in Russia, definite traces of Mongol administrative, financial, and even judicial systems. For a Mongol Code of law existed already at the time of Genghis Khan. The methods of taxation enforced by the *Baskaks* were drastic but efficient. A commercial route by caravan linked Sarai with Asia, bringing to Russia not

[11] Vernadsky (*see* Bibliography).

only tea, silk, and other Chinese products, but also Chinese civilization. Last but not least, recent excavations in the Sarai region have revealed the remnants of advanced Mongol technology — such as ceramic kilns, canalization, central heating, hydraulic power mills, dams, mints; specimens of merchandise from foreign lands, which the Mongols used for decorating their homes, were also found in those excavations. For though their way of life was still nomadic, the khans' court had acquired an almost stable aspect. Even following their defeat at Kulikovo it could have seemed that they had come to stay forever. Actually, however, the yoke which had weighed so heavily on Russia was broken under Dimitry. Not only was the enemy weakened, he was losing ground by a process of absorption. The invader was slowly disarmed and ceased to be an alien body threatening the land he had invaded. The Russian princes were no longer forced to kneel before the khan, nor did they pay him the large amounts of tribute previously exacted. They even "infiltrated" the khan's capital, Sarai, where a Russian diocese was established in 1261. One of the khans, Ouzbeg, married a Greek princess, and his daughter married prince George of Russia.

On the other hand, long after the military and financial control of the Mongols began to decline, their influence left its imprint on various branches of Russian life and customs. A number of Mongol words were incorporated into the Russian language — words dealing with administration, finance and communications, animal life, horses and horsemanship. In short, Mongol expressions defined material objects and the practical order of things which the conqueror superimposed on the original Russian pattern. Another important factor was the intermarriage of Mongols and Russians and the gradual integration that followed. Many Mongols became part of the Russian people. While some of the invaders remained pagans or Moslems, many were baptized and founded Christian families. They were completely Russified and their names acquired Russian endings and inflections.[12] Those who

---

12 B. Nikitine, who made a study of this subject gives a number of well-known Russian family names of Mongol origin. Among them we find the name of the famous pianist and composer Rakhmaninov (*see* Bibliography).

were former khans, changed their title to that of prince or boyar.

The process of integration went on until the sixteenth century, when the Mongol empire declined and the lords of Sarai lost all control over Russia. Their influence is doubtlessly a factor in the development of the Russian nation, its culture, art, and language.

However, the Byzantine tradition was even more closely tied up with Medieval Russia; we cannot but see its predominance not only during the "Golden Age" but even under the Mongols. At the height of their power the Sarai rulers, as we have seen, were pagan and later acquired a strong Moslem strain. Yet neither paganism nor Islam prevailed in Russia — but the firmly anchored and deeply rooted Church of St. Vladimir and St. Sergius.

If, in the beginning, strict Byzantine ecclesiastical tradition was transmitted to Russia, we know that already in its "Golden Age," Kiev had asserted its own creative and independent spirit. This spirit was kept alive mainly through the Church first in Kiev, then in Vladimir and Moscow; thus the Church rose from her ashes together with her people.

We may, therefore, conclude by saying that the Russian national mind and character have been formed almost simultaneously by several decisive influences; they were shaped by all these elements during the middle ages, in the days of struggle, defeat, chaos, or victory. The factor of the Church presented continuity, thus offering a foundation for Russia's further development.

CHAPTER FIVE

The Pageant of the Kremlin

RUSSIAN history, as we have already seen, often took sharp turns, sometimes proceeding by leaps and bounds. Eons seem to divide the scene of Mongol havoc and devastation from the "white walls" of Moscow gleaming under a cloudless sky. This sky was to be filled with triumphant rays of light, then once more obscured by heavy clouds of tragedy.

In this oft changing panorama, the continuity of the Church, as already mentioned, remained a striking element. However, this does not mean that the Church and its seat, transported to Moscow, did not share the storms and struggles which so often interrupted the "Pageant of the Kremlin." On the contrary, as years went by, the fate of Church and State became ever more closely linked. Moscow was now the seat of the grand prince, who *de facto* ruled vast territories, and it was also the seat of the metropolitan whose primacy was recognized by all the prince's subjects. This primacy was undefined, since Russian prelates were still under the authority of the patriarch of Constantinople. But the Moscow Church was acquiring more and more the character of an autocephalia (autonomy). The prince and the Metropolitan together with Monastic support (St. Sergius) had freed Russia from Mongol pressure, and the people regarded them as the builders of Russian strength and independence. The very fact that not only Prince Dimitry, victor of Kulikovo, had acted with the blessing of a great saint, but that his successors turned for advice and approval to the Church, made it an essential factor in the nation's life.

However, Russia was not as fully stabilized as might appear

on the surface. There still remained vast areas which were not subject to the "hat of Monomakh," as the Moscow crown, received from Kiev, was called. As a matter of fact, Kiev itself was not under the Moscow sway, but was part of the Lithuanian State. Toward the middle of the fourteenth century, the Lithuanian princes had occupied a considerable part of Western Russia. Many cities of the region, including Kiev and Chernigov, weakened by Mongol invasion, were easily conquered by their strong and well-armed neighbors. Often Lithuanian alliances were sought by Russian princes against the Mongol lords. Soon the Lithuanians held all Russian principalities west of the Dnieper as well as other territories stretching to the Black Sea. When in 1386 the Lithuanian grand prince Yagailo was offered the Polish throne and accepted it, he was converted to the Roman Catholic faith together with his nobility. Part of the Russians followed their example, but most of them (especially the vast majority of the people) remained Russian Orthodox. West Russian regions, together with Lithuania, were gradually drawn into the Polish (Western) orbit, and their destiny was in many ways different from what constituted so clearly, already at that time, the world of Moscow. Kiev had a metropolitan of its own, even at the time when the Moscow prelates still called themselves "Metropolitans of Kiev" *in partibus*. Actually two political and ecclesiastical authorities divided Russia. Kiev was now part of the Western diaspora, being geographically and politically close to the latter's boundaries.

From Lithuania, and more so from Poland, the Catholic World came in contact with Western Russia; its presence was to be from that time on almost constantly felt, not in Kiev alone but in Moscow as well. This meant that Latin influences reached Russia indirectly. They were made manifest in the field of theology in its Thomistic presentation, and of the humanities which had reached a high degree of development in the west. Russia, which had been cut off from them almost entirely by the Mongol "iron curtain," could now benefit from them. But the proximity of another, in part alien, "Westernized" people, created tensions which increased as both the Moscow State and the Moscow Church became firmly established and centralized.

This tension grew when political and military conflicts arose between Russia, Lithuania on the one hand, and Poland on the other. As to religious dissensions, they became strong and dramatic enough when the Russian Orthodox and the Catholics started disputes (at the time of the Council of Florence and later). The conflict was further complicated at the time of the Reformation. The Eastern Churches, as we know, were not directly affected by this crisis. But they did receive some of its impact at a distance. Russia too was stirred and her Church challenged to enter into the great spiritual disputes as they kept arising.

Kiev became an important meeting ground for these various currents. It still retained under the Poles and Lithuanians much of the religious and cultural pattern of Yaroslav's Golden Age. It was not Latinized. In later years it frequently took the side of Moscow against Poland or remained neutral. When in the eighteenth century Kiev was joined to the Russian territory, it did not need to be "Russified," for it had the same faith, the same language,[1] the same Byzantine liturgy as Moscow. Even the Ruthenian Uniates who were to recognize the authority of the Holy See in 1591, retained their rite. However, despite this obvious cultural and spiritual unity, the two people, great and little Russians (or Ukrainians, as they are more often called today) did not entirely merge; and conflicts arose between them at every critical moment of their history.

Another territory which remained for some time outside the Moscow diaspora was the land of Novgorod, that is the vast area subject to this important Northern commercial center. Though Novgorod, like all other Russian territories, was governed by a prince, it had a long tradition of independence. Novgorod was a city of merchants, who were both wealthy and astute; they traveled far along the great waterways to Byzantium and across the lakes and rivers of the north which led to economic expansion.

---

[1] With but comparatively few phonetic and idiomatic differences, which grew when the modern classical Russian language was definitely formed at the end of the eighteenth century.

Yaroslav the wise had granted them a special charter: they had the right to elect their own officials, including the *posadnik* or mayor. The townsmen were actually invested with powers greater than the prince who, in fact, could retain his crown only with the citizens' approval. Novgorod had its assembly or *Veche* at which State and economic problems were dealt with and which was held in the market place. The *Veche* was summoned, whenever such problems arose, by the ringing of a bell. It was the first pattern of a free Russian democracy.

This city, which kept out of feuds and intestine quarrels, was also spared the devastations inflicted by the Mongols on other Russian cities. The invaders had almost reached the gates of Novgorod, but turned back because of the marshes which surrounded it. It was Novgorod, which, led by Alexander Nevsky, defeated the Swedes and the Teutonic Knights. Because it was a busy port, it became a member of the Hansiatic League. Last, but not least, the citizens of Novgorod chose their own Archbishop who exercised his authority not only in ecclesiastical, but also in civil and in judicial affairs. He had his court of justice and it was he who settled local disputes which neither prince nor mayor could resolve. If scenes of violence broke out, as they often did — for the citizens of Novgorod were headstrong and turbulent — the archbishop came out in solemn procession with cross and banner, fully vested, to pacify the mob.[2] The magnificent Cathedral in which he officiated was, like the Kiev basilica, dedicated to St. Sophia. Novgorod had its own school of church architects and icon painters.

Thus, this city, one of the most ancient in Russia, could well be proud of its independence and of the high degree of its cultural development. Its citizens came to consider it as a commonwealth in its own right, as a sovereign, and almost — as a living person. They called it: "Lord Great Novgorod."

As Moscow grew, developing not only its own centralized government but also its own culture, it would not admit such a

---

[2] Political or economic disturbances were fought out on a bridge spanning the river Volkhov. These combats sometimes took the form of riots or were fought out singlehanded.

neighbor, or such a rival as Novgorod. The lordly city was partly conquered, partly absorbed at the end of the fifteenth century by the Moscovite state. Moscow also took over the Northern hinterland which had been for so long the "warehouse" of the Novgorodian merchants. Now Moscovite settlers and monastic colonizers replaced them. The abbeys of Solovki on an island off the White Sea shore and of Valaamo on Lake Ladoga became the outposts of the Church.

However, the spirit of the Veche, of the Novgorod "freedom bell" did not die out; it was transferred to other places, took other forms and names. It came to be known as the *Volnitza*, which means a bold, dynamic, unbridled spirit — limitless as the Russian Steppes.

It is against this background of the *Volnitza* and of conflicting forces of the periphery, that we must see the gradual hardening of Moscow rule. It is no longer the management of a small "estate" saved by a prudent administrator from national disaster. It has become the nation itself. True, documents of that time do not as yet refer to this nation as *Rossiya* (Russia) but as *Russkaya Zemlya* (the Russian Land), the word "land" in Russian meaning in this case not so much a country as the Latin "terra."[3] But this land was acquiring from year to year the features of a strong and already *de facto* autocratic State. Not alone Novgorod, but other, formerly independent, territories like the principalities of Perm and Riazan became part of the Moscow domain; they were now all governed according to a system in which, as we have seen, the Mongol bureaucratic pattern supported by armed force could be clearly traced.

*   *   *

A parallel of the "hardening" is also found in the Church of that time. If the first Metropolitans of Moscow offered the example of great sanctity, their successors were more concerned with building up their power than with developing the spiritual life of the faithful. Paradoxically enough the Russian land, which had a spiritual flowering during the early medieval period (before

---

[3] To denote a country the word *"Strana"* would be used.

the Mongols), entered the "dark ages" after Kulikovo. Instead
of spreading Christian culture as the monks of Kiev had done,
the Church did little in the fifteenth century to promote it, being
mostly concerned with ritual and the pomps of ceremonial; and
there she zealously re-established her prestige. The study of theology was but a secondary preoccupation; Christian morals were, so
to say, "taken for granted"; they were taught according to elementary rules based on quotations from Scripture, which had
become mere aphorisms and proverbs; they could be endlessly
repeated and copied out by scribes and pharisees.

This situation was the more deplorable because the aftermath
of the many feuds which had torn Russia, as well as of the crude
methods applied under the Mongol rule, had led to a corruption
of morals in every class of Russian society. Brutality, struggle for
power, the coveting of riches and titles, the fast growing habit of
solving every conflict by force, such were the characteristic traits
of the ruling class — the boyars, the military commanders, the
governors of towns, and other officials. As to the people, they
had been so long mistreated by the Baskak (the Mongol tax col-
lector) and later by the Russian administrators who imitated the
Khans' methods, that they either lived in fear and trembling,
or rebelled, while others sought a compensation in cheating and
robbery. Such was the sad picture which must be placed, alas,
next to the Kremlin's brilliant panorama. The Church herself,
shaken by the tragic events of the preceding century, was unprepared to meet the moral challenge. Still less could she deal with
the vast religious problems which were raised outside her borders,
but with which she soon became directly concerned.

In 1439, the Council of Florence marked the return of the
Patriarch of Constantinople to the Holy See of Rome. Metropolitan Isidore represented Russia at the Council and signed its decrees. When the news of his adherence to Rome reached Moscow
it aroused a turmoil. The clergy, the people, and the grand prince
himself regarded the decisions taken by the Patriarch of Constantinople as an apostasy. Unaware of the theological implications of the Council and being completely unprepared to meet

them, the Russian Church could only turn away from them. She had been for such a long time cut off from the Christian world, including not only Rome, but also Byzantium that she had lost almost entirely the ecumenic spirit and had lived in splendid isolation. She had jealously guarded the Christian heritage received in pre-Mongol days, and this had demanded great heroism and devotion. Indeed, it meant preserving against tremendous odds Scripture and Tradition, Patrology, the decisions of the seven Councils, the sacraments, and the liturgy. But it also meant perpetuating, as in a tightly sealed vessel, all the germs of hostility between East and West born from the days of Photius to the final separation of Caerularius. That such a separation could cease and unity be restored seemed to the Russian Orthodox a temptation to be rejected, a deadly peril to be avoided, the snare of the devil himself. This was moreover the ruin of Byzantium's unique and hitherto *undefiled* authority.

Until then, we must remember, Russia had virtually not been under any other authority than that of her Mother Church. Rome was far away, and if not completely alien, was almost unknown.[4] The many points raised by Caerularius in the eleventh century (and the Russian Church still lived in that century) had been, as we have seen, not so much dogmatic as relating to liturgy and custom. But to the Russian religious mind these issues seemed as vital and sacred as the points of dogma on which Photius had insisted. The Council of Florence had pronounced against both the dogmatic and the nondogmatic objections of the Eastern Church; it had maintained the *Filioque* and the teaching about purgatory, rejected by the East. And it preserved the use of unleavened bread, the celibacy of priests, fasting on Saturday,[5] and

---

[4] Historians often point to the Latin missionaries, like St. Boniface, St. Bruno, Piano di Carpini, and others who visited Russia in the middle ages. They also recall the relations of Russian princes with Rome, or the mention of the Holy See in ancient Russian documents and even legend. Without seeking to minimize the value and interest of such contacts, we should not look upon them as signs of an actual and durable rapprochement. The curtain between Russia and Rome was but occasionally raised and remained mostly drawn. This explains the shock felt in Moscow at the time of the Florentine Union.

[5] Fasting on Saturday was at that time prescribed by the Western Church and later kept only on ember days and on the Easter Vigil.

the other rules which the Christians of the East did not observe. The difference of rites and of canonical law also seemed irreconcilable. That these problems should find a peaceful solution never even entered the field of speculation, until the decrees of the Council were signed at Florence. When this event took place, Russia had to face a possible union as something quite unexpected generally speaking. And because of this very fact the primacy of the Pope, so long ignored by Russia, was reaffirmed as alone able to operate such a union. This emergency was not only uncalled for but unwelcome. The decisions of the Council were received in Moscow with indignation, and by many — even with horror. Upon his return from Constantinople, Metropolitan Isidore was deposed and fled to Kiev. Some time after these dramatic events, Constantinople too rejected the Florentine Union. But even having thus "redeemed" herself at the eleventh hour, the Byzantine Church had lost face in the eyes of Russia. The Patriarch of Constantinople, who had betrayed Orthodoxy, ceased to be the undisputed authority he had formerly been. The Russian Church no longer wished to depend on him, for it was Moscow and not Constantinople which had withstood "temptation" and guarded the pure faith. Until the Council of Florence, the metropolitan of Moscow was nominated by the patriarch of Constantinople. After the fall of Isidore, the Russian bishops themselves in 1449 elected his successor, metropolitan Jonas. Constantinople was informed of the election but was not requested to confirm it. Byzantium accepted the *fait accompli* without protest. This was the beginning of Russia's *autocephalia.*[6]

The second event which changed the destinies of Moscow and became at the same time a great landmark of world history, was the conquest of Constantinople by the Turks in 1453. Moscow regarded this catastrophe as a just punishment for the even temporary acceptance of the Florentine Union. But here much more than ecclesiastical affairs or even questions of dogma was at stake. Byzantium, which blended Church and State into one, was a theocracy in the fullest sense of the word. It was the *Second*

---

[6] As pointed out by A. Schmemann (*see* Bibliography).

Rome, both as an empire and as an Ecclesia. Now that it was no more, Moscow alone seemed worthy to accept its heritage. Soon the Moscow State was to call itself "The Third Rome."

The flowering of the Russian nation as a political and economic entity was also hastened by the rapid decline of Mongol power. Already for a number of years, and even decades, the khans had been losing their hold on Russia. This was not so much a capitulation as a withdrawal into the Asiatic hinterland. The Mongol forces gradually melted away. There still remained a few "islands" of their former empire. One of the islands was Sarai, which from a nomad camp had grown into a city; today this city figures on the map as Astrakhan, the main Russian port on the Caspian sea. Another important center was Kazan, founded upstream on the bank of the Volga. This city also remained in the hands of the Mongols after their main armies had receded. Astrakhan and Kazan were conquered in the mid-sixteenth century by Tsar Ivan the Terrible. However part of the population of the two cities remained Mongol or "Tatar" as the Russians called and still call their former conquerors. Under Soviet rule, this city has become the capital of the Tatar Autonomous Soviet republic. There are many Tatars, most of them Moslem, among its inhabitants; they have their mosques and minarets next to the Russian Orthodox churches.[7]

The Mongol yoke having been definitely broken in the early sixteenth century, Russia emerged; she was enjoying her newly gained power and freedom, while proud Byzantium was humbled and her imperial dynasty brought to ruin. Moscow did not hesitate to accept the magnificent inheritance.

This inheritance received from the fallen empire was strikingly exemplified when, in 1505, the grand prince of Moscow, Ivan III, married Sophia Paleologue, the niece of the last Byzantine emperor. After her uncle's death on the ramparts of besieged Con-

---

[7] The Moslem quarter of a city on the Volga has been vividly pictured in the novel of the Russian writer, Sergei Maximov, who was a skipper on the Volga boats and later came to America. This novel, *The Unquiet Heart,* gives a cross section of the population of the middle-Volga area, rarely described in modern Russian fiction.

stantinople, Sophia had fled to Rome, where she had been reared as a Catholic princess under the auspices of the Holy See. But the young girl was still attached to her Byzantine memories. When the marriage was arranged, it was believed in Rome that Sophia would bring the Catholic faith to Moscow. Instead, it was Byzantium which she helped to revive at her husband's court. As a reigning princess of Moscow she had to return to the Greek-Orthodox faith and was wed in the Kremlin Cathedral. Many scholars, artists, and high ranking nobles from Constantinople accompanied Sophia to her new country. Soon the court of Ivan III resembled the splendors of the Paleologues. The prince adopted the Byzantine double-headed eagle — the emblem of the Basileus and also of the highest hierarchy. And just as in Byzantium, Church and State were blended more and more intimately in Moscow, until they too formed a *theocracy*.

But in this blending of the secular and the ecclesiastical power, it was the secular arm which began to predominate. Ivan III no longer called himself grand prince, but tsar (caesar).[8] He was vested in the regalia of the Basileus, and his boyars donned the ceremonial dress of the defunct court of Constantinople. The Church also stiffened its protocol, as if to enhance the Tsar's prestige, but not to dominate it. The magnificent cathedral of the Assumption which Ivan built inside the Kremlin and which was designed by the Italian architect Fioroventi, was to serve rather for official ceremonies and pageants than for popular worship. From this cathedral the great procession issued on Palm Sunday; it was called the "procession of the ass," and was something like a pageant and a mystery play — the Metropolitan riding on a snow-white donkey, and cheered by the crowd, waving palms, in commemoration of Christ's entry into Jerusalem. The tsar was on foot, leading the ass by its gilded bridle. But the metropolitan well knew that despite this show of humility, the secular ruler was the master; it sufficed to recall the fate of Isidore, deposed and banished by the grand prince, and of other prelates who

---

[8] Officially this title was adopted by Ivan's grandson, Ivan IV (*see* Chapter Six).

had been imprisoned or otherwise punished by the secular arm.

Thus theocracy was becoming more and more autocratic. This did not mean, however, that the Russian Church had lost her spiritual influence. It was present as a moderating factor in the affairs of men and State. It reminded the Russian people that beside and above the walls of the Kremlin there was *another* world where both men and State were judged *sub specie aeternitatis*. Last but not least, the living forces of the Church were hidden in the wilderness, where the seekers of silence continued their search for purification and salvation following the example of St. Sergius. But this voluntary retreat from the world caused a division in Russian religious consciousness. The faithful wondered whither they should turn — to the hermits, the "black robes," who had preserved intact the highest religious and ethical values, or to the secular, so-called "white clergy," which had been drawn into the vortex of worldly struggles and ambitions. Instinctively the devout Russian — boyar or humble serf — sought the advice of the monk in his "desert." The higher hierarchy, the bishops and metropolitans were monks, since no married priest could be consecrated as a prelate. The hierarchy, therefore, was respected, not only because of its exalted position, but because it too belonged to the monastic world. But even among the "black robes," monks and prelates, conflicts arose toward the end of the fifteenth century. The defenders of a harmonious theocracy were troubled by the open defiance of unexpected opponents.

The first clouds appeared on the horizon with the rise of two heretical sects: the *Strigolniks* and the *Judaisers*. Both sects originated in Novgorod. They denied the divinity of Christ, the Incarnation, the veneration of the saints, and were against the priesthood and the prayers for the dead. These were probably faraway echoes of the teachings of Western sects, which for the first time stirred the Russian masses and even the clergy. As we have seen, the Church had not been sufficiently armed with dogmatic theology. She was unable to argue with the dissenters. Their teaching began to spread, owing in part to the rebellious and dynamic character (a spiritual "volnitza") which it repre-

sented. Moreover the preachers of the heresy were men of strict
piety fanatically dedicated to their cause. The sects even attracted
a member of the higher hierarchy. When the heretics were punished by imprisonment, torture, and death at the stake, a great
ascetic and mystic, Nilus of Sorsk, implored the Church to show
mercy.

*   *   *

Nilus was himself suspected of heresy, but he never strayed
away from his Mother Church. However, he did start a movement
which for a time became a matter of bitter conflict. This was the
time when Russian monasticism not only developed rapidly but
became flourishing and when certain religious communities were
extremely prosperous. They owned many acres of lands cultivated by the "monastery" serfs, and great riches poured into their
coffers. Such prosperity and economic power scarcely recalled the
poor and humble life of St. Theodosius. Even the Abbey of the
Holy Trinity had become a resplendent shrine from which the
spirit of St. Sergius seemed to be absent.

Opposition to monastic wealth came from some of Sergius'
disciples who had preserved his spirit. These were the monks of
strict observance, devoted to contemplation, who had left the
security of the Moscow area, and once more fled into the "wilderness." These "seekers of silence" built their separate cells or her-
mitages for small communities in the vast almost uninhabited
lands which lay on the eastern bank of the Volga. They were
therefore called the Transvolgians. By their life of destitution
and mortification, as well as by their open criticism of the rich,
they defied the conformist monastic pattern. The defiant school
was led by Nilus, abbot of the Transvolgian hermitage of Sorsk.

The leader of the established, wealthy monasteries was Joseph,
abbot of Volotzk. The religious communities which he inspired
and directed were well ordered, governed by severe discipline;
but this discipline imposed the letter rather than the spirit of
the monastic rule. Asceticism was observed, but the splendors of
the liturgy outshone the ceremonies of the prince's court itself.
Solitude and silence were often ignored or had to be neglected

because of the throngs of pilgrims and penitents, including boyars loaded with gifts, who poured into the abbeys. The churches with their gilded cupolas and mighty pillars were often more imposing than the Kremlin palace; the monastery buildings with their halls and refectories seemed more fit for a banquet than for the scant meal of the hermit.

It was against this magnificence that Nilus of Sorsk hurled his reproaches. He reminded the Josephites (as the followers of the Volotzk abbot were called) of the words uttered by St. John Chrysostom: "If a man wishes to donate sacred vessels or other furnishings to a church, tell him to give them to the poor . . . for no one has ever been condemned for not decorating a church."

It was in this spirit that Nilus wrote the *Tradition to the Disciples,* the rule of perfection he gave to his brethren. "The Tradition," which is a treatise of moral and mystic asceticism, may be considered as one of the most remarkable early Russian spiritual writings. Not only does it set down the rule of absolute poverty and strict mortification but it also teaches the method of "the Prayer of Jesus" or *Hesichast* as practiced by the mystical school of the monks of Mount Athos.[9]

At an ecclesiastical council held in Moscow in 1503, Nilus openly rebuked the Josephites. He entered into a thundering dispute with the abbot of Volotzk, who was also present at the Council. To Nilus' attacks Joseph answered by defending ecclesiastical wealth on social grounds. He argued that the riches accumulated by the Church as well as the land she owned served the poor, since they were dedicated to acts of corporal mercy. And this was true, nor was it an overstatement; for the contents of the monastic granaries and all other food grown or collected by the Josephites were generously distributed to the needy who flocked to their gates. Many a time the Volotzk abbey came to the rescue of famine-stricken populations.

Thus Joseph's arguments were justified and the social service he rendered can scarcely be denied by modern historians and sociologists. Neither can the abbot of Volotzk be justly accused

---

[9] *See* Part Two, Chapter Thirteen.

of any moral blemish or dogmatic error. Joseph was a remarkable figure of his time, no less remarkable, in fact, than his opponent, Nilus of Sorsk; and together they were canonized. If he finally won in the practical, earthly contest, he did not do so at the expense of spiritual riches. Joseph did maintain in Russian monastic life great principles of liturgy and Church discipline, combined with an active social role which the Russian monk continued to play. On the other hand, the Josephites have come down in Russian history as the symbol of ecclesiastical wealth, and of a certain prosperous and "mundane" aspect of the Church. While Nilus of Sorsk, on the contrary, is the Russian ascetic and mystic *par excellence*. Besides the "Tradition" and the method of prayer it advocates, another brief document written by Nilus has been piously preserved. This is his last will or testament, in which he recommends his brethren to bury him without honor; let his body be cast away in the wilderness to be devoured by the beasts and birds of prey. For, as Nilus wrote, "this body has greatly sinned before God and is unworthy of burial."[10]

Commenting upon St. Nilus, Prof. George Fedotov points out the unusual and extreme character of the hermit of Sorsk. He is a man of "sharp contradictions," he is "terribly aware of sin" (as we see in his "Tradition"), and so "enraptured with Divine Love" that his soul escapes the world, "burying itself in a pit." Nilus' repudiation of aesthetic values in worship "verges on iconoclasm," and in this he is "unique among Russian saints," for all of them usually associated monastic life and the beauty of liturgical art. As Prof. Fedotov further points out, Nilus has a great love of tolerance, he protests against the punishment of heretics. As to his humility, it is also remarkable; he does not wish to be called a teacher or abbot by his disciples: they are his "friends." He does not speak of admonishing them but of "sharing the spiritual experience."[11]

Somehow, there is no place in the "Pageant of the Kremlin"

---

[10] English translation of "The Tradition" and of "The Will" is included in *A Treasury of Russian Spirituality* (*see* Bibliography).
[11] *Ibid.*

for the man who stripped himself of everything in life and sought ultimate indignity in death. In Nilus of Sorsk we find the true spirit of the Desert Fathers, or, if we think in terms of our own time, it is the heart aflame of a Charles de Foucauld.

CHAPTER SIX

The Tragedy of the Kremlin

IN THE reign of Ivan III's successor, Basil III (1505–1534), a monk from the city of Pskov whose name was Philotheus formulated the religious implications of Moscow political philosophy. He expressed this theocratic ideology in a letter addressed to Basil which ran as follows:

> The church of the ancient Rome fell because of the Apollinarist heresy;[1] the gates of the church of the second Rome, of the city of Constantine were broken by the axes of the sons of Agar;[2] and so today the holy ecumenic, apostolic church of the new, the Third Rome of your sovereign empire shines forth brighter than the sun because of her Orthodox faith in all the regions below the sun to the very confines of the universe. Oh, most pious tsar, may your power be aware that all the Christian Orthodox lands are drawn into thy single empire. Thou art the only truly Christian sovereign in the entire world. . . . For two Romes have fallen, but the Third Rome stands, and a fourth shall never be.

Thus emerged from an obscure monastery cell the mystic idea of "Russia-Third Rome." From Philotheus' text, officially recorded in the Moscow chronicles, a number of conclusions were drawn which influenced Russian religious and political thought. Or, perhaps, more correctly speaking, Philoteus expressed the Eastern religious and political myth of his time.

The text is quoted in all Russian history books; many scholars, Russian and non-Russian, have analyzed from every angle these lines of exalted praise and allegiance.

---

[1] This heresy of the fourth century, to which Philoteus attributes the "fall of Rome," had been actually many times condemned by the Holy See. The author merely found a vague pretext, not having any convincing explanation to offer.

[2] A biblical expression meaning the Turks.

Let us briefly sum up the result of this analysis. Some historians — a majority in fact — repeatedly point out that Philotheus' idea determined the entire pattern of Russian autocracy and nationalism; the idea of the Third Rome gave birth to a peculiar Russian *messianism*. Others declare that the Moscow rulers adopted this messianic ideology in order to justify or even "sanctify" their own worldly ambitions: the centralization of power and the extension of their influence to the Western Slavs who had previously been under Byzantine guidance but were now subject to the Turks. Still other historians see in the application of the Third Rome ideology the means of a gradual transfer of ecclesiastical authority to the State.[3] Having been entrusted not only with secular duties but also with the mission of defending the *only true Church,* the prince was, like his Byzantine predecessor, entitled to all the powers necessary for such a task. His role was on the same level as that of the hierarchy; it was founded on the firm belief that the ruling sovereign was indispensable to the Church as the Church was indispensable to the ruling sovereign. The "sacral" nature of the Byzantine emperor's power transferred to the Russian crown is clearly expressed in another historic letter. Some fifty years before Philotheus, the Patriarch of Constantinople, Anthony, writing to grand prince Basil I, defined as follows the role of the prince whom he already calls tsar, and places him so to say *within* the Church:

> The holy tsar occupies a high place in the Church. He is not like the other local princes and lords. From the beginning the tsars secured and confirmed piety in the entire world; the tsars convoked ecumenic councils. They reaffirmed in their laws the observance of

[3] The problem of "Moscow-Third Rome" is discussed by Robert Lee Wolff in *Daedalus,* journal of the American Academy of Arts and Sciences, Spring, 1959. This number is devoted to an "introduction to the issue 'Myth and Mythmaking.'" Mr. Wolff's article, entitled: "The Three Romes, The Migration of an Ideology and the Making of an Autocrat," presents many interesting points for the analysis of this ideology. We regret, however, that the author has centered his attention on the political "myth" and has not shown the *religious* and *universal* implications, which, according to F. Dvornik, preceded the autocratic distortion and do not necessarily lead to it. Russian religious messianism also reflecting the "Third Rome" ideology has no connection with the political and autocratic "migration."

that which has been said in divine and holy laws concerning true dogma and the good management of Christian life. They have done a great deal against heresies. . . . In every place where there are Christians, the tsar's name is mentioned in prayer by patriarchs, metropolitans and bishops, and this privilege belongs to no other ruler. It is impossible for Christians to have a Church and not to have a tsar.[4]

It was not only to Russia that this idea of the tsar-Church relation was brought by Byzantium. Bulgaria, which was also imbued with Byzantine culture, had anticipated Moscow. The fourteenth-century Bulgarian tsar, John Alexander, was represented in a painting as crowned by Christ. His capital, Trnovo, was at that time invested with a religious mission, prefiguring Moscow-Third Rome.[5]

Hence we see that this ideology is not peculiar to the Russian mind alone. It is linked to the very principle of the Christian empire, as pointed out by Fr. John Dvornik, when he said:

> . . . the attitude of all Orthodox Churches toward the State, especially the Russian Church is dictated by a very old tradition which has its roots in early Christian political philosophy. . . the Christian emperor was regarded as the representative of God in the Christian commonwealth, whose duty it was to watch not only over the material, but also the spiritual welfare of his Christian subjects. Because of that, his interference in Church affairs was regarded as his duty.[6]

This idea of the Christian ruler's sacred mission as crystallized in Byzantium still retained, however, a universal significance. When Constantinople fell, Moscow took pride in her own survival, which she considered providential. She was now steering her own ship, keeping her two self-appointed skippers — the metropolitan, head of the Church of All Russia, and the tsar, the protector of all Russia. Soon the Russian ship was alone to ride the waves. John Alexander's sacral heritage did not survive the de-

---

[4] As quoted by Schmemann, *ibid.*

[5] M. de Taube, *A Propos de Moscou-Troisieme Rome*, Editions Russie et Chretiente, No. I, 1947 (*see* Bibliography).

[6] Speech of Fr. Dvornik's at St. Procopius Unionistic Congress. Quoted from the *Byzantine Catholic World*, Sunday, July 12, 1959.

cline of Bulgaria, and other Christian princes of the East fell one by one under the Turkish yoke. Moscow meanwhile could go on boldly reaffirming that she "would not pass." But this reaffirmation was soon to lead to negative results: the predominance of the secular and the national over the spiritual and universal. The very foundations of the Church as suprapolitical and supranational were no longer taken into account. By asserting her independence from the Patriarch of Constantinople, the Russian Church had lost the universality proclaimed by the Nicene Creed. She now spoke in the name of Moscow-Third Rome, which as yet was not even an empire.

*   *   *

All these various interpretations and commentaries seem valid, especially the one offered by Fr. Dvornik. Russia did adopt and transform in one way or another the ideal of a Christian kingdom reflecting the city of God. If the tsars' search for temporal power found in this teaching a convincing argument in their favor, the monk in his cell still saw in the Third Rome a promise for *all*, of a religious transfiguration so dear to the Christians of the East. Later, Russian religious thinkers, poets, artists, also conceived their people's messianic future as a transfiguration in Christ. But, finally, just as medieval princes, so the modern autocrats — the communist dictators — tried to lend to their atheist philosophy the glamor of a mystic idea, the "brave new world" according to Karl Marx. In neither case, it seems to us, can the Third Rome ideology be treated as a mere "slogan of expedience," as modern historians often try to present it.

In 1549, Ivan IV, later known as "the Terrible," was officially crowned *Tsar* (though, as we have seen, the title had been already assumed by his grandfather); or rather, Ivan himself placed "the hat of Monomakh" on his head, according to the Byzantine ritual of coronation.

This first grand episode in the history of the Russian tsars was brought to the screen by the famous Soviet movie-director Eisenstein, in the opening scene of his picture (part one): "Ivan the Terrible." Like Eisenstein's earlier mentioned picture "Alexander

Nevsky," his "Ivan" is also accompanied by Prokofiev's score. But if the symphonic music for "Alexander" expresses the triumph of a just and valorous prince, how sad are the chants and symphonic patterns inspired by "Ivan the Terrible." The defiant young prince presented in the coronation scene is gradually turned into the cruel and perfidious madman. The "holy Tsar" ideal is transformed into a nightmare.

Ivan's coronation was the gesture of an autocrat. First of all he dealt with Byzantium, rejecting the offer of the Patriarch of Constantinople to attend and bless his ascent to the throne. Ivan sent word to the Patriarch that the presence of the Metropolitan of Moscow would suffice for the ceremony. The head of the Russian Church therefore anointed Ivan and sang the *Mnoguiye Leta* (*Multi anni*) of the coronation *Te Deum*.

For a time it seemed that the Church of Moscow-Third Rome was firmly established. Ivan himself encouraged this idea. Unbalanced and perverted as he already began to appear, he was attached to the Church and impressed by her, as long as she remained obedient. And in the beginning at least, the Church supported him. The ruling Metropolitan Macarius needed the tsar's help; he was concerned with the immediate religious and ethical problems of the day: the struggle against the heretics continued to be one of his preoccupations. There was also the urgent necessity to amend the morals of a country which, as we have seen, had fallen to an extremely low level. This was the gross and brutal way of life, known as *tatarstchina, tatar barbarism,* reminiscent of the khans' depravity. But in order to amend this way of life, the Church herself had to be reformed. Pomp and ritual were not enough. It was necessary to teach sound moral theology; it was necessary to print more books and to correct the existing copies, for many errors had found their way into holy writ, the liturgy, and didactic works, too hastily translated from the Greek and copied by incompetent scribes. In the days of Basil III, a learned monk, Maxime the Greek, had tried to correct these errors. But since, in doing this he had turned to Roman sources, he was accused of being a Latin and imprisoned. Under Ivan, the Russian master-printer, Fedorov, had brought out the first printed books, but they still contained many errors inherited from the manuscripts. Such a situation could not be changed immediately. In fact, it was to lead a century later to the first serious crisis inside the Russian Church.

Meanwhile, Macarius hastened to give the Church more spiritual strength and a better administration. In 1553 he convoked an ecclesiastical conference attended by many prelates. This conference became known as the *Stoglav,* the council of "One Hundred Chapters" — these were the chapters of a report prepared by the members of the conference; it contained all the reforms, instructions, and directions considered necessary, as well as the theological arguments to be used in forthcoming disputes with heretics and with the dissenters who followed the teaching of the late Nilus of Sorsk.

Besides the discussions and decisions of the *Stoglav,* which Macarius directed, he undertook a new compilation of the lives of the saints. This compilation called *Chetyi-Minei,* which became the official calendar of the Russian Church, also contained all the texts, homilies, and hymns for every saint's feast.

Macarius composed, moreover, the *Stepennaya Kniga* or "Book of Degrees," listing all Russian princes generation by generation. This book was founded on material offered by the ancient chronicles; it not only contained genealogy, but also expressed the political philosophy of the theocratic State. Macarius ruled the Church during her most prosperous years. The neighboring princes whose territories were falling one by one under Ivan's sway, swore allegiance to the Church of Moscow. And it was to Moscow that they brought their miraculous icons and the relics of their local saints. The Russian capital became the immense shrine of a powerful national church.

However disturbed Ivan was during the later part of his reign, his early years on the throne were fortunate, and revealed his spirit of shrewdness and decision. The cities of Kazan and Astrakhan were conquered, and thus the last "islands" of Tatar influence were subdued. The Mongols who remained after the Khan's withdrawal lived with the Russians on friendly terms, and mingled even more freely than before. Ivan's last wife was a Mongol princess. One of his chief boyars who was himself to become a tsar of all Russia, Boris Godunov, was of Mongol descent. This mixture of race and culture produced a fine intellectual strain. At that time, many former Tatar noblemen took Russian names or Russified their own. They sat in Ivan's court, became members of his council, and were soon indistinguishable from the other boyars. There was no race hatred in ancient Russia. As to the Church, she readily baptized the heathens or Moslems, though the latter did not so easily yield to the Christian faith as the former.

Another important event which took place in the time of Ivan was the conquest of Siberia. The immense lands beyond the Ural Mountains were occupied by the adventurous Cossack, Yermak, and by his armed bands in the pay of the wealthy Novgorod merchant, Stroganov. Conquest was followed by colonization and Siberia became a new apanage conceded by Stroganov and Yermak to the Tsar. Soon afterward, the Church extended her work to these new lands, converting the heathens and serving the colonists who began to settle rapidly in the territory which had been in previous centuries but a vast wilderness, inhabited by a few nomad tribes.

Once more we can see Church and State working in close co-operation, whether in the Kremlin council halls or in the settlements of Siberian pioneers. As the French historian Rembaud[7] points out regarding this period of Russian history, the Moscow State presented a remarkable unity of government, language, and faith; from the North Sea to the heart of Siberia the people obeyed the same laws, spoke the same tongue, worshiped in the same Church.

This was also the time when the life of the Moscovite sovereign was ruled not only by court etiquette, but by a ritual closely resembling the liturgy. The mass and vespers, Te Deums and Memorial services were continuously sung in the Kremlin Cathedral with all the Byzantine pomp introduced by Sophia Paleologue.

----
[7] *See* Bibliography.

The Tsar was vested like a high priest in robes of gold bedecked with jewels, wearing a gold or richly enameled icon on his breast, and looking himself like an icon. He could scarcely be distinguished from the metropolitan, who was always at his side.

During these early years, Ivan manifested strong religious inclinations, which seemed sincere and even edifying. He had done much reading and studying and had a thorough knowledge of Scripture. That his intellect was keen and alert was attested by the Polish Jesuit Posseven, who visited Ivan's court and argued with him on theology and dogma, without gaining his point, as he himself admitted in his "Relations."

Unfortunately, after making such a glamorous debut, Ivan's character began to deteriorate. His passions overcame him; his mind sickened; he developed sadistic instincts and a persecution complex nigh to hysteria. His faith following more and more crooked lines gave way to religious mania. It was then that Ivan became known as "the Terrible." He began to use the Scriptures and the religious philosophy of the "Book of Degrees," in order to satisfy his insane rapacity and to crush his opponents. Executions and tortures alternated with the ringing of the Kremlin church bells and religious processions. Ivan himself donned the monastic habit, though obviously no prelate would give him the tonsure. His closest retinue also masqueraded as monks. These were his henchmen, the *Opritchniky,* as they called themselves, which meant the "outsiders," a "police extraordinary" whom the tsar trusted more than his bodyguard. He had recruited the Opritchniky from all ways of life: adventurers, sadists, minions of his court, stray Poles and Lithuanians, Mongol executioners. Blood flowed daily on the Red Square in front of the Kremlin. Ivan began to destroy his closest boyars and advisers, for every single one was suspected of treason.

However, with his uncanny astuteness, Ivan sought to impress the masses with the idea that he was "on their side" against the "treacherous boyars." He denounced the latter as "enemies of the people" who exploited the poor and prevented the tsar from being near to his faithful subjects. This clever political maneuver strikingly resembles the one used by Stalin during the purges. But in Ivan's time such a maneuver was easy because of the very nature of the sovereign's supposed mystical role. Thus it was that at one time, angered by the growing opposition of the boyars, Ivan suddenly left Moscow, retiring to a nearby monastery with his Opritchniky. Panic reigned in the deserted capital, while the citizens spread terrifying rumors: had the tsar forsaken them, to be crushed by their enemies? Thousands of men and women flocked to the monastery gates. They were led by the metropolitan himself, the acolytes carrying icons and banners. On their knees the people implored Ivan to come back.

At the end of the first part of his picture, Eisenstein masterfully presents this unforgettable scene, conveying the tense atmosphere enveloping both the tsar and his people and almost reminiscent of Greek tragedy. The second part shows Ivan at the height of his insanity. . . . The tsar returned to Moscow with his henchmen and blood flowed once more on the Red Square.

Now all Russia trembled. Who dared oppose this monstrous power? But in this dark age two men stood up, symbolizing heroic moral and spiritual resistance.

One of them was Prince Andrei Kurbsky, Ivan's most cherished and talented commander who had conquered the last Mongol strongholds on the Volga. Though heaped with honors, Kurbsky could no longer suffer the spectacle of imprisonments and bloodshed. The other was Philip, metropolitan of Moscow, Macarius' successor, who openly and severely rebuked the tsar in the name of the Church.

Kurbsky had fled Moscow to join the Lithuanian and Polish armies, at that time at war with Russia. From the city of Volmir, the rebel prince wrote a series of letters to the tsar, charging him with many crimes which he himself had witnessed and could speak about with authority. "Those who have been slain by you," wrote Kurbsky, "stand by the throne of God and ask for Vengeance."

The messenger who brought Kurbsky's letters to the tsar was tortured and executed, swearing allegiance to his master to his

Boris and Gleb, the "morning stars of Russia." Their character as "passion bearers" is the keynote of Russian sanctity.

Two crowns. At the left is the globe crown of a 17th-century tsar. At the right, the 13th-century "hat of Monomakh." The chain is of 13th- or 14th-century workmanship.

Sovfoto

Old Moscow, from a painting by A. Vasnetsov.

The "white walls of the Kremlin."

Red Square, Moscow, seen from the walls of the Kremlin.

SCENES FROM THE
LIFE OF ST. SERGIUS

*Vision during Mass. A
cloud of fire descended on
the chalice.*

*Our Lady, accompanied by
two Apostles appears to
St. Sergius.*

*St. Sergius and his brothers
in the bakery.*

St. Sergius tames the bear.

Sovfoto

St. Sergius' monastery of the Trinity, Zagorsk.

The famous painting of the Trinity by Andrei Rublev.

Icon of the Virgin, by the 15th-century Theophanes the Greek.
This painting is in the Cathedral of the Assumption.

The Cathedral of the Assumption, Moscow, famous coronation palace of the tsars. Behind it, to the right, is the Church of the Twelve Apostles.

A typical altar setting in a small church.

The Crucifixion. This is one of the best icons of the Passion of our Lord.

A late 14th-century icon of St. George. Now in the Russian Museum, Leningrad.

Our Lady of Vladimir. One of the best loved icons of the Blessed Mother.

Religious articles presented to various churches by 17th-century tsars and boyars. Gold, enamel, and precious stones ornament these sacred objects.

Blessing of the paschal cakes in the patriarchal cathedral in Moscow. The photograph was taken on Easter Sunday, 1957.

The "icon corner" in the home of a 17th-century nobleman.
Every home had its "icon corner," even though not as elaborate as this one.

last breath. But Kurbsky himself was out of reach. All Ivan could do was to answer his letters with solemn indignation and blind fury. In his letter to the prince he used all the subtle sophisms borrowed from his library of mystico-political writings. He invoked the Holy Trinity as having placed him on the throne: he reminded Kurbsky of all the illustrious and holy rulers who had preceded him, from St. Vladimir, who had baptized Russ, to Alexander Nevsky and Dimitry Donskoy, who had saved her from the invaders. The "Stepennaya Kniga" gave a religious tinge to the Ryurikovitchy genealogy. Therefore Ivan's final argument was that to rebel against the holy tsar was not only high treason but also heresy.[8] Kurbsky was out of reach, and could not be punished, but metropolitan Philip was at hand and easier to crush. Ivan imprisoned him in a monastery cell and ordered him to be silent. Yet, paradoxically enough, the tsar came to seek the prelate's blessing for a campaign he was planning against the city of Novgorod (which long before had lost its freedoms). The metropolitan refused to approve this campaign, declaring: "Only the good are blessed." He was murdered in his cell, and Ivan proceeded with his plan, not only humbling, but devastating Novgorod.

*   *   *

After Ivan's death in 1584, Russia, deeply shaken by the reign of terror, was on the decline. Of the tsar's three sons, one had perished, beaten to death by his father in a fit of insane rage. The other, little prince Dimitry, had been murdered in mysterious circumstances. It was generally believed that the assassin had been sent by Boris Godunov, who was planning to mount the throne. Prince Fedor, Ivan's son who survived and reigned (1584–1598), was sickly and feeble-minded; he could not reflect the splendors of the "Third Rome." However, Fedor's time was marked by an important date in the life of the Russian Church. This was the election of the first Russian patriarch in 1589.

---

[8] The Kurbsky-Ivan correspondence is not only a historic document but also a literary monument. Both the tsar and his commander were excellent stylists and capable of arguing their points with brilliance. Kurbsky's letters are, moreover, what we might call the first Russian political writing, as he himself is the first Russian political émigré.

It was Tsar Fedor who initiated the negotiations in order to reaffirm, so to say, at its highest level the prestige of Moscow's ecclesiastical authority. The request raised no objections on the part of the four ruling Eastern Patriarchates: Constantinople, Antioch, Alexandria, and Jerusalem. The final permission was granted in the name of all four by the senior (*primus inter pares*), the patriarch of Constantinople. He gave his blessing to the tsar, requesting him to call a council of Russian prelates. The latter met in the Cathedral of the Assumption in the Kremlin and was presided over by the Greek Patriarch who had come to Moscow especially for this occasion. Three candidates were chosen and their names presented to the tsar. He was to draw one of the names, this being the final choice made by divine providence. The name drawn by the tsar was that of Job, metropolitan of Moscow. There followed the ceremony of solemn consecration performed by the head of the Greek Church. Metropolitan Job was placed on the *ambo;*[9] beside him Tsar Fedor was seated on his throne. Job recited the profession of faith, exchanged the kiss of peace with the patriarch and assembled prelates, and was then led in to the altar, supported by two bishops, while the choir intoned the solemn *trisagion,* or "thrice-holy" chant: "Holy God, Holy Mighty One, Holy Immortal One, have mercy on us." The Greek prelate placed the Gospels on Job's head and made the sign of the cross over him. Thus was installed the first Patriarch of Moscow and all Russia.

As we see, there was no conflict between Constantinople and Russia over the election and consecration of Patriarch Job. On the contrary, it seems to have been welcomed by the heads of the other Churches not in union with Rome. In the eyes of these Churches, autocephalia was an inevitable and normal phenomenon. Nonetheless, the Greek hierarch was still considered as the senior, the *primus inter pares,* and therefore Russia did not obtain the

---

[9] An elevated platform in front of the iconostasis, i.e., outside the altar gates. The celebrants stand on the *ambo* during various parts of the liturgy. It is also used for other ceremonies, for delivering sermons and for certain announcements. *Ex cathedra* pronouncements of the Eastern Churches not united to Rome are made "from the ambo." The tsar alone of all laymen could be seated on this platform.

spiritual leadership to which the "Third Rome" seemed to have entitled her. She may have suffered some disappointment in this realization. But the Russian Church could not foresee that her newly established patriarchate was to face many a difficulty, brave many a storm, and bear the heaviest crosses as yet sent to the "Third Rome."

Already Tsar Fedor's reign was marked by a dramatic event; it concerned Russia's Western territories. As we have seen, the Kiev metropolia together with the other Southwestern dioceses had separated themselves from the destinies of the see of Moscow and technically remained under Greek jurisdiction. As Polish influence grew in those regions, and mainly during the Jesuits' fast-spreading activities, the Southwestern provinces were gradually drawn into the Catholic orbit. Ever since the Council of Florence and the flight of metropolitan Isidore to Kiev, a movement of reunion with Rome had been started and intermittently continued there.

In 1595, six years after the establishment of the Moscow patriarchate, five Southwestern prelates, headed by Michael Ragoza, metropolitan of Kiev, met in the Lithuanian city of Brest-Litovsk and petitioned the Holy See for permission to return to communion with Rome. Permission was granted on January 23 of the same year. This act, known as the Union of Brest-Litovsk, led to the formation of the *Uniate* Church, in reunion with the Catholic world, and preserving the Byzantine rite. In those days, the Uniate territories were ruled by Poland and Lithuania, so that Moscow could neither interfere in their Church affairs nor influence them directly. The Russian Orthodox clergy, however, shocked and distressed by this Catholic manifestation at Moscow's very gates, directed their efforts toward the task of regaining their prestige. This was achieved in part by Peter Moghila, the learned Russian Orthodox prelate who had studied in Rome and who skillfully turned the weapons of Latin theology and scholastic argumentation against the Uniates. Kiev returned in 1533 to Russian Orthodoxy when Moghila became ruling metropolitan of that city. In 1686, the Southwestern lands became part of the Moscow State, but the conflict between the Uniates and Orthodox persisted and is even today far from being resolved.

*   *   *

The Ryurikovitchi dynasty which had ruled Russia for over seven centuries became extinct when Fedor died in 1598, leaving no heirs. According to Russian custom dating from the early middle ages, a new ruler could be elected by public acclaim. A council was called in Moscow for that purpose and elected Fedor's closest adviser, related to him by marriage: this was Boris Godunov, whom many suspected of having assassinated the child, Dimitry. Actually this was the beginning of a long period of political and military crisis known in Russian history as "the time of trouble."

From Poland there appeared a pretender, claiming that he was the son of Ivan the Terrible, Dimitry, who was supposed to have been slain but had actually been saved from the assassins. The "false-Dimitry," whose origin even today remains unknown, was a former novice, a fugitive from a Russian monastery, Grigory Otrepiev by name. He was supported by the king of Poland who speculated on the fall of Boris and by the Jesuits, active at that time in Poland, who hoped to bring the Catholic faith to Moscow. The pretenders' army broke into Russia at a time when the tsar seated on the throne was tormented by remorse, recalling the youthful Dimitry's death. Thus at least is Boris Godunov presented by the Russian poet Pushkin in a historic play. The famous composer, Musorgski wrote his opera "Boris Godunov" on Pushkin's libretto. Those who have attended a performance of this opera will recollect the tragedy it so colorfully relates: Boris crowned in the Kremlin, then dying from despair and remorse while his country is threatened by the pretender's army. Alas, this is but another dark chapter of Russia's history when the Catholic cross was brought to her borders by a foreign invader. Here is one of the scenes of Pushkin's "Boris Godunov":

> *A House in Cracov. The Pretender and Fr. Chernikovsky,*
> *a Jesuit:*

Pretender: Nay, father, it will not be hard. I know

The spirit of my people;
Piety with them is not extreme, their tsar's example
To them is sacred. And their tolerance
Makes them indifferent. I warrant you
Before two years my people all, and all
The Northern Church will recognize the power
of Peter's vicar.

Jesuit: May Saint Ignatius aid thee
When other times arrive. Meanwhile, Tsarevich,
Hide in thy soul the seed of heavenly grace;
Religious duty bids us oft dissemble
before the impious; the people judge
Thy words, thy deeds; God only sees thy motives.[10]

In Pushkin's presentation, founded on thorough historical research, the Jesuit obviously believes that the young man who
claims the Russian crown is Dimitry, Ivan's son, so to say, arisen
from the grave. Therefore he calls him *"tsarevitch,"* i.e., "Prince
and heir apparent." He also believes that this rightful successor
to the Moscow throne will bring the Roman faith to Russia. Yet
he begs him to be patient and carry out his plan with prudent
consideration. But Dimitry does not wish to "hide the seeds of
grace." He is quite sure that "his people," as he calls them already,
will be easily converted to Catholicism, provided Poland helps him.
The young Polish girl, Maryna Mnishek, who also believes in
him and who flatters his vanity, urges him to seek the crown
without delay. Russia herself is divided; while some of the boyars
muster around Tsar Boris, others are drawn into the pretender's
orbit. Boris is panic stricken. It is the Church which steps forward
to dispel his doubts. In a solemn speech, the Patriarch tells Boris
that the child Dimitry is truly dead and buried and that a miraculous cure was performed near his uncorrupted body. Dimitry is
now an "angel of the Tsar in Heaven" and a "miracle-worker."
This refers to the true sequence of events which led to young
Dimitry's canonization granted by the Russian Church to young
children, innocent victims of cruelty.

Boris is reassured by the Patriarch's testimony. Dimitry is dead;

---

[10] A. Pushkin, Works (*see* Bibliography).

there can therefore be no living heir to the Ryurikovitchy. But
soon, instead of fear, it is remorse that is awakened in the tsar's
troubled soul. At the gates of the Kremlin Cathedral, a "fool in
Christ," the idiot Nick, accuses Boris; this is how Pushkin presents
the scene: the people laugh at Nick while awaiting Boris, who
attends the liturgy.

> *Square in front of the Cathedral in Moscow*
> The people: The tsar, the tsar is coming.
>   (the tsar comes out of the Cathedral; a boyar in front of him
>   scatters alms among the beggars.)
> Idiot: Boris, Boris, the boys are hurting Nick.
> Tsar: Give him alms! What is he crying about?
> Idiot: Little children are hurting Nick. . . . Have them
>   killed, as thou hadst the Tsarevitch killed.
> Boyars: Go away fool! Seize the fool!
> Tsar: Leave him alone. Pray for me, poor Nick. (Exit)
> Idiot: (calling after him) No! No! It is impossible to pray
>   for tsar Herod; the Mother of God forbids it.[11]

In order to feel the full impact of this scene, we must recall
that "fools in Christ" in Russia were no ordinary beggars, nor
were they idiots; they were men dedicated to God, voluntarily
adopting the manners and speech of the half-wit and the garb of
the poor outcast. "Fools in Christ" were therefore both scoffed
at and venerated. The beautiful Moscow Cathedral of St. Basil
the Blessed is dedicated to one of these fools who was canonized
by the Byzantine Church. Another "fool in Christ," St. Isaac the
Recluse, who lived in the eleventh century, was a Russian merchant. He retired to the Kiev monastery of the Caves, where he
worked as cook and server. Because of his feigned "foolishness,"
the brethren laughed at him; one day he was told to go out and
catch a crow. Isaac bowed low, went into the monastery garden,
caught a crow with his bare hands and brought it to the brethren.
After that he began to be respected, but wishing to behave like
a half-wit, he insulted the abbot, the monks, and the laymen, and
was often beaten.

There are many other stories about the "fools in Christ." Two

---

11 *Ibid.*

Englishmen, Gorsey and Fletcher,[12] who came to Moscow in the reign of Ivan the Terrible, describe one of these "fools," who rebuked and insulted the tsar, crying out that "he drank the blood of the Christians and devoured them." He threatened Ivan with punishments, and a thunderstorm broke out. The Tsar was so frightened that he asked the fool to pray for his salvation. This beggar was called "holy Nick." It is probable that Pushkin transposed the episode described by Fletcher, to the time of Boris Godunov. In this transposition, he masterfully expressed the psychological aspect of tsar versus people, of pride versus Christian humility.

One of the most dramatic scenes of Pushkin's play and of Musorgski's opera is the death of Boris. Both text and music are full of tragic forebodings. And indeed, after the death of Godunov, Dimitry seized Moscow. He brought with him his Polish bride, his motley retinue, and Latin customs which he tried to impose on the people. He was accepted for a while by men of highest rank, but the common people rose against him. He was overthrown and murdered. Utter ruthlessness marked many episodes of "the time of trouble." Patriarch Germogen was murdered by the invaders because he was the leader of Russian national resistance. There were two more pretenders, each of them assuming by turn the name of the slain child, Dimitry; each was unmasked and chastised. Then once more we see the close alliance between Church and people. After Germogen's murder, his successor, patriarch Philaret, headed the patriotic movement which was to liberate Russia and restore order in a half-devastated country. The Church struggled for survival, with the support of two men of exceptional energy and virtue; Prince Pozharsky, a military commander from Moscow, and Kozma Minin, a tradesman from Nizhny Novgorod. Mustering a national militia and gaining the entire people's trust and co-operation, Philaret, Pozharsky, and Minin freed Russia and rebuilt a crumbling nation, purified and purged of Ivan's evil memories as well as of the bitterness aroused by the pretenders. A "National Council" was convoked,

---

12 Fletcher was Queen Elizabeth's ambassador to Moscow.

attended by the representatives of various strata of Russian society, from boyar and military commander to officials and tradesmen, in a word, by the very men who had contributed to the liberation of Russia.

Patriarch Philaret, who before entering monastic orders was a boyar by name of Theodore Romanov, would have been elected tsar had it not been for his "black robe" which forbade him to wear the crown. While still in the world he had been married and had lost his wife during the "Time of Trouble." His son, Michael Romanov, was still a youth, and far less influential than other candidates, most of them titled or high ranking noblemen. But the Council elected Michael as a tribute to his father. Thus the Romanov dynasty was founded. Michael was placed on the throne, while Philaret became *de facto* ruler of the Moscow State. The patriarch was a wise and prudent administrator; Michael a well-educated and deeply religious youth. Father and son co-operated to rebuild Russia.

This almost complete fusion of Church and secular power could not obviously last for long. Under Michael's successors the picture changed once more; great progress was achieved, new cultural values were created, while many of the old ones were for a time still piously preserved. But many conflicts were to arise once more between tsar and patriarch, as well as within the Church herself. The tragedy of the Kremlin was not over.

CHAPTER SEVEN

The Church on Trial

AS SOON as the "Time of Trouble" ended, Moscow reaffirmed once more the ideal of the Third Rome. The beginning of the reign of Michael's son, tsar Alexis, was one of the most harmonious periods in Russian history. Here the very word "harmony" often used by Russian historians to describe this period must be understood in its Platonic sense as something at the same time exalted, wise, and aesthetically beautiful.

Alexis himself was called — in contrast to his dreaded predecessor Ivan — *The Most Quiet Tsar*. He knew how to blend traditional devotion with cultural and social interests. He was surrounded not by the turbulent and envious boyars of Ivan's days, but by men both prudent and learned, experienced in the affairs of the State, and in technical and economic problems. These problems had arisen after the military and political disasters brought about by the "false Dimitrys." Education was at a low ebb; it was practically nonexistent if compared to the cultural resources of other European countries of that time. The same could be said of technology, which had proved especially deficient in the military field during recent wars. Alexis realized that to amend these defects, it was necessary to turn to the West for initiation. Thus began the process of Russia's "Westernization."

The task of changing Russia into a modern Western State is usually attributed whole-piece to Peter the Great, i.e., to a period some ten years after Alexis' reign. It is indeed true that Peter undertook a number of radical reforms which broke the mold of ancient Moscow, creating a new empire after the model of other European nations. But medieval Russia's "iron curtain" had already been lifted by Alexis. The preceding centuries of isolation, it must be remembered, were due first to the Mongol occupation, then to the fear of Western neighbors who had rapidly developed, causing Russia to lose her Southwestern provinces.

To this fear must be added the dread of foreign religious influences, first Catholic, then also Protestant; the tide of the Reformation had reached Moscow's border lands, and the Russian Church was extremely suspicious of outlandish "infiltrations." Foreigners were not easily admitted to Moscow unless as ambassadors or other accredited visitors. There was no "cultural exchange" to speak of.

Alexis called in foreign technicians — military engineers, makers of arms, various craftsmen, physicians and pharmacists — and invited them to settle in Moscow, but only in order to exercise their trade or profession. They were segregated in a special district of Moscow reserved for them. Little attention or none was paid to their religious convictions, though most of them were Lutherans.

Besides the foreign technicians, many scholars and theologians came to Moscow from the Southwestern territories which, as we have seen were under the Polish sway. These scholars were Russian-Orthodox, and had studied in the Divine Academy of Kiev founded in 1631 by Metropolitan Peter Moghila. Like Maxime the Greek in the fifteenth century, so Peter Mohila had used Latin scholasticism to argue with Catholics and to uproot Latinism. This method, paradoxically enough, offered Russian religious thought a strong Catholic foundation. Kiev scholars studied not only in their newly founded Academy but also in Rome. Some of them had even embraced Catholicism to get a better training, then reverted to the Russian-Orthodox faith as soon as that training was completed. Nevertheless, they retained their Catholic formation and brought to Moscow a knowledge of the Catholic Church and a respect for her which until then had not existed.

The Latin clerics introduced to Moscow not only books of piety and dogma, but also Latin verse and drama: the latter being the first theatrical productions to replace the "Procession of the Ass" and archaic mystery plays. Russian verse was composed for the first time, according to the Latin syllabic pattern.

Tsar Alexis himself valued Western culture and appointed one of these Latinized clerics, Stephan Yavorsky, as tutor to his young son Peter. A number of well-educated boyars also followed Western cultural patterns. They placed foreign books on their library shelves and even hung foreign paintings on their walls, a thing unheard of when only icons were permitted in the home. Some of these noblemen, like Prince Galitzin and the boyar Fedor Rtistchev, were not hostile to Catholicism; they promoted Roman ideas, as well as the Kiev scholars who propagated them. At that time, the Greco-Slavic-Latin academy, the first institution of higher learning offering humanities, was founded in Moscow.

The influence of Catholic devotional works also reached Russia in the second part of the seventeenth century. This influence is strongly felt in the writings of the Ukrainian monk, Demetrius Tuptala, who in the early eighteenth century became Metropolitan of Rostov, and was canonized some fifty years after his death. St. Demetrius of Rostov was an outstanding scholar and the author of books of piety. One of them, a new version of the *Tchetii Minei* or the calendar of the Saints, differs in many ways from the calendar previously compiled by metropolitan Macarius. St. Demetrius borrowed considerable material from the Latin Lives of the Saints. He followed Western hagiographical patterns in presenting his calendar which is contained in several volumes and is still used by the Russian-Orthodox both in the U.S.S.R. and abroad.

The spirit of Catholicism is also found in St. Demetrius' devotional writings: instructions to priests and laymen about prayer, recollection, the liturgy, the mastering of the passions and the avoiding of sin. This spiritual advice is given by St. Demetrius according to a method which is more Roman Catholic than Russian-Orthodox or Greek. The color and wealth of his style, the many meditations on the humanity of Christ, and his realistic description of Christ's life are something unusual in Russian books of piety. St. Demetrius often insisted on frequent communion and on the adoration of the Holy Sacrament, not usually practiced in the Eastern Churches (except by Uniates).

Demetrius of Rostov was extremely popular among his flock. He could teach with subtlety but also with simplicity, as he does, for instance in this brief advice for daily practice:

> From early morning be a seraphim in your prayer, a cherubim in your deeds, an angel in your conduct.

Admiration and love of St. Demetrius even in today's Russia is reflected in the *Journal of the Moscow Patriarchate.* The official organ of the Russian hierarchy presented an article by Bartholomew, Archbishop of Novosibirsk and Barnaoul, devoted to Demetrius' writings. The author especially praises the Saint's instructions entitled *The Spiritual Alphabet,* containing his admonition to priests to be mindful of their flock and at the same time to be attentive to their own spiritual perfection. He also points to St. Demetrius' continual insistence on the necessity for the pastor to *instruct* and *guide* the faithful; writes Archbishop Bartholomew: "He never left a single Mass without giving an instruction, recalling the words of the Apostle Paul: 'For even if I preach the gospel, I have therein no ground for boasting, since I am under constraint'" (1 Cor. 9:16).[1]

Sermons and other church instructions in the U.S.S.R. being strictly controlled by the Government, the article of the Archbishop of Novosibirsk is of particular interest; it shows the importance attached to instruction by Russian prelates today.

Besides works of piety, Demetrius of Rostov also wrote dramatic works. His play *The Nativity* is vivid and colorful. Speaking of this remarkable author, the distinguished literary critic, D. S. Mirsky writes that he was "the most exquisite fruit of the cultural revival" of his time.[2]

*   *   *

The attraction for the West felt by the Russian seventeenth-century elite was reciprocated by Western interest in Russia. This is exemplified by the strange and fascinating story of a priest, Yury Krizhanitch. Though born in the West and having at first learned about Russia only by hearsay, this adventurous voyager

---

[1] *Journal of the Moscow Patriarchate,* No. 1, 1949.
[2] D. S. Mirsky, *A History of Russian Literature* (*see* Bibliography).

not only came to Russia, breaking through the "iron curtain," but has influenced Russian culture, as well as Russian political and religious thought.

Yury Krizhanitch was a Croatian, born and educated in Zagreb. He was a Western Slav, of Latin formation. He later studied for the priesthood in Vienna, Bologna, and finally in Rome, where he entered the College of St. Athanasius, which was established by the Congregation *De Propaganda Fide* to train missionaries for the Slavonic lands. Immediately after his ordination, Yury Krizhanitch wrote a treatise entitled *Bibliotheca Schismaticorum,* which is still preserved in Rome in one of the Vatican libraries.

From these early days, the young Croatian priest was preoccupied with the problem of reunion. He expressed, in his first work, the basic idea that, in spite of the Schism, the Slavs were still linked to the Universal Church by patristic tradition, by the sacraments, and by Apostolic succession. Therefore, Krizhanitch declared, both Eastern and Western Slavs were not actually schismatic, but merely "separated Brothers."

In his treatise, Krizhanitch insisted among other things upon the observance of the eastern rite among the Slavonic peoples. He vigorously defended his ideas, but he had yet to encounter many difficulties before he could actually follow his extraordinary vocation. Among all the Slav people with whom he was concerned, he was most interested in Russia. He read all that was written about Moscow by Catholic missionaries, travelers, and scholars. He was aware of the fact, that under Tsar Alexis, Moscow had attained a very high degree of culture and spirituality, and he felt that Catholics should know about her flowering. He was, moreover, inspired with a deep, fervent, and disinterested love of Holy Russia and dreamed of going there. But no plans had been made for him in that field, and the holy Congregation did not consider the young Croatian priest very seriously. Krizhanitch persevered in his own project, joined a foreign embassy en route to Moscow, and arrived there, not as a priest, but as a diplomatic agent.

He took advantage of his position to have a look at Moscow and its influential circles. A Catholic priest, entering Russia as

such, would not have had these opportunities, in fact he would
not even have been allowed to enter.

Yury Krizhanitch made the best of his stay in Moscow. He
sent reports to Rome, hinting that he was in touch with some
Russians who were in favor of the Catholic faith. He was, it is
believed, received in private audience by the Patriarch. He acquired in Moscow as many Russian books as possible concerning
the many controversies which were then raging between Russian-
Orthodox and Catholics, between Russian-Orthodox and Protes-
tants, among Russian-Orthodox themselves, at that time torn, as
we shall see, by internal discords.

When Krizhanitch returned with his embassy to Western
Europe, and reported at Rome, he met with little encouragement.
The information he brought back from Moscow was practically
disregarded.

Some time later, Krizhanitch was named to a bishopric in
Galicia, where Catholics observed the Eastern rite. Thus, he was
thoroughly trained in Eastern liturgy. But his primary interest was
to go back to Moscow. Not being able to obtain his superior's
permission, he once more visited Russia on his own initiative, as
scholar, interpreter, and former diplomatic agent. He offered his
services to the tsar as court-librarian and grammarian. He obtained
a modest subsidy from the Russian crown, and could have lived
safely in Moscow had not the Moscovite officials discovered that
this scholar and interpreter was actually a Catholic priest. Yury
Krizhanitch was arrested and exiled to Siberia, where he spent
fifteen years. Though restricted in his priestly capacities, he was
permitted to pursue his scholarly works, and was employed as a
clerk in local administration. During the long years spent in
Russia, Krizhanitch composed a grammar and a lexicon in which
he attempted to blend all Slavic languages into one, in order to
create a common tongue, a kind of Slavic *esperanto*. He also
wrote a general treatise on Russian affairs, entitled the *Politica*.

In this work Krizhanitch made a few main points which were,
in his days, and are still in our time, of considerable interest.
Generally speaking, he followed the lines of the "Third Rome"

idea, in the sense that he too proclaimed Russia's special mission. But he insisted that this mission would be attained only through the improvement of Russia's culture, technology, and government according to Western patterns. In another of his works, Krizhanitch carefully listed Russia's natural resources and economic potentiality. He described Siberia, the land of as yet scarcely explored wealth, where he lived so long as an exile and which he studied with remarkable care. In all of these writings, composed in the "all-Slavonic" tongue of his own invention, we find the scholarly and at the same time stubborn and impatient mind, who wanted to embrace not only Russia, but all the Slavs. For Krizhanitch dreamed of bringing together the Slavonic world under the scepter of the tsar, but only provided the tsar would undertake the necessary reforms and give the people the just and ordered government which he found lacking. He may indeed be called "the father of panslavism," not of an aggressive idea aiming at conquest and domination, but rather of a plan for the peaceful progress of a Slavonic "united nations" organization.

Krizhanitch sent his *"Politica"* to the Kremlin, where it produced no reaction. The book was stored away in an attic of the palace. It is believed, however, that the project was later discovered by young tsar Peter and may have inspired his own vast plans of reform.

After fifteen years, Yury was permitted to leave Siberia; we cannot follow him through the later years of his extraordinary career. Let us simply conclude, that he returned to western Europe, entered the Dominican order, and died as a chaplain in besieged Vienna, tending the sick and wounded.

We can see why this adventurous Croatian priest, who found no support and paid dearly for his devoted mission, is so important for Russian history of the late seventeenth and early eighteenth centuries. For he expressed in his clear and dynamic theory so much that Russia needed and finally achieved. But Krizhanitch is also important for a certain religious trend which was followed by Russian Catholics. This trend was to seek a way of bringing back Russia into the universal family of Christian nations, at the

same time preserving her own traditions and her own deep aspirations. This is why one of the most famous Russian Catholics,
Vladimir Solovyev, composing his "Profession of Faith," which
gave one of the keynotes of ecumenism, turned to the man whom
he considered his precursor, calling him "The great Krizhanitch."[3]

*   *   *

As we see from the severe treatment of a Catholic priest in
Moscow, under tsar Alexis, a deep feeling of distrust predominated
in Russian-Orthodox minds concerning all that came from Rome.
This distrust extended also, though in a far less acute way, to
the Greek and Ukrainian clerics who often came to Moscow.
Many prelates from Southwestern Russia were influential, but
they were considered as outsiders and became objects of envy in
the eyes of the Moscow clergy. Distrust and bitterness were at the
core of a dramatic conflict which soon arose between the leaders
of the Church. This was the *Raskol,* or inside schism.

When Tsar Alexis mounted the throne, restoring Russia's "harmony," the Church turned once more to her immediate tasks.
As in the days of the *Stoglav council,* the improvement of *mores*
and the integrity of the magister became the object of the clergy's
main preoccupation. The Time of Troubles had left the Russian
people in a state of considerable moral confusion. Krizhanitch had
pointed out as much in his *Politica,* accusing the government and
its bureaucracy, as well as private individuals, of many a sin
skillfully hidden behind the pompous decor created by the "Most
Quiet Tsar." The Church herself had become lax, closing her
eyes on these sins. Monasticism was helpless, being too remote —
when keeping to strict observances — or too absorbed in worldly
matters — when it was too closely associated with the lords of the
Kremlin.

The need of reform was strongly felt. It was initiated by a
group of secular priests, the so-called "white clergy," led by Archpriest Neronov, a man of exceptional moral character. The group
took the name of the "zealots of piety." They had the support of

---

[3] Solovyev's profession of faith is included in the Nota Bene to his work
Russia and the Universal Church (*see* Bibliography).

the Tsar and of Archbishop Nikon, already known as an out-standing prelate and later to be elected patriarch. The "zealots" preached both by word and by example: they insisted upon intensive prayer, fasting, penance, and the exercise of charity. They forbade all amusements and dissipations, even those not necessarily sinful. The "zealots" have often been compared to the Jansenists who at that time had started in France a movement which strikingly resembles that of Neronov's followers. The Tsar's own spiritual director, Stephen Vonifatiev, and a former country priest by the name of Avvakum were the champions of this moral reformation; they went so far as to dare rebuke the hierarchy and the Tsar himself, when they saw him failing.

The movement of the "zealots," despite all its rigors, was hailed by many as a salutary manifestation of Christian virtue. But it was soon challenged by one of its former most ardent promoters.

In 1662, Archbishop Nikon was elected to the patriarchal throne. He was a man in many ways remarkable. The son of a peasant of half Finnish, half Russian origin, he became an exemplary monk and then a strong-minded and authoritarian prelate. Nikon had been initiated by the learned men of Kiev to the organization of the Roman hierarchy; from the Greek scholars he knew the methods of the patriarchate of Constantinople, which even under Moslem domination were strictly disciplinarian. Nikon himself inclined toward discipline.

One of the first orders issued by Nikon was the correction of the liturgical books. Let us recall that this measure had been already applied a century earlier, by Metropolitan Macarius. But the correction had not been completed and new errors had crept into the various texts, hymns, rubrics, and the like, used during the liturgical year. There were, moreover, errors in the Church ritual — for instance making the sign of the cross with two fingers instead of three,[4] and singing two instead of three alleluias. These distortions had occurred when the liturgy was brought to ancient Russia or later and had never been corrected.

---

[4] The Slavonic Sign of the Cross differs from the Latin — it is made with three fingers put together.

The revisions ordered by Nikon and immediately put into practice called forth violent objections from his former friends, the "zealots of piety." Neronov, Vonifatiev, Avvakum, and other priests condemned these changes not only as "newfangled innovations," but as actual heresy. They likewise rose against certain practices of laymen, which had nothing to do with the liturgy, but which were outlandish and therefore objectionable; the smoking of tobacco and the shaving of beards. All these things were rejected by the "zealots" and publicly condemned.

Nikon answered by drastic measures. The "zealots" were excommunicated, imprisoned, or banished. Scenes of unheard of violence took place when the rebellious priests were seized in church, dragged into the street, carted off to prison and shorn, a punishment considered as the ultimate humiliation. Nikon himself tore the priests' headgear off Neronov's head. The patriarch's men ripped a monk's cassock off his back as he stood in church holding the chalice. Another monk who witnessed this scene spat in Nikon's eyes, took off his shirt and hurled it into Nikon's face. But lo and behold, the shirt spread and covered the paten on the altar. The monk was beaten, put into chains, and locked up in a monastery.

Archpriest Avvakum who vividly described these scenes in his autobiography was himself arrested and banished. The former country priest, appointed to one of the great Moscow cathedrals because of his many talents, was a man both obstinate and fanatically minded. He was moreover a gifted writer. The autobiography which he composed during his long years of banishment in Siberia is a remarkable human document written in the vernacular. Avvakum is considered a master of style which even Russian writers of our day seek to imitate.[5]

Archpriest Avvakum is one of the most colorful figures of these stormy years of Russian Church history; and he is also one of the most tragic ones, despite the many spirited and even at times humorous pages in his autobiography. After years of banishment, prison, poverty, and endless other tribulations, the obstinate

---

[5] *Life of Archpriest Avvakum,* by Himself (*see* Bibliography).

Avvakum was burned at the stake still crying out his accusations against Nikon's reforms.

That the archpriest and a few men of his type should suffer persecution for reforms which actually concerned the outward signs of the liturgy and the passing fashions of the day, may seem surprising; still more surprising is the fact that Nikon's necessary and wise policy led to such bitter strife in which thousands of priests and laymen participated, and which became known as the *Raskol.* The dissenters, who called themselves *Raskolniky* or *Starovery,* i.e., "Schismatics" or "old believers," opposed Nikon's reforms as stubbornly and desperately as Avvakum. Many of them suffered severe punishments and all were excommunicated by the Patriarch's decree. But Nikon's very severity and autocratic methods only fanned the flame of dissent which rapidly spread throughout Russia and Siberia. The Russian people's rebellious spirit, the spirit of the *volnitza,* that freedom-loving temper which had been crushed in Novgorod, now reappeared in the *Raskol.* But even this would not suffice to explain the Raskolniky's passionate protest. In order to understand this tragic split in the Russian Church we must recall its deeper meanings. One of them is that since the Third Rome had received Byzantium's heritage, it considered every part of this heritage sacred, inviolable, and to be jealously guarded. No word or gesture of the liturgy could be altered without the approval of an ecumenic council. Such an attitude may be said to be formalistic, but we should not forget that the eastern Liturgy is deeply symbolic; it not only praises God but also teaches. Thus, for instance, the two fingers used for the sign of the cross conveyed the dogma of the two natures of Christ and was a refutation of the Monophysite heresy. The Greeks argued that the three fingers they prescribed meant the Trinity, and the two remaining ones Christ's two natures.

But this explanation did not sound convincing to the ears of the Old Believers, who had never heard of it. The second reason for the Raskol was the fact that Nikon had entrusted the correction of books to Greek and Ukrainian, latinized scholars. The latter, it was said, formed his immediate entourage bringing foreign ideas and customs to the Moscow patriarchate.

Despite these various interpretations, the Raskol is an extremely complex phenomenon. It is even more difficult to comprehend if we follow its further development.

The dissidents, completely cut off from their mother Church, had to depend on the priests who had led the Raskol or had joined it. Their number sufficed in the beginning, but later it was considerably reduced by executions, death, or life imprisonment. To insure the ordination of new priests the Raskolniky had to seek dissident bishops outside Russia, in Poland or in the Far East, but they were few and scattered. A considerable group of dissidents decided to remain without priests, and consequently without the sacraments, except baptism, which can be performed by a layman, and marriage, since the priest is only a witness in the wedding ceremony, and does not perform it. In the latter case, the dissidents encountered serious difficulty, since marriages in Russia had to be registered by the parish in order to be legal. Thus it was that many old believers, who were married and had children, lived outside the law.

Some groups could still receive communion from dissident monasteries which sustained them by sending them consecrated bread and wine. Others were deprived even of this solace and were satisfied with prayers in their private oratories, and secret shrines, before ancient icons hidden away in their homes. These Old Believers, who called themselves the "priestless," were more fanatical, the more bitterly opposed to Nikon.

One of the strangest and most terrifying manifestations of the Raskol was the wave of extreme fanaticism exhibited when groups of dissidents went to voluntary death by throwing themselves into the fire. Entire villages perished in the flames, the victims crying out that "it was better to die than to serve the antichrist." According to available statistics, some twenty thousand Raskolniky died in these conflagrations from the beginning of the schism to the end of the seventeenth century.[6]

---

[6] P. Miliukov, *Outlines of Russian History* (*see* Bibliography).

It was also during that fateful period that the great monastery of Solovky, on the White Sea shore, one of the strongholds of Russian piety, rose against Nikon. The monastery was built on an island protected by thick walls and the arctic wastelands. From Solovky the Holy Eucharist was brought and distributed to the priestless, some of them living hundreds of miles away. In order to break the resistance of the Solovky monks, the tsar sent an army which kept them under siege for seven years.

The Raskol very nearly broke up the Russian Church, splitting her into two bitterly opposed camps. Persecutions and excommunications continued for many years. Meanwhile Nikon's own prestige began to decline. His authoritarian nature, his criticism of high ranking noblemen and of the tsar himself caused his downfall. He was deposed and banished and another patriarch, more docile to the secular power, was elected in his place.

The dissensions between the established Church and the Old Believers were never solved. For more than a century the conflict remained bitter, with intolerance shown on both sides. Then gradually there came a time when a sort of coexistence was tolerated. Persecution ceased and the anathemas were withdrawn. The Old Believers were allowed to practice freely; even the priestless were forgiven. Their marriages were legalized provided they called a priest to witness the ceremony. According to statistics of the late nineteenth century, there were some thirteen million Raskolniky in Russia of that time.[7] The Raskolniky's moral convictions inspired respect. They were hard-working and thrifty people; their abstinence from drink and tobacco, their exemplary family life were noteworthy. When the persecutions were over, many old believers settled in Moscow and in other big cities. They became merchants, factory owners, and businessmen, mostly in the textile and silversmith industries. On the eve of the 1917 revolution several families of Old Believers were millionaires and patrons of the arts. The Moscow Art Theater, the Tretiakov Picture Gallery, the collections of the French impressionists and of other modern paintings were created by a cultured elite of

---

[7] *Ibid.*

Old Believers. Revolution destroyed or drove out of Russia the descendants of these great families. Those who survive still keep their ancient faith. The peasants, the workers, the craftsmen, some of them icon painters who through many generations had belonged to the Old Believers, remained in Russia; they too continue to adhere strictly to their dissident Church. A compromise has been arranged between them and the Moscow Patriarchate, which does not condemn them. Like all other religious groups in the U.S.S.R., they are allowed to worship by the Soviet government provided they are not subversive.

As in tsarist days, the Old Believers still form a minority but they preserve most faithfully not only the precepts of their dissident Church, but also their customs and their distinctive character — stubborn, severe, and independent. The Raskol has always been considered as a phenomenon of great importance in Russian history and Russian Church life. Moreover, amateurs of art have studied the icons of the Raskolniky, as the most ancient and most traditional of all. Liturgists have analyzed their chants; amateurs of literature praise the *Life of Avvakum*. Psychologists have seen in their dramatic conflict a projection of the typical Russian traits: a soul divided and extreme in its inner life and outward manifestations. Dostoyevsky chose the name Raskolnikov for the hero of his great novel *Crime and Punishment*, because he wanted to portray a *Raskol* or conflict of the human mind. Last but not least, sociologists have traced the origins of the Russian revolutionary movement in this schismatic trend. The Soviet Government created therefore special archives in which most valuable material concerning Old Believers is preserved. The late professor Bonch-Bruyevich, a prominent communist scholar, was for many years director of these archives.

However we interpret this historical and religious event, we should not, it seems to us, attach too great and exceptional a meaning to its various aspects and manifestations. Though severely tried, the Russian Church once again remained unshaken. She drew the majority of the people toward her; she then offered a peaceful haven even to her rebellious children, without forcing them to give up what they held true and sacred. Since no question of dogma had ever been raised in the Raskol, such a *status quo* was not only possible but welcome.

The *Life of Avvakum* marks the epilogue of the ancient period of the Russian Church. The beginning of the modern age was close at hand, heralded by the cultural flowering under the "Most Quiet Tsar." The advent of Peter was to bring great and definite changes in the spirit and structure of the Third Rome.

CHAPTER EIGHT

From the Kremlin to Saint Petersburg

WHEN Peter became tsar, in 1682, he was crowned in Moscow in the Cathedral of the Assumption and his throne stood opposite the throne of the patriarch. He lived in the Kremlin "of gleaming stone" where his father, the "most quiet tsar," had ruled. In 1700, when the patriarch Adrian died, the tsar did not think fit to have the head of the Church re-elected. In 1703, Peter's new capital, Petersburg (today Leningrad) was founded on the banks of the Neva. A new palace was built in Western style by Western architects. So was the new Cathedral, St. Peter and Paul. There was no throne for the patriarch.

Such was the setting in which the history of modern Russia starts. Peter wanted it to become a modern epic. To accomplish this metamorphoses, he hastened the process which was initiated by his father and turned deliberately westward. He sought in Europe the cultural and technological improvements which had been recommended by Yury Krizhanitch in his *Politica*. These improvements comprised military and naval techniques, engineering and shipbuilding; industry, commerce, education, and the arts. Peter also changed the old way of life and threw tradition to the winds. He replaced the boyars' rigid byzantine robes by western apparel, cut off their beards, placed wigs on their heads, and gave them dutch clay pipes and tobacco. He invited them to balls, insisting for the first time that women attend parties.[1] For greater speed and convenience in matters of administration and the writing of official orders, he modernized the Russian

---

[1] Before Peter, women rarely appeared in public; they were restricted to their quarters. A married woman welcomed guests, but did not join them at meals.

language and replaced the old Slavonic letters by a modern alphabet.

We further know that Peter fought the Turks and the Swedes, first losing, then winning famous battles on land and sea. For his military operations he exhausted and literally bled his people. For his reforms, he used crude and ruthless methods. His forced westernization of Russia has been often compared to Stalin's forced collectivization.

This parallel should not, however, be carried too far, for it easily becomes a cliché. History rarely "repeats itself." In spite of Peter's too sweeping, too drastic actions, he did not want to subdue the entire world to an abstract social and political ideology, as do the communists. He did not keep down the iron curtain which divided Russia from the West; on the contrary, he removed it and, as Pushkin wrote, he "opened a window on Europe."

It has been often discussed whether Peter's reform benefited Russia or, on the contrary, crippled the development of a normal process. In Russia there long existed and probably exist even today two schools of thought: the "Westerners," who defend these reforms, pointing to their remarkable achievements, and the "Slavophiles," who defend the heritage of ancient Slavonic cultural and religious tradition *versus* Peter's hastily built and roughly hewn new world. Both camps have strong arguments in favor of their theory.

Without seeking to solve this dilemma, we must admit that there is one aspect of these reforms which strikes us as unfortunate. This is the suppression of the patriarchate and the reform of Russian Church administration.

Peter was not irreligious. When he founded Petersburg, he brought the relics of St. Alexander Nevsky to his new capital and built a monastery and cathedral in his name. Alexander was a warrior-saint, who had defeated the Swedes before Peter and was very much to the tsar's own liking. But Peter feared the Church, which was hostile to his reforms and which exercised, as we have seen, a power almost as great as the tsar's. True, patriarchs could be deposed and banished, as Nikon had been, but their throne was never empty for long. During his journeys abroad, to Germany and England, Peter had observed the organization of Protestant churches which were obedient to the State and whose hierarchies had no authority either spiritual or political comparable to those of Rome or Moscow. Since the Russian patriarch had died, an opportunity was offered to let the patriarchate die with him. But how was the Church to be administered? Peter turned to the Russian clergy to solve this problem. There were at that time a number of priests who were not opposed to Peter's pro-Western policies and who, on the contrary, welcomed them. The leader of this group was Feofan Prokopovich, Archbishop of Novgorod. A stanch supporter of the tsar, Prokopovich was a highly educated man, who had received a Latin — in other words, Western — formation in the Kiev Divine Academy. Like St. Demetrius of Rostov, he was an author and playwright, and was moreover a great orator. His most famous speech was his funeral oration at Peter's death, when he summed up the tsar's achievements in which he himself had taken an active part.

Together with Feofan Prokopovich Peter developed a State system which scarcely reflected the Third Rome ideology. For now there was a *secularized State* in which the powers of the Church were reduced to administrative functions. And even these were strictly circumscribed. For that purpose, Peter entrusted Prokopovich with the writing of the "Church Regulation" which set down the rules of the new ecclesiastical machinery. Instead of the Patriarch, the Russian Church was to be governed by the *Holy Synod,* a collegiate body of prelates. The project was communicated to the other Eastern patriarchs who approved it and officially recognized the Holy Synod as their "brother." Thus, the new institution was canonically sound and could arouse no objections. In order to ensure his control over it, Peter appointed a civil official, the *Chief Procurator of the Holy Synod,* to represent the State. The "Church Regulation" defined the new status as follows:

> The fatherland need not fear from the synodal administration the same mutiny and disorder as occur under a single ecclesiastical ruler.

The Regulation stated in so many words, that "the people being ignorant, did not know the difference between the spiritual and the secular power" and were too impressed by "the greatness and fame of the supreme pastor." They considered him as a "second sovereign" and believed that the Church was "another superior State." This, the Regulation went on to explain, "often led to dissensions and even mutiny among the people and stirred hostility to the sovereign" under the guise of religious fervor. But, Prokopovich said reassuringly:

> When the people understand that the synodal administration is established by monarchical decree and the decision of the Senate, they will be discouraged and will give up hope of winning the support of the church dignitaries for their riots.

The Regulation, immediately put into practice, dealt a terrible blow to the Russian Church. In fact she was paralyzed and tied down for two centuries, and was only revived when the patriarchate was restored in 1917, at the time of the Bolshevik revolution. Strangely enough the patriarch's empty throne was occupied once more, when the tsar's throne became vacant. Had Peter been able to see this, he would, no doubt, have wondered at history's paradoxes.

Though the suppression of supreme ecclesiastical authority had been deliberately willed by the Tsar, he seems to have had no qualms of conscience about it. The recognition of the Synod by the leaders of the other Eastern Churches made his position secure in the eyes of the faithful. He had, moreover, as we have seen, the support of part of the clergy, and of its most influential and best trained representatives, like Prokopovich. If he encountered hostility it was from men who were losing their influence. There were among them the Old Believers, who had risen against Peter from the very beginning of his reforms, since they interpreted them as another version of "foreign heresy" and had proclaimed that he was Anti-Christ. But Peter had not hesitated to crush the opposition ruthlessly, sending to the torture chamber and death his own son, Alexis, who had become the leader of his enemies.

In his "taming of the Church" Peter could argue that he respected her divine mission, not interfering with her magisterium nor tampering with her dogmatic structure. But he went much further in his "secularization" when he set up special pageants and buffooneries, in which his courtiers masqueraded as caricatures of priests and his chief jester as the pope. In these gross impersonations of anticlericalism we can see the precursor of communist antireligious propaganda — *i.e.*, an attack against the Church ordered *from above* and suffered by the people in silence.

Russian-Orthodox historians have pointed out the tragic effects of Peter's legislation. "Through the establishment of the Synod," writes Fr. Alexander Schmemann, "the Church becomes one of the departments of State, and up to 1901 its members called the tsar 'the chief judge of this divine college.'" And Fr. George Florovsky points out that after the creation of the synod, the Russian clergy became a "class of scared priests," while an "ambiguous silence reigns in the higher spheres," and the best clerical elements retire "to the inner desert of their hearts."

Generally speaking, the creation of the Synod was rooted in Western Protestant influences far more than in the Byzantine or Russian theocratic tradition. For in this tradition, Church and State contributed together to the government of the Christian people. Peter disassociated these two factors. As Father Schmemann points out, this was the establishment in Russia of *Western absolutism,* which had emerged in history from the conflict of Church and emperor in Europe. Peter had admired absolutism in France. He had, as we have seen, observed the secularized political structure which had been evolved in England and Germany. The new structure of the Russian State was actually Protestant, but this new element was so well disguised, that many convinced Russian-Orthodox did not see it until after Peter's death. The tsars were still solemnly crowned and anointed as in the days of Ivan and Alexis. Symbolically, the coronation continued to be performed in the Assumption cathedral in Moscow, where for a few hours the sovereign of a secular state appeared in *sacral* robes. This was the ambiguous situation which Fr. Florovsky speaks of; it presented side by side not tsar and Church, as the Byzantine and Moscow States had done, but the tsar and an ecclesiastical bureaucracy.

The fatal consequences of Peter's Church reform became even more apparent after his death. The "tears, sweat and blood" of the so-called early "Petersburg period" were over. Russia entered the family of European nations, no longer as a poor relation, but as a triumphant empire. Under Peter's successors, European culture was even more eagerly and rapidly absorbed than in the stormy days of the reforms. This was the age of European "enlightenment," the age of the Encyclopedist, when reason prevailed and science invaded "the dark corners" of superstition. This was the triumph of a philosophy, which preached *deism,* the cult of a Divine Architect or of a pantheistic God, instead of the crucified and resurrected Christ.

Enlightenment also came to Russia, and deism replaced the faith which had inspired St. Sergius and St. Demetrius of Rostov. This does not mean, however, that the Christian outlook on life completely vanished from the Russian cultured world. It lived on in many ways, acquiring modern dress, but preserving much that was essential. Thus, for instance, a lofty religious inspiration can be found in the "Ode to God," written by Gavrilo Derzhavin, one of the first and greatest Russian poets, who replaced the poor syllabic verse borrowed from the Latin by a monosyllabic typically Russian meter. In the "Ode to God" you may trace the influence of the encyclopedists and the fascination reason held for the enlightened Russian; but there is also fear and even awe of the almighty which is nearer to the "caves" and "deserts of the hermits" than to the eighteenth century scholar's study:

> In its sublime research, philosophy
> May measure out the ocean-deep — may count
> The sand or the sun's rays; but God! for Thee
> There is no weight or measure: — none can mount
> Up to Thy mysteries. Reason's brightest spark,
> Though kindled by Thy light, in vain would try
> To trace Thy counsels, infinite and dark;

And thought is lost ere thought can soar so high,
Even like past moments in eternity.

Neither the genius of Peter, whose memory was still so vivid,
nor the splendors of the court of Catherine the Great, whose
poet laureate Derzhavin had become, could eclipse the power
and glory of Him whom the poet calls Potentate:

Thou from primeval nothingness didst call
First chaos, then existence: — Lord! on Thee
Eternity had its foundation; — all
Sprung forth from Thee: — of light, joy, harmony,
Sole origin: — all life, all beauty Thine.
Thy word created all, and doth create;
Thy splendour fills all space with rays divine.
Thou art, and wert, and shalt be! Glorious! Great!
Light-giving, life-sustaining Potentate.

In the "Ode to God" we also find the cult of science spread by
the Encyclopedists, and even of what we would call astrophysics
in our day:

A million torches lighted by Thy hand
Wander, unwearied, through the blue abyss:
They own Thy power, accomplish Thy command,
All gay with life, all eloquent with bliss.
What shall we call them? Piles of crystal light, —
A glorious company of golden streams, —
Lamps of celestial ether burning bright, —
Suns lighting systems with their joyous beams?

But Derzhavin's is not a materialistic universe. After this magnificent description of the "celestial bodies," the poet exclaims:

But Thou to these art as the noon to night.

Yes! as a drop of water in the sea,
All this magnificence in Thee is lost: —
What are ten thousand worlds compared to Thee?
And what am I then? Heaven's unnumbered host,
Though multiplied by myriads, and arrayed
In all the glory of sublimest thought,
Is but an atom in the balance, weighed
Against Thy greatness, is a cypher brought
Against infinity! Oh! what am I then? Nought!

Then once more Derzhavin raises man to his true dignity, bestowed on him by God:

> Nought! Yet the effluence of Thy light divine,
> Pervading worlds, hath reached my bosom too;
> Yes! in my spirit doth Thy spirit shine,
> As shines the sunbeam in a drop of dew.
> Nought! yet I live, and on hope's pinions fly
> Eager towards Thy presence; for in Thee
> I live, and breathe, and dwell; aspiring high,
> Even to the Throne of Thy divinity.
> I am, O God! and surely THOU must be![2]

However lofty, deism could not satisfy the need of spiritual food felt by so many cultured Russians of the age of "enlightenment." Some of them sought in Catholicism the way out of their dilemma. It is interesting to recall that at the time of Empress Catherine the Jesuits came to Russia and paradoxically enough, Russia, which had been so hostile to Roman priests and so afraid of "latinism" let them settle down in Petersburg without raising any obstacle. This took place during the period when the Society of Jesus was dissolved by the Holy See and its members expelled from many other countries. Empress Catherine was in conflict with the Vatican and chose to ignore the papal bull. It never reached Petersburg, and the Jesuits who had their community established there did not receive it. They could pursue their activity and later opened a college.

Under Catherine's successors there were conversions to the Catholic Church among a number of distinguished Russians belonging to great families, like the princes Galitzin and Volkonsky. Because of these conversions, Tsar Alexander I became wary of Jesuit influence; their college was closed and the fathers expelled from Russia in 1815. Nevertheless, Catholicism continued to attract the Russian religious mind. Conversions, though few, were mostly among men and women of exceptional moral character and outstanding intelligence.

---

[2] The above translation is by Sir John Bowering, a contemporary of Derzhavin; it interprets excellently the lofty thought of the Russian poet, but cannot render the magnificence of Derzhavin's style (printed by Regina Laudis, O.S.B.).

The best representatives of the Russian-Orthodox faith withdrew to faraway monasteries to lead lives of prayer and contemplation outside the "enlightened" world. As we shall see, there were many great ascetics and two great saints among them. But notwithstanding this fact the "church regulation" had a disastrous effect throughout Russia. It produced a vacuum which was soon filled with false prophets, false gods, and a variety of sects.

The entire history of the religious, or pseudo-religious, currents which invaded Russia in the eighteenth and the nineteenth centuries has not yet been written. While most of the cultured elite followed Voltaire (with whom empress Catherine corresponded) or worshiped at the shrine of deism, some idealistic young men adopted the mystic and humanistic teaching of Scottish freemasonry. The Protestant Bible Society of England established headquarters in Petersburg and was permitted by the Holy Synod to distribute cheap editions of the King James bible in Russian translation. Protestant influence also began to initiate religious trends among the peasants. Many sects became popular, drawing a considerable number of followers; the Baptists, the Evangelists and the Molokans, the Dukhobors, the Stundists, the Mennonites, the Huepfers, and others.

There appeared, on the other hand, extreme mystical movements, also mostly among peasants; they stemmed from the priestless and other radical religious groups, which considered themselves God-inspired, visited by the Holy Ghost, receiving "sacred books" from heaven, like the Mormons, or founding celibate communities like the Shakers. The most extreme of these sects were the *Skoptzy,* who mutilated themselves to avoid sin, and the *Chlysty,* the flagellants, who have a long and complex history. The leaders of this sect called themselves "Christs," and the women called themselves "Mothers of God." Their chapters, called "ships," held vigils to await the "visitation of the spirit." During these vigils the members of the sect formed a circle, sang, danced, whirled, and fell into trances. Dramatic prophesies were uttered by the "Christs" and "Mothers." Extreme asceticism was observed together with weird sexual practices and obscure orgies which made the Chlysty one of the most repulsive and uncanny sects ever known in Russia. At one time, the Chlysty had followers in Moscow and Petersburg, and their influence penetrated even into aristocratic and highly educated circles. One of their prophetesses, Tatarinova, had a considerable following. This sect was often pursued and punished by law. Russia's best preachers and experienced theologians tried to argue with them. But they persisted in their dark cult.

The Skoptzy and the Chlysty represent, as we have said, the extreme and most heterodox of the Russian sects. The other movements mentioned had no such perverse and malignant a character. They lived according to evangelical principles and established rural communities for collective work and prayer. They were convinced pacifists and refused to obey the State laws. They were arrested and tried, but sought refuge in faraway areas of the far North or Siberia, or emigrated to Canada and the United States. It will be remembered that the famous writer, Leo Tolstoy, took an interest in the sects, whose ideology was so near to his own pacifism and anti-State theories. He soon had his own followers among the intelligentsia and among the people. As a rule Russian intellectuals had a liking for the *sectanty* (members of sects), respected their convictions, and were often inclined to share them, or sympathize with them.[3]

At the end of the nineteenth century, there were from thirteen to fourteen million *sectanty* in Russia, according to available statistics.[4] This is but a minority compared to the many millions of Russian-Orthodox who belonged to the established Church or to the Old-Believer groups. But the influence of this minority should not be ignored by those who seek a deeper understanding of the religious life of Russia.

The persistence and influence of the sects can be traced even today in Soviet Russia, where we find a large group of Baptists who have their churches. Many visitors, especially protestant

---

[3] The well-known religious philosopher, Nicholas Berdyaev describes his meetings with the *sectanty* in his book, *Dream and Reality*.
[4] P. Miliukov, *ibid.*

leaders of Europe and America, have attended Baptist services in Moscow and even preached at them.

A great number of *sectanty* were arrested in the days of Stalinist persecutions because they were pacifists and refused to obey the State. They were sent to labor camps, but even there they offered passive resistance, refusing to work for a State institution. Members of various sects participated in the famous strike at the Vorkuta labor camp in the 'fifties. This has been attested by eyewitnesses, who were later liberated and related their experience. However, these descriptions give us no clues by which the sects could be identified. They may have presented a mixture of various religious trends, and there seem to have been Tolstoyans among them. After the Vorkuta strike, when the fate of internees was somewhat eased, the sectanty were permitted to work in the infirmary, a type of activity which did not conflict with their convictions. According to many reports, the members of the sects were said to be the most stubborn inmates of labor camps.

* * *

Like the *Raskol*, the sects are a paradoxical phenomenon in the history of the Russian Church. They show us that religion in Russia was not an ironclad *totalitarian* ideology, as it has been often defined. The "Third Rome" rapidly deteriorated under the impact of Peter's reforms and Catherine's enlightenment. We note that the sects arose precisely at the time when the cultured Russian elite turned away from the Church, and Russian monasticism, harshly rejected, retired to the desert. The monks, as Dostoyevsky so often pointed out, had the people with them. Together they clung to the old traditions, preserved the liturgy, and worshiped at ancient shrines. But even monastic life was half paralyzed by secularization. Religious communities were subject to severe laws, and their activities restricted. A minority of the people found no solace in the established Church and turned to the sects and their extreme teachings. It was thus that a tragic estrangement began to develop between the ruling class and the people. The tsars, the noblemen, the intellectuals lived their own lives and considered the people as the victims of obscurantism, as ignorant and uncouth peasants led by a "scared" clergy. Or else the peasants were members of strange and often morbid religious movements, to be either condemned or laughed at.

Meanwhile the established Church was more and more subjected to the Holy Synod. The Procurator who had been first appointed as a mere controlling officer and observer, now became a high official with the rank of minister. This hypertrophy of the secular arm and the withering of ecclesiastical authority came to its climax in the late nineteenth century during the reign of Alexander III. The procurator of the Holy Synod was at that time Pobyedonostzev. He was the epitome of the darkest reactionary forces ever centered in Russia in the person of a high official directly responsible for the spiritual welfare of his country.

CHAPTER NINE

The New Era

POBYEDONOSTZEV combined vast culture with Machiavellian shrewdness; he was a mixture of almost fanatical faith (in a Church he was called to supervise) and cynicism as to the means to be employed by his administration. He was a pharisee who impressed sincere Christians by a sort of exalted conviction of his correctness. Even Dostoyevsky fell under his sway for a time, and his extreme pronouncements about the national mission of the Russian Church and her absolute righteousness date from his association with the procurator. The latter, whom they called "the tsar's grey eminence," had a fanatical belief in a "Third Rome" of his own creation, so unlike the noble conception of the monk Philoteus, that we should not even seek to compare the two ideologies. This religious absolutism followed the pattern of the tsar's political absolutism. It created in the eighteen nineties an irrespirable atmosphere which bred the germs of future revolutions. Thus were born in many a heart the hatred of both State and Church, as well as the internal political and social schisms which ended in 1917 in communism.

Pobyedonostzev's fanaticism made him a stark enemy of the religious minorities in Russia. This included all the sects which he cruelly persecuted. It included also the Jews, favoring the spread of antisemitism to a degree until then unknown in Russia. The "tsar's grey eminence" tormented the Catholics by rendering their legal situation extremely difficult, especially for new converts. But strangely enough he translated the *Imitation of Christ* into Russian. This translation is not only most accurate but perfect in style, for Pobyedonostzev was a brilliant writer.

It is believed that despite his temporary connection with the Procurator, Dostoyevsky realized how distorted his mind was and depicted him in the "Brothers Karamazov" as the Grand Inquisitor.

*   *   *

However dark and paralyzing the "synodal period" was for the Church and her life, this life did not cease to develop, resisting, on the one hand, the tide of secularization, and on the other hand, the pressure of Pobyedonostzev's administration. Father Alexander Schmemann is quite right when he writes:

> In spite of a very wide spread opinion, the "synodal period" can in no way be considered as a decline, as a withering of spiritual forces. First of all the deep and wide culture, which was gradually created in the Church, and which distinguished these times from the previous "Moscow period" is too often forgotten.[1]

Father Schmemann reminds us, in his impartial analysis of these times, that not only the Russian secular development, but also the Russian magisterium was influenced by Western culture; and this meant, where the Church was concerned, the penetration of Latin theology and the Latin methods of teaching into spheres which up to then had been more or less closed to such influences.

> No matter whether it was through the West, through Latin or German books, but the great, long forgotten tradition of thought, of disinterested search for truth and of ascetic devotion to it, was revived once more in Russia Orthodoxy.[2]

And Father Schmemann further reminds us that this period was marked by a great monastic revival and by a new flowering of sanctity. Indeed, it was at the time of Empress Catherine and her infatuation with Voltaire that Bishop Tikhon of Zadonsk gave up his see and retired to a monastery, to become a humble monk and a man of prayer and mortification. He was a profound and gifted writer, a remarkable spiritual director, and an experienced psychologist. His letters and spiritual advice to priests and laymen are, like those of St. Demetrius of Rostov, among the

---

[1] *Op. cit.*
[2] *Ibid.*

best of Russian religious writings. After Bishop Tikhon's death
he was canonized by the Russian Church.

St. Tikhon's spiritual way and devotions were strongly marked
by Western influences. Summing up the characteristic traits of
this remarkable pastor, G. Fedotov writes:

> His spiritual life has two faces: the thought of death and the
> vision of the celestial world. He meditated constantly on this
> "double eternity." The fear of eternal torments was a mystical
> reality for him to as great an extent as were the visions of Christ,
> the holy Virgin, and the angels. In both these objects of contempla-
> tion, Tichon is the son of the Western Baroque rather than the
> heir of Eastern spirituality. Especially uncharacteristic of Russian
> religion is his continual concentration on the sufferings of the
> Crucified Savior. He had always before his eyes the icons — or,
> rather, pictures — portraying the various moments in the tragedy of
> Golgotha. These were obviously pictures after the Western pattern,
> the Eastern Church knowing no sacred models for them.[3]

St. Tikhon, also, is portrayed in some of Dostoyevsky's famous
pages: Reading in *The Possessed* the interview between Stavroguin
(the hero of the novel) and the prelate to whom he intends to
confess his crime, the reader finds not only the main characteristics
of the saint but even his name. Dostoyevsky's Bishop Tikhon, who
is the very opposite of the Grand Inquisitor, remains a fictional
character, but we know from the great writer's notebooks that
he had a great devotion for the real bishop, the saint of Zadonsk.

*   *   *

St. Seraphim of Sarov, who is considered by many as Russia's
greatest saint, also belongs to the "synodal period." He lived at
the time of Pushkin which marked the flowering of Russian
culture: poetry, prose, political and social thought, philosophy, and
higher education, all that the human intellect could produce in
so short a time, were created in the days of St. Seraphim. And
yet the echoes of the modern world scarcely reached the cell in
the "desert" of the Sarov woods, where this hermit lived and
preached, bringing to the people a very different sort of enlightenment.

---

[3] *Op. cit.*

St. Seraphim spent thirty-one years in solitude and in extreme mortification. For a thousand nights he prayed standing on a stone; he lived on a scant diet of vegetables and berries and encountered many dangers, from the attack of robbers to that of the wild beasts. Like St. Sergius he tamed both the bears and the devils who tempted him. After these long years of spiritual training he emerged from his lonely cell, or rather opened its doors to the people. Many men and women in the neighborhood or even in faraway districts heard of the hermit and came to consult him. Sinners repented, erring souls received his advice most devoutly and went away reformed. Those who wept were comforted and those who sought the truth found it at Sarov. But the proud were humbled and the hardened criminals reproved.

What was the secret of St. Seraphim's teaching? It was contained in a few words, for he called this way of perfection the "acquisition of the Holy Spirit." This could be done through simplicity, a complete dedication to God, and constant prayer. Though St. Seraphim practiced the prayer of Jesus taught at Mount Athos, he also recited a sequence of prayers, closely resembling the rosary.[4]

Seraphim had a great devotion to our Lady. He called her the "Joy of all Joys" and died kneeling before one of her icons. The Saint of Sarov left his followers not only a heritage of traditional piety and devotion, but a new and dynamic way of perfection. It was perfection through severity, but also through joy, through simple and morally sound advice and mystic ecstasy, when his soul soared in pure love of God. During one of his conversations with his disciple Motovilov, he reached such ecstasy that he seemed transfigured and aflame with dazzling light. Motovilov, who was a layman, reported his conversation with the saint and the transfiguration which he witnessed. At the same time, Seraphim remained in the eyes of the Russian people a

---

[4] The Eastern rite rosary dates back to the seventh century. It is usually made of wool in which there are 100 knots with a larger knot at each tenth. At the end is a cross also made of knots. Beside woolen rosaries, there are also rosary beads; there are 25 beads to a "decade." Usually 100 ejaculations and several other prayers are recited in the sequence, also a number of Hail Mary's are repeated.

man both meek and humble, who, like Therese of Lisieux, taught
not the "royal road" to heaven but the "little way" open to the
poor in spirit. For many years after his death he remained almost unknown to the majority of the faithful, nor was there room
for his teaching in the glamorous Petersburg circles. But his
teaching was piously preserved by his close disciples and by the
nuns of a monastery which he visited as spiritual director. This
monastery, Novoye Diveyevo, became the pattern of Russian
ascetic women's communities. Prayer, contemplation, charity, such
was the teaching St. Seraphim left to the nuns of Diveyevo.

St. Seraphim was canonized in 1903, i.e., on the eve of
World War I and the Russian Revolution. His cult began to
spread rapidly. In fact it seems to have developed very much
like the devotion to the Little Flower in France. It was as if
the world needed great modern saints to meet the challenge of
great modern tragedy. The Little Flower's miracles spread not
only throughout France but throughout the whole world. St.
Seraphim's spiritual help to those who call upon him accompanied thousands of Russians whom the revolution drove out of
their native land. Today the icon of the Sarov hermit is found
in many a Russian home all over the world. Fr. Tyszkiewicz, S.J.,
speaking of this remarkable representative of Russian spirituality
says: "Saint Seraphim of Sarov is among all relatively recent
Russian saints, the one best known, best understood and best
loved in all deeply religious Russian circles."[5]

*   *   *

Let us also point out that it was during the "synodal period,"
that an important historio-philosophical movement, was created
in Russia by a group of writers and thinkers, known as the
Slavophiles. This group headed by Ivan Kireievsky and Alexy
Khomyakov was opposed to the idea, most common at that time,
that Russia had benefited from the reforms of Peter the Great.
Though themselves highly educated men, imbued with Western
culture, the Slavophiles defended the principle that Peter had
destroyed authentic Russian spiritual values replacing them by

[5] S. Tyszkiewicz, S.J., and Dom Th. Belpaire, O.S.B., *Ascetes Russes* (*see*
Bibliography).

a completely secularized scale. Both Kireievsky and Khomyakov were fervently attached to Russian Orthodoxy and based their historical and philosophical theories on its teachings. Khomyakov founded a school of Russian-Orthodox lay theologians. He developed the theory of *Sobornost*, in other words, an ecclesiology which had for its foundation the Koinonia, or communal unity of the first Christians (Acts 2:42). *Sobornost*, which comes from the Russian word *sobiratj*, to gather, and which can be translated by the word *communion* or *unity*, is, in the eyes of Khomyakov the foundation of the Church. For the Church *is* unity, that is a free association of men in Christ and in His charity. The official Church did not immediately accept Khomyakov's doctrine, and would not even permit its publication for a long time. But it was finally recognized by modern theologians as the best definition and projection of the spirit of Russian Orthodoxy and of the latter's deepest religious experience. Khomyakov's work on *Sobornost* had a great influence on the further development of Russian-Orthodox thought.

The religious philosopher, Vladimir Solovyev, a brilliant member of the Russian-Orthodox Church, who later became a Catholic, also lived in those days. Solovyev's major works, *God and Godmanhood* and *Russia and the Universal Church* were neither understood nor welcomed by the Holy Synod. In fact, the second of these books could not be published in Russia as long as Pobyedonostzev was Procurator. But the Christian philosophy these works contained was known by the Russian intellectual elite; it stimulated their writings and had a profound influence on Russian twentieth-century religious thought.

Solovyev, it will be remembered, centered his philosophy on universality, on *oneness* in Christ. This was an outlook very near to that of Khomyakov, but Solovyev's *Sobornost* reached out much further; it was no longer Russian only; it embraced the entire world. During the last period of his life, Solovyev was deeply concerned with the ecumenical problem, with the reconciliation of East and West, divided by the schism. He believed that Russia belonged to the Universal Church despite the schism. We have told of his interest in Yury Krizhanitch, whose views on Russia he shared.

"There was a glorious time," wrote Soloviev, "when on Christian soil, and under the banner of the Universal Church, the two Romes, that of the West and that of the East, were joined in the name of one common aim: the establishment of Christian Truth. In those days, their peculiarities, the peculiarities of the Eastern and of the Western character, did not exclude, but completed each other. This unity was precarious because it had not yet gone through the ordeal of becoming aware of itself, and so it was broken. The great quarrel between East and West, which had been solved within the Christian idea, was renewed with even greater violence within the limits of historical Christianity. But if the separation of the Churches was historically necessary, it is even more necessary morally for Christianity to put an end to this division."[6]

Let us not forget that it was also in the "grand inquisitor's" age that Dostoyevsky wrote his great novels so deeply imbued with the spirit of the meek and gentle Christ beloved by St. Seraphim.

We may truly say that Russian religious thought, expressed by great writers and philosophers, all of them laymen, was born in the nineteenth century and is typical of these times. It expresses a Christian revival which flowered in the days when Russian society was torn between atheism and official pietism; it had nowhere to turn until a few men like Khomyakov and Solovyev began to speak of the God-Man, of communion and universality in Christ.

*   *   *

Scarcely more than a decade after St. Seraphim's canonization, the "synodal period" drew to its tragic end. The events that led to it belong to Russian political and social history and we leave them to specialists in this field. We have, however, attempted to bring out some of the spiritual causes of this decline: the secularization of many branches of Russia's life which had formerly been deeply penetrated with religious aspirations; the tragic break

---

[6] *Russia and the Universal Church*, see Bibliography.

between the people and ruling class and between ruling class and the Church. To this must be added a weakened hierarchy, deprived of its head, and a clergy either "scared" or insecure in the general confusion.

In February, 1917, the "token" structure of the Third Rome crumbled in three days. As we have seen, the Moscow Patriarchate was providentially restored in the very midst of the storm. Let us briefly recall this event. Even before the end of the Romanov dynasty many changes had marked the life of the Church. In 1906, after the first revolutionary outbreak and the granting of a constitution, there was a new spirit in the Holy Synod itself. Most of its members were progressive and the Procurators who succeeded Pobyedonostzev were eager to efface the grim memory of the "grey eminence." The democratic provisional government, which ruled for eight months after the Tsar's abdication and up to Lenin's rise to power, proclaimed full religious freedom for all faiths *sine conditio*.[7] It desired, moreover, to restore to the Russian Church its true spiritual authority. Upon the Holy Synod's own request, a council was convoked; it was composed according to the rules of Eastern autocephalous Churches of bishops, priests, and laymen, representing 66 dioceses, and met in Moscow in July, 1917. The council voted during the crucial period when the provisional government had been swept away by the tidal wave of communism. Once more, as in the days of Tsar Fedor, candidates were nominated and lots were drawn by an old monk. He drew the name of Tikhon, Metropolitan of Moscow, who became the eleventh patriarch of all Russia and was consecrated November 21, 1917, in the Cathedral of the Assumption. By that time, Lenin and the Bolshevik Party had become Russia's absolute masters.

The newly elected patriarch was to encounter many a trial and brave many a storm. His first proclamations were directed in energetic and even violent terms against the "satanic forces" of bolshevism. Religious demonstrations were held in Moscow and Petersburg. "Never before or since have I seen such a solid

---

[7] The separation of State and Church was announced at the same time.

mass of people," declared one of the eyewitnesses of the procession held in the capital around the Alexander Nevsky Abbey.[8]

What followed was tragedy: Not only had Tikhon to resist Lenin's atheist and materialist State; he also had to oppose the new religious group, who combined the ancient trends of the Church with a number of innovations. These radical reforms made the group more acceptable to the new regime, but were contrary to dogma and tradition. The members of the clergy adhering to this movement and known as the "Innovators," founded the so-called Living Church and their own hierarchy. They joined forces with the Soviet government to evict Tikhon. The patriarch was arrested and interned, while his opponents established good relations with the men in power. The majority of the people, however, did not accept the Living Church and wanted Tikhon at the head of the hierarchy. The patriarch was to be tried in court; but the Bolsheviks, aware of the mood of the faithful, decided to compromise. They forced Tikhon to make a statement for the press recognizing his "faults," i.e., his antagonism to the Soviet regime, and promising co-operation with it. In July, 1923, Tikhon was released and was allowed to resume his functions as acting patriarch.

When Tikhon died in April, 1925, his "testament" was published in *Pravda*, the official communist organ. In this document, the Patriarch once more stressed the necessity of compromising with the government. Little by little he had succeeded in gathering religious forces around his see, thus preparing the downfall of the Living Church. However, his concessions were severely judged by many, especially by Russians who had fled abroad and who could not follow closely the development of events. Others declared that Tikhon's statements were a forgery. Western observers also disapproved of the patriarch or disbelieved his declarations.

It must be remembered, however, that Tikhon had no choice; if he wanted to save the Church from utter destruction, he had to obey. His concessions were made, certainly not in order to

---

[8] Miliukov, *ibid.*

preserve his own life, but only to protect his flock and all that remained of faith and morals in a world doomed to paganization.

It must be also stressed that Tikhon made no concessions in so far as dogma was concerned, nor did he undertake any changes in the liturgy. On the contrary, he prescribed its strict observance to counteract the Living Church. Thanks to him, the Innovators' movement did not last long.

After Tikhon's death, the Bolsheviks forbade the re-election of a new patriarch. But they allowed the nomination of a *locum tenens*. The prelate who assumed this task was metropolitan Sergius of Nizhny Novgorod.

Though once again the Russian Church was without a head, there was a legal status which permitted her to continue her main functions. And this Sergius' "skeleton hierarchy" did despite new and tremendous difficulties.

Having failed to promote the heretical Living Church, and being on the other hand unable to cut off the remaining healthy branch of the Church, the communist government launched its policy of militant atheism. Priests were accused of conspiring against the regime. The "Association of the Godless" was created to track them down, denounce and persecute them. Twenty-eight bishops, and 1200 clerics and monks were arrested, and executed. The ancient monastery of Solovetzk on the White Sea shore was turned into a vast prison and was soon filled with members of the clergy, among whom were several Catholic priests. Many died from sickness and exhaustion, being condemned to hard labor in the arctic cold. Only a few who were later liberated or escaped lived to tell the tale of horror. But providentially perhaps, the very setting of the historic abbey inspired the prisoners and helped them to carry their cross. Many of them were assigned quarters in what had been formerly a great cathedral, with beautiful frescoes peeling from the walls.

The priests and monks who were not arrested suffered terrible privations. They were placed in a special category of soviet citizens, the lowest one, which was deprived of ration cards. And they were assimilated *a priori* to the "enemies of the people." They were forbidden to celebrate the liturgy and their churches were closed.

It was at that time that many priests went underground in order to continue their mission. They hid in the woods, like their forefathers had done in the days of the Mongol invasion. Disguised as peasants and workers they lost themselves in the crowd of ever moving, ever anxious populations driven from town to town by civil war, famine, and epidemics. They were called the "wandering priests."

The story of these priests has often been told, but it should be retold over and over again: they brought the sacraments to the people whose churches were closed and whose pastors were gone: confession, communion, marriage, baptism — all these were secretly performed. There were also laymen who wandered throughout Russia, reading Scripture and giving responses to the priests. These devoted clerics and faithful kept up the flame of a Church which truly was "Living," the Church of the catacombs which nobody could destroy.

The Christians suffered long years of persecution in Russia. But in 1937, two decades after the October revolution, the head of the Godless Association, Yaroslavsky, published an official report. This report stated clearly that the communists' antireligious policy had failed, and that there were millions of practicing Christians in Russia, whom nobody had counted, but who were actively participating in religious life. The Godless Association had not taken into account the simple fact that it was no use closing churches and pursuing priests, because the latter did not need any churches, nor could they be tracked down in their underground.

From that day on, godless persecutions ceased and were replaced by "godless propaganda," but this "peaceful method of persuasion" also failed. When World War II broke out and Hitler invaded Russia, the people rose to her defense; but they wanted their religion to be freed from chains and their churches reopened. This process took place gradually, as the priests came out of their underground. In 1943 a council was convoked to elect a patriarch, and its choice was the former *locum tenens,* Metropolitan Sergius.

This election and the events that immediately followed marked a new period in the history of the Church in the U.S.S.R. Paragraph 123 of the Constitution proclaimed already in 1936 *freedom of religion* for all the peoples of the Soviet Union; it had never actually been applied until the forties and fifties, but is now more widely put into effect. It must be stressed, of course, that *complete* freedom of religion does not exist in Russia in the sense that these words should be and are understood in noncommunist countries. The Church in Soviet Russia cannot teach children religion; only when a Soviet youth or girl have attained their majority have they a right to be instructed by a priest. Sermons are strictly supervised and no philanthropic or other activities usually associated with Church organizations are permitted in the U.S.S.R. The only privilege that the Church enjoys is *freedom of worship.*[9] Though old churches are allowed to reopen or new ones may be built, they are heavily taxed and the building costs are extremely high.

Despite all these restrictions, however, we find the following figures given by trustworthy sources for the year 1959:

There are 35 to 50 million practicing Russian-Orthodox in the Soviet Union, distributed among seventy-three dioceses, with 33 thousand priests, 5 thousand religious (including monks and nuns). There are three seminaries; the most important one located in the abbey of St. Sergius and the Trinity has about two hundred students. Moscow has about fifty churches open. These churches as well as the shrines of St. Sergius and of the Kiev Caves are well attended, often crowded, and filled to capacity on great feast days.

Here are a few observations made by Catholics who visited Moscow.

Jacynth Ellerton writes:

---

[9] This law applies to all denominations — Russian-Orthodox, Protestant, Catholic, Moslem, Jewish.

We went into a church. Here all was changed. Here were the
Russians I was used to in the West. Hundreds of them packed
tightly together. Here they were relaxed and at home. Here there
were strong old faces full of expression. It has been reported that
some of the younger women who have begun to go to church have
said that only there do they feel truly themselves. Here was radi-
ance. Among the lovely glittering lights and the new gold leaf, the
icons, and the brightly coloured carpets, the tablecloths covered in
roses, the tureens of holy water and in the slow shapely liturgy
they were happy at last. . . .
We spent a good deal of time with the church leaders. We visited
churches and Theological colleges. We went to a monastery and
to the patriarchate. There was a great deal of very frank conversation. I could only listen and hope to understand.

When such scenes are described, we often hear the objection:
only old men and women go to church. A recent report which
refutes such objections is brought to us by another Catholic,
Jacques Nantet, concerning his visit to the Zagorsk Abbey:

. . . every day, even during the week, the six churches within
its precincts are very busy, whilst on Sundays one finds quite a
crowd, made up mostly of women, young and old, but also including plenty of children and men of all ages.
The presence of these children is most significant, for it shows
that many men, even if they do not go to church themselves,
nevertheless are willing that their children should receive religious
instruction.
For both men and women the average of attendance is highest
in the 18–30 age group. After thirty it falls, especially among men,
but it would seem to rise again among the over-fifties.

Mr. Nantet writes that there are many vocations in Russia "from
agnostic circles or working-class families."[10]

*   *   *

One more question remains and it is not an easy one to
answer: how far is the Russian Church, in the person of her
patriarchs and in her entire body, subservient to the Soviet government? Just as in the days of Tikhon, certain statements of the
Moscow hierarchy seem to convey the impression that the Kremlin

---

[10] Jacynth Ellerton, "A Catholic in Moscow" in *Eastern Churches Quarterly*,
1959, XII; Jacques Nantet, in *Blackfriars*, July-Aug., 1959.

"party lines" are blindly followed. There are also reports which
either openly state or suggest that the status of the Church under
communist rule is very much the same as it was in the days of
Pobyedonostzev: a hierarchy deprived of its authority and forced
to do what it is told; a clergy which is either debilitated, "scared,"
or worst of all, obliged to render services to the secret police.
Such accusations are shocking, because they involve thousands
of priests and young men preparing for priesthood. Even were
these reports founded on particular factual incidents they would
not and could not indict the entire Church. We have seen that
while many faults were committed in the days of the "grey
eminence" there were also in this time truly admirable monks
and pastors and saints like Seraphim of Sarov and Tikhon of
Zadonsk. These two great mystics lived in the days of absolutism,
whose defects they knew. They were neither subservient nor rebellious, for their "conversation was in heaven" — not in the hall
of worldly fame. We have seen on the other hand that even in
the days of a triumphant Third Rome, the Church often *led
the way*. She spoke the truth to tsars and potentates and inspired
Russia's life not by thundering sermons, not by impressive demonstrations, but by a deep, one might say God-given, prudence.
And, most important of all, not once did she reject the dogma
she had given Russia at the dawn of her life.

It seems to us that the example of the past will offer us a
key to the dilemma of the present. Instead of repeating, as some
critics do incessantly, that the Church in Russia is directed by
the Communists — could we not venture instead to say: it is
perhaps the Russian Church which, in some almost invisible way,
leads communism against the latter's will to its defeat. For "every
valley shall be filled and every mountain and hill shall be brought
low."

It remains for us to show why such a metamorphosis is possible. We have often pointed in this book to the remarkable continuity of the Russian *Ecclesia,* a continuity that remained un-
broken for one thousand years while prelates were crowned or
uncrowned, thrown into jail, murdered, or placed on the throne

opposite the monarch's. Should this continuity cease because of fifty years of trials? A half century may be enough to undo a political regime, to bring a social system to an end; but for the Church this is but a fleeting moment. There are in the life of the Russian Church some profound and timeless elements which constitute her strength: these are her great devotions, her liturgy, her love of prayer and contemplation which have so often "filled the valleys" of her tears. In the second part of the present book we shall try to give a picture of these invaluable spiritual treasures.

PART TWO

The Russian Church in Tradition and Life

CHAPTER TEN

Great Devotions of the Russian People

WE HAVE followed the course of Russian history through many periods, each of them different, marked by triumph or disaster and sometimes by both simultaneously. As the panorama unfolded we saw that at the crucial hours of struggle, suffering, and chaos, one factor remained and asserted itself with extraordinary force. This was the Church. So let us recall an ancient Russian legend: "The holy City of Kitezh."

When the Mongols invaded Russia, the legend tells us, Kitezh was a thriving community, with a large population. The city stood on the shores of a beautiful lake, and the citizens who were very pious built many churches and shrines. The bells of Kitezh could be heard far away in the countryside. The Mongols surrounded the city and its inhabitants were doomed. Then it was that a saintly young maiden, Fevronia, prayed God to save Kitezh. Her prayer was heard, the lake rose and its waters engulfed the city, with all its people, houses, churches, and shrines miraculously preserved. And thus Kitezh was saved and continued to live its mystical life, in peace and joy, at the bottom of the lake. It was said that the bells of its churches could still be heard as their deep voices rose above the waters.[1]

After the communist revolution, the legend of the holy city survived, and the people were continuously coming to the shore of the lake to listen to the bells. The Soviet police sent down divers to prove that there was nothing at the bottom of the lake, but could not stop the bells of Kitezh from ringing in the hearts of the people. Thus the mystic city has become the symbol

---

[1] Rimski-Korsakov wrote an opera on the Kitezh theme.

of all that is dearest to holy Russia: the great devotions which the Church preserved in the days of the Kremlin as well as in the days of the underground, for where love is, there God is. There are many devotions, many customs and traditions engulfed under the stormy waves of revolution, but still mysteriously alive. We shall describe a few of them in these closing chapters. Let it be remembered that they are all centered in Christ, our Lady, the saints, and the liturgy which daily praises them.

CHRIST

As in the Western, so in the Eastern Church, Christ is daily brought to the faithful in the holy sacrifice of the Mass, in the liturgy, instructions, days of fasting and on feast days, in the humility of oral or silent prayer and in the sublime heights of mystical experience.

The Eastern Church presents Christ in many aspects, and though all of them are true to dogma and tradition, they are different in many ways from those of Western Christology.

This is symbolically featured in the very pictures which represent our Lord and in the prayers which the Eastern religious mind composed to praise and implore Him.

Christ is often and very forcefully pictured in Eastern religious art. The Byzantine icons present Him as the PANTOKRATOR; that is as Emperor, all-powerful ruler, and judge. This formidable aspect is shown, for instance, in the recently uncovered mosaics of St. Sophia in Istanbul, or in the famous Pantokrator of Ravenna. This is the image of Christ "IN MAJESTY," of CHRIST RISEN, GLORIFIED, and ASCENDED TO HEAVEN.

Therefore He is pictured as mature, bearded, usually with rather severe features, holding in His right hand the book of judgment, or with His hand raised in blessing.[2] He is indeed the "Heavenly Emperor," in other words, CHRIST THE KING,

---

[2] *The Eastern Churches Quarterly* offers, in its 1952 Spring issue, a very interesting and exhaustive article on the Eastern Conception of Christ, in other words on the PANTOKRATOR. The author of this article is Dom Edmund M. Jones, a Benedictine Monk of the Congregation of Monte Oliveto, Louvain, Belgium (*see* Bibliography).

and He is usually portrayed by Byzantine painters on the walls of the church or inside its dome; for indeed such a triumphant, glorified, *majestic* Christ, can only extend His blessing to mankind from heaven.

Since Christianity came to Russia from Byzantium, it was from Byzantium that Kiev received the icon of the PANTOKRATOR. This severe and even awesome judge became, so to say, the CONSCIENCE of the Russian people. The eye of God was now present in every Russian home, and the SEVERE IMAGE of the heavenly Judge was there to remind every man of his immediate duties as a Christian. Indeed, it can be said that the presence of this heavenly judge — either in Russian homes, or shining from the domes of churches and cathedrals — was rather terrifying. But little by little, the Russian people were less terrified than *attracted* BY CHRIST. For indeed, what Christianity brought to Russia was not only the idea of celestial triumph and judgment. Christ meant a great deal more to these newly baptized people. He meant love, charity, compassion; He meant suffering and humiliation and crucifixion, in order that mankind might be saved; and above all Christ meant gentleness and meekness. He stirred the Russian people's conscience far more through the Beatitudes than through the terrors of the last judgment.

Hence, very soon the Russian concept of Christ became somewhat different from the Byzantine concept. The image of the PANTOKRATOR was replaced by the Icon of our Saviour, also holding a book in His hands, it is true but with the open pages of this book showing the words of St. John's Gospel — "*A new commandment I give unto you; That you love one another. . . .*" The ideal of the loving, the meek, the humiliated Christ, appears in earliest Russian religious writings. This ideal is reflected in the life of St. Theodosius, the founder of the famous Abbey of the Caves. When Theodosius was a youth, long before he became a monk, he declared that he wanted to imitate Christ, who according to St. Paul, "emptied Himself, taking the form of a servant" (Phil. 2:5–7). This is the *Kenosis*, meaning "self-emptying" in Greek.

St. Theodosius typifies the Russian concept of the humiliated and crucified Christ. As a child, he insisted on sharing the labors of the peasants in the fields, and gave away his clothes to beggars. When he was abbot of the Caves, he strictly observed holy poverty, and offered his own mortifications and strenuous manual labor as an example to his brethren.

St. Sergius, as we have seen, also pursued this life of mortification, poverty, humiliation, so that when he too, like St. Theodosius, became abbot of a famous monastery, he was often ignored, scoffed at, and insulted by people who imagined themselves devout Christians. The example of Christ, and prayers to the "most sweet Jesus," form the center of Russian religious life. Hence we find, very early in Russian devotional practice the ejaculation to Christ, known as "the Prayer of Jesus": "Our Lord, Jesus Christ, have pity on us, sinners." This prayer is indeed very short, but it is repeated by devout Russian Christians, over and over again, just as the Hail Mary is repeated by Christians in the West.

We have seen that the Prayer of Jesus was practiced in the fifteenth century by Nilus of Sorsk. Describing the spiritual state achieved through this devotion, Nilus of Sorsk says:

> Of a sudden, the soul is infused with joy, and this incomparable feast paralyzes the tongue. The heart overflows with sweetness, and while this delight endures, a man is drawn unwittingly from all sensible things. . . . When a man is conscious of this sweetness flooding his entire being, he thinks that this indeed is the kingdom of heaven and can be nothing else. . . . One who has discovered this joy in God, not only knows no stirring passion but is forgetful of his very life, since the love of God is sweeter than life, and the knowledge of God sweeter than honey, and the honey-comb and love is born of it.[3]

And so we may say, indeed, that veneration of Christ Jesus, and especially of Christ humiliated and crucified, is the center of Russian spirituality. We have mentioned a few outstanding religious teachers, and saints of the Russian middle ages. Let us now recall the famous Russian writer, Fedor Dostoyevsky.

"I affirm," wrote Dostoyevsky, "that our people were enlight-

---

[3] Fedotov (ed.), *A Treasury of Russian Spirituality* (*see* Bibliography).

ened a long time ago, by accepting Christ and His teaching.
The people know everything. . . . They learned in the churches
where during centuries, they heard prayers and songs that are
better than sermons. . . . Their chief school of Christianity was
the ages of endless suffering endured in the course of history
when abandoned by all, oppressed by all, working for all, they
remained all alone with Christ the Comforter, whom they received then in their soul and who saved them from despair."

And here is a brief, but impressive quotation from the great
Russian religious thinker, Vladimir Solovyev:

"The Russian people believe in Christ and in Our Lady: these
are the foundations of everything."

*   *   *   ˙

Among so many Russian devotions to our Lord we do not
find that of Christ the King, because this is a recent Western
devotion. But, as we have seen, Russians have worshiped for
many centuries the sovereignty of Christ in the Pantokrator.

The Russians do not have the devotion to the Sacred Heart
since this too is a Western devotion, initiated at a time when
the East had been cut off for many centuries from the West.
However, the Russians have such a deep love of that which fills
the heart of Jesus — mercy — that they have their way of ex-
pressing it in words and forms which would have delighted St.
Margaret Mary Alacoque had she known of them.

Russians are deeply aware of the meaning of Redemption. It
is one of the central themes of their piety. They very often speak
of Christ as the Saviour and many churches are called by this
name.

We have already seen the importance of the kenosis in Russian
Christology. Contemporary Russian thinkers and theologians have
brought out especially in their writings the *kenotic* aspect of
Christian life and culture from the earliest days to nineteenth
century authors in Russia.[4]

We must not think, however, that this ideal of the humiliated,
merciful Christ is the projection of a sentimental and emotional

---

[4] Nadejdo Gorodetzky, *The Humiliated Christ in Modern Russian Thought.*
See Bibliography.

temperament. The Russian Christ is not a figure of sweetness on a picture post card. He is sad, austere, and He is also demanding. He is the Christ presented as He was in the days of the Fathers by St. Maxim the Confessor: for him, the merciful Christ is still the legislator, holding up to us the new commandment,[5] "Love ye each other."

Even under the communist regime we find remarkable examples of devotion to Christ. The poet Serguey Esenin, who was a peasant, had for a time joined the bolsheviks then turned away from them in revolt. Speaking of the failure of godless propaganda, Esenin wrote that because of these attacks, the peasant will "more desperately cling to Christ."

OUR LADY

The Russian people have a very great devotion to the Blessed Mother. Indeed, this is one of the deepest devotions of the Russian Church. However, the Eastern liturgy and private prayer to our Lady are not like those of the West. Thus, for instance, we often hear the question: is the Rosary recited in Russia? Do the Russians recite the Hail Mary? The answer is that, both in official and private devotions, the Hail Mary *is* daily recited by the Russian Orthodox. However, they are not acquainted with the rosary, a devotion which did not develop fully until after the schism. Neither do Russian Orthodox use beads,[6] except monks, nuns, and specially devout people, i.e., mostly pilgrims.

Another difference which marks Marian devotion in Russia is that only the first part of the Hail Mary is recited both by the Russian Orthodox and by Russian-Catholics of Eastern rite. This first part of the prayer is more ancient than the second and was recited before the schism, when there was but *One Church.*

---

[5] I. H. Dalmais, "La Doctrine Ascetique de St. Maxime le Confesseur" in *Irenikon*, Ier trimestre 1953. 3.

[6] The beads were mostly used in Greece and in the Near East. In Russia they were replaced by a knotted cord of black wool or leather, as used by the early hermits. This cord has many knots but they do not represent Hail Mary's or other prayers as we find in the Rosary. They mark a series of various devotional prayers, among them "The Prayer of Jesus." There are also prayers to our Lady included in this private devotional cycle (*see* Chapter Thirteen).

Most important among Russian devotions to Mary is the *Acathist* or "Hymn to Our Lady" which is in itself a whole set of prayers, comparable to the Little Office of Our Lady in the Western Church. The Acathist Hymn was brought to Russia from Byzantium, where it was composed, probably in the sixth century. It is a collection of scriptural readings presenting all the pre-figures in which Mary was described in the Old Testament, as well as a sequence of troparions, and other chants, songs of praise and litanies. There are twenty-four various chants in the Acathist, presented in four parts and forming a special service celebrated in church or recited privately. In the Acathist we have the entire story of our Lady, first prefigured in the Old Testament and then related in the Gospel: from the Annunciation to the Visitation, to the Nativity and the Purification; then following Christ's life on earth and Mary's own role as intercessor before her only-begotten Son.

Let us quote from the nineteenth chant of the Acathist:

Nineteenth Chant

Thou art the castle of virgins and of all those who have recourse to thee, O Virgin and Mother of God: for the Creator of Heaven and earth prepared thee, O pure one, and came to dwell within thy womb, and taught us all to cry out to thee:

Hail, candid pillar of virginal innocence;
hail, open gate of salvation to come!
Hail, sweet occasion of nature's renewal;
hail, flowing well of the bounties of God!
Hail, O restorer of those born in shame;
hail, O reviver of those without sense![7]

The Eastern liturgy has placed our Lady, the *Bogoroditza* at the center of mystical life. Let us here stress that in the Eastern Liturgy the Blessed Virgin Mary is often called *"Bogoroditza"* (*Theotokos*, in Greek), which means "The One Who Gave Birth to God." In other words she is proclaimed the *Mother of God* in answer to the heresies of the early Christian centuries. This is also an answer to the Protestant approach, which avoids calling

---

[7] Byzantine missal (*see* Bibliography).

Mary the mother of God. In the Eastern Liturgy, the dogma of our Lady's motherhood is continually brought out, both in vocal prayer and in chants.

The Acathist is officially read on several occasions of the Church calendar or can also be said privately, in monasteries or in the home, although the length and complex nature of these prayers do not make them accessible to the ordinary faithful. However, the praise of our Lady is uttered continually at Mass, vespers, and other services of the Proper. On Sundays and at other times throughout the year, we always hear the hymn to Mary:

> It is indeed fitting and right to bless thee, O Mother of God. Ever blessed and most sinless One, and Mother of our God. Honored above the Cherubim and beyond compare more glorious than the Seraphim: Who without stain gave birth to the Word of God. Truly Mother of God, we sing thy praise.

Each Marian feast has its own hymns — troparions, kontakions, and canticles. The Eastern church calendar has a Marian feast for every day throughout the year, i.e., 365 feasts, relating either to the life of our Lady on earth or to the miracles she performed after her assumption. Thus each day the Church stresses the crucial significance of our Lady's intercession, of her help in man's tribulations and struggles on earth. It can truly be said that Russians constantly pray to Mary, either in the Acathist and other prayers, or in the brief ejaculation:
"Holy Mother of God, save us!"

*   *   *

The Immaculate Conception and the Assumption are not dogmas of the Russian Orthodox Church. However, they were recognized by the Eastern Church, before, as well as after the Schism. Experts in theology and in the teachings of the Eastern Church have elaborated on this theme.

The Assumption was often depicted in ancient Russian iconography. One of the earliest representations of this event is on the door of the Cathedral of Souzdal, erected in the thirteenth century. And yet our Lady being taken to heaven is not clearly stressed in Russian Orthodox teaching; this teaching rather uses the word "Dormition," that is, the *falling asleep* of the Blessed Virgin.

In the Proper of the Mass of the Dormition (August 15), i.e., Feast of the Assumption in the West, we find the following troparion:

> In thy maternity, thou didst retain thy virginity, and even though thou hadst ascended to heaven, thou didst not forsake the world: O Mother of God, thou hast passed to Life, since thou art the Mother of Life: through thine intercession, save our souls from death![8]

Many crucial events from the life of our Lady are depicted in the Russian icons. Most of them represent Mary holding the Infant Jesus in her arms. Several of these icons are particularly venerated in Russia; one of them, Our Lady of Iberia, was long preserved in a chapel in the very heart of Moscow. This icon mysteriously vanished from the chapel at the height of the godless persecution, but has recently been rediscovered and re-established as a sanctuary in Moscow. The other famous icons of the blessed Virgin are: Our Lady of Vladimir, Our Lady of Kazan, and an icon of the Assumption, the most ancient Russian relic, preserved in the city of Kiev. There is also Our Lady of the Sign, and the beautiful Pietà, or burial of our Lord, with the Bogoroditza lamenting over her son. This is a masterpiece of ancient icon painting.

Throughout many centuries our Lady performed miracles in Russia. She did not appear herself, as she did at Lourdes, La Salette, and Fatima; she worked her miracles by means of her icons. This is why Our Lady of Vladimir, of Kazan, of Iberia, became the center of popular devotion, since they were, and still are, considered miraculous. According to official Russian ecclesiastical registers, published before the revolution, there were over two hundred miraculous icons in Russia, which were venerated by the local population and attracted many pilgrims. These icons were often copied, reproduced, and distributed all over Russia.

Some of the icons bear the name of the locality where they

---

[8] *Ibid.,* Byzantine missal.

were found or where the miracle was performed Vladimir, Kazan, Iberia). Others bear the name of the special help they gave. Thus, for instance, there is Our Lady of Immediate Help, Our Lady of the Unexpected Joy, Our Lady The Prompt Listener, Our Lady of the Living Fount, Our Lady the Consoler of My Grief, Our Lady Salvation of the Sinner, Our Lady Salvation of Those Who Drowned at Sea, Our Lady the Purifier, Our Lady the Unfading Flower, Our Lady Who Shows the Way (*Odygitrya*, in Greek), and many others.[9]

One of the most venerated Russian icons is Our Lady of Vladimir, which was enshrined in the Cathedral of the Assumption in the Moscow Kremlin. During the revolution the so-called "godless gangs" looted the cathedrals and churches and removed most of the icons. Some of them were destroyed, others were preserved, one might say, miraculously. Among these were Our Lady of Vladimir. After antireligious propaganda had subsided, archaeologists and art experts in the U.S.S.R. began to defend Russian religious treasures. They proved to the Soviet government that some of these art treasures were priceless, among them the icon of Our Lady of Vladimir. So this ancient icon was preserved and re-established, not in the Cathedral of the Assumption, where it belonged, but in the Tretyakovsky picture gallery in Moscow. This may have troubled many a devout soul, who wanted the icon back in its cathedral, but God's ways are mysterious. Our Lady of Vladimir, W. Ryabushinsky tells us,[10] has been stripped of its robes of gold and silver and jewels, so that the original painting — which for many centuries had remained hidden, has now reappeared in all its beauty. The famous icon, which is now in the Moscow art gallery, produces even a stronger effect than

---

[9] Our Lady of Perpetual Help, venerated in the West, is not a Russian icon; its origin is probably Italo-Byzantine, i.e., painted in Venice under Byzantine influence. We find in Eastern iconography an image of Our Lady similar to the image of the Virgin of Perpetual Help, under the name of "Our Lady of the Thumb." This refers to the fact that in both the Western picture and the Eastern icon, we see the Infant Jesus holding on to his mother's thumb as he contemplates with awe the instruments of his future passion, held by the two angels.

[10] "Russian Icons and Spirituality," in *The Third Hour*, issue V, 1951.

in the days when it was in the Cathedral. W. Ryabushinsky writes: "One might say that the Queen of Heaven, divesting herself of her regal robes, had issued forth from the cathedral to preach Christianity in the streets, where all could see her — the believers, as well as those who do not as yet know Christ."

Let us picture to ourselves these men and women and children in the Moscow art gallery, filing past the holy image of the Bogoroditza, the holy mother of God. To some of these visitors she may be familiar, because they have seen reproductions of this icon in so many homes, as Pope Pius XII declared. Our Lady of Vladimir may be a revelation, a great discovery, or a rediscovery of Russian art and culture's religious sources. Perhaps some faraway memories begin to stir in them, the typically Russian religious trait: thus devotion to our Lady is reawakened by the icon; for is not the fact of its having been saved from destruction a miracle in itself?

As soon as the Soviet government granted a certain measure of freedom to the Russian Church many other icons were brought out of the underground and placed either in churches and shrines or in museums where they are visited once more by the people. As early as 1949, the Church calendar, published by the Moscow patriarchate, listed the miraculous icons venerated in Russia. These amount to 250, bearing the names of the various localities or of their special meaning as described above. Once more, the Russian people pray to our Lady of "Unexpected Joy," Consoler of My Grief, Salvation of the Sinner, and the others, as they used to long ago.

The Russian icons are not only venerated in the U.S.S.R. Two of them have come to America, brought with the Russian refugees after the revolution; these are the miraculous icons of Our Lady of Kursk and Tikhvin, which are both preserved, each in its own shrine in New York.

ST. NICHOLAS

St. Nicholas was born in the city of Lycia, in Asia Minor, in the early fourth century, and died about the years 345–352. He was ordained to the priesthood in his early youth, and later became Bishop and then Archbishop of Myra; he took part in the Council of Nicea, which condemned Arianism; under Emperor Diocletian he was imprisoned, persecuted, and even tortured for his faith. Some eight centuries after his death, Italian seagoing merchants brought over the Saint's body to their own land, and from those days on, the relics of St. Nicholas have been piously preserved at Bari, Italy, where many pilgrims, Catholics, and Greek and Russian Orthodox, come to pray and to ask for his intercession.

St. Nicholas was, and still is, a great miracle worker. He is often represented in pictures, standing near a tub, with three children emerging. These children are said to have been saved by St. Nicholas and miraculously brought back to life, after they had been killed by robbers. That is actually the origin of Santa Claus and of his love of children, including the distribution of Christmas toys. This miracle of the children in the tub occurred in France. There is a beautiful sculpture in the Chartres Cathedral, commemorating this event. When St. Nicholas performed this miracle, the golden legend tells us, he was on his way to Regensburg, Germany, in company of an Irish monk, Maurice. But where was he coming from? He was coming, so the story goes, from the Russian city of Kiev. St. Nicholas seems to have been at various times, in various parts of the world. Some of them he visited during his life on this earth, others after his death, and since he seems to have had a great predilection for holy Russia, the Russians have always loved St. Nicholas. One of the legends about the Archbishop of Myra tells us that when, after his death, the Italian merchants took his body to Bari, the soul of St. Nicholas accompanied them, and flew above the ship which carried his relic. But during the voyage the Saint's soul decided to fly in a different direction, not to the Mediterranean, not to Italy, but to Russia; it found a few steppingstones in the middle of the sea . . . these steppingstones which had been left by St. Andrew, the Apostle, who, as we have seen, was believed to have been the first evangelizer of the Russian land. And thus it was that

St. Nicholas came again to Russia, where he abides until the present day.

This story about the saint's soul journeying to Russia along "Saint Andrew's way" reflects the Russian people's poetic and religious instinct. It also shows that St. Nicholas means to them as much as St. Andrew the Apostle does. One might even say that the devout Russians are more familiar with St. Nicholas than with St. Andrew. They feel at home with him, confide in him, invoke him constantly, and keep his icon in their homes. He protects them against every sort of evil: fire, sickness, famine, but especially against dangers at sea and during other forms of travel. In the East St. Nicholas is the patron saint of travelers, just as St. Christopher is in the West. He protects shipwrecked sailors, fliers, and automobilists. No devout Russian will start upon a journey without a medal of St. Nicholas, and before the revolution, his icon was seen in every railroad station.

The Russian people love the Archbishop of Myra because he was an extraordinary man, an *extraordinarily kindly man.* He is described in ancient Russian religious documents as *"The Rule of Faith and the Image of Meekness."* His power, his authority, were truly supernatural, and yet he used neither power nor authority, but kindness.

It is a worthwhile task to collect the various stories connected with St. Nicholas in Russian religious tradition. A great number of these stories have been preserved by *Russian folklore,* mostly *oral.* Every Russian-born Christian has heard about St. Nicholas and his miracles from his or her early childhood. His icons, his medals, the invocations addressed to him, the constant reminder of his kindliness, all these are part of a Russian religious education. But this is not all. There are, in Russian religious thought, even in contemporary Russian literature, quite a number of writings devoted to St. Nicholas, and founded on Holy Russia's golden legend. There is, for instance, a book about him entitled *Moscow's Favorite Legends.* The author of this book, Alexis Remizov, who died in Paris in 1957, was a remarkable writer, one of Russia's best stylists, and a deeply religious man. Remizov describes in the beautiful style which was his, the various episodes of the life of St. Nicholas and also what the saint did and continues to do after his death. He also tells us about St. Nicholas visiting the Russian countryside together with Elijah, the Prophet. In Russia, Elijah is venerated and feared; since he was taken to heaven in a fiery chariot, he commands the weather and especially thunderstorms, cloudbursts, and hail. So the Prophet, as the legend goes, had a formidable aspect, and was in an angry mood. But St. Nicholas was mild and even tempered; he was very old, and leaned on a staff, and meekly followed the angry prophet through the Russian fields. Now, the Prophet wanted to punish a peasant who was a sinner, and threatened to destroy his crop with thunderstorm and hail. St. Nicholas took pity on the man, and advised him to sell his field to another peasant before it was destroyed. So the man sold his field to a neighbor, and it was then destroyed by Elijah. Seeing that he had punished the wrong man, who was not a sinner at all, the Prophet hurriedly worked a miracle, restoring the crops to their former shape, so that the field became once more golden with ripe wheat. St. Nicholas then told the sinful peasant to buy back his field; it was he who had sown, and he who should harvest. And this "competition" between saint and prophet went on and on. Then the wicked peasant was told to repent, and to take a loaf of bread to the angry prophet. He was to carry it on his head. And he was to take another loaf to St. Nicholas, the *Merciful One,* and this loaf he was to hide under his coat. The two loaves were taken to be blessed at Sunday Mass. And seeing the peasant's humble devotion, the prophet Elijah realized that his anger was in vain, and that St. Nicholas had indeed been the more saintly of the two, because he had shown mercy. And the peasant was forgiven by the Prophet.

It seems that St. Nicholas often "competed" with other holy men. For here is another story about him, this story is told by the great Russian religious thinker, Vladimir Solovyev. One day St. Nicholas was visiting some peasants with another saint whose name was Cassien. On their way, the two saints saw a cart and horse bogged down in deep mud. "Let us help the driver," suggested St. Nicholas. But St. Cassien protested, saying, "If we soil our garments in this mud we shall not be able to enter paradise." But St. Nicholas, heedless of his shining garments, waded into the mud and pulled out the driver and his cart. His garments were covered with mud, while those of St. Cassien had remained immaculate. When they stood before the gates of heaven, St. Peter came out and had a look at them: one soiled and muddy, the other shining white. And Peter let Nicholas enter first; and Cassien, only as second best, was allowed to humbly follow the saint who had helped a poor man at the cost of his archbishop's robes.

There are many other stories about St. Nicholas. He is often shown under the protection of Michael the Archangel, commander of the heavenly hosts. Under the Archangel's protection, St. Nicholas worked many miracles in Russia. Some of these Russian legends about St. Nicholas paint an even more moving picture: they describe the Archbishop of Myra journeying through the Russian land, in company of Christ Himself. The merciful, the meek, and kindly St. Nicholas is the symbol of Christ's love for the long-suffering Russian people.

CHAPTER ELEVEN

Liturgy and Art

NEARLY all Russian devotions are closely linked to the liturgy. This means that the people do not associate religious life so much with individual piety as with the *Opus Dei*.

Liturgical worship does not exclude, of course, private devotion: the Our Father's and the Hail Mary's recited silently before the family icons, and the reading of the Gospel and the Psalms at home. The devout have special lecterns in their rooms on which the psalter is placed, with a candle lighted for morning and evening recollection.

One of the customs most often individually observed is the sign of the cross made and repeated on many occasions; inside the Church it marks the most solemn moments of the Mass. It is not made by all of the faithful together, as is done in the West, but by each in his own time and at his own choice. (This is why, to the Russians, the Latin strictly regulated behavior at Mass seems almost mechanical, and the ringing of the bell by the altar boy sounds like an interruption.)

The sign of the cross is, of course, made before and after meals, as in all other countries. But it is also made before leaving on a journey or upon returning to a familiar place; it marks the beginning and end of work and of learning good or bad news, entering a house on an important visit, while the eyes are fixed on the family icon, passing by a Church, seeing a funeral procession, or hearing of a person's death. The sign of the cross is also made on the occasion of a solemn statement, at moments of fear or misgivings, when in danger, fighting a temptation or in fervent supplication. When saying good-by to a friend, or visiting the sick, or putting a child to sleep, a Russian will trace the sign of the cross over him, or do so from a distance, on the threshold of a room or on the porch of a house. These are familiar gestures. Even under the Bolsheviks, Russians have not forgotten to make the sign of the cross, as we see from soviet movies and plays. But these customs would soon become meaningless, as they may to atheists, if they did not come from the great fount of the *Opus Dei.* Just as in the West, the Eastern liturgy is centered on the Eucharistic Offering. As in the West, too, the daily office is an important part of worship; but in the Latin rite it is observed almost entirely by priests and religious, while in the Eastern rite it is familiar to laymen also. Vespers and matins are celebrated in all churches and acquire great solemnity on the vigil of feasts.

We know that the Byzantine liturgy varies from the Latin one both in form and in structure. There are nevertheless some very striking similarities, as the division of the Mass in several parts — Mass of the catechumens, of the faithful, consecration and communion (the offertory alone is not found in the Byzantine rite, being replaced by the preparation of the Holy Species before the liturgy starts). Very impressive is also the similarity of the canon. Then once more each liturgy proceeds in its own way.

The greatest difference between the Western and Eastern Mass is that the latter is *in the vernacular.* We have seen that the liturgy was brought to Kiev from Byzantium in the native, Slavonic tongue. Greek is used in many other branches of the Eastern Church. There are also Masses in Arabic, in English, German, French. Modern languages are used more and more by the Russian-Orthodox in Western Europe and America, because of the families of émigrés and of displaced persons who in the third and even as early as the second generation do not understand Slavonic.

The main characteristic of the Eastern liturgy is its symbolism. It vividly pictures, not only the Eucharistic sacrifice *per se,* but also the meaning of the given period of the liturgical year and of the feast of the day. The liturgy also portrays the life of Christ;

it recalls it in its processions, in the closing and opening of the altar doors, in the very movements of the celebrants. Thus for instance, the priest's "little entrance" with the Gospel recalls the teaching life of Christ; the "big entrance" with the holy species symbolizes the entrance of Christ into Jerusalem; the drawing of the curtain over the main altar doors during vespers is a reminder of the infant Christ in His mother's womb, etc.

No doubt, not all the faithful who attend the liturgy in Russia know the meaning of these symbols; only liturgists can explain them fully. Nevertheless the people *learn* during worship; it is a sermon, a meditation on the Mysteries, and a lesson on Scripture.

At vespers, the choir sings about the feast of the coming day; the lector reads a number of psalms, and the fragrant holy oils with which the faithful are anointed on the vigil of the great feasts symbolize the good odor of Christ. The icon of the feast is placed in the center of the Church, so that each can learn about it. This was important in the days when the Russian people were illiterate. Today, the exposition of the icon of the feast is again important, since oral religious instruction is limited for adults and forbidden for children. The hymn and antiphon also tell of an event in the life of Christ, our lady, the angels, and the saints.

We shall speak, therefore, in this chapter about the two main expressions of Russian liturgical art: icon painting and religious music.

ICONS AND ICON PAINTING

In the act of consecration of the human race to the Immaculate Heart of Mary, written by the late Pope Pius XII in May, 1943, there is a special paragraph concerning Russia and the Russian Icon.

> Queen of the most holy Rosary . . . give peace to the people separated by error or by discord, and especially to those who profess such singular devotion to thee and in whose homes an honored place was ever accorded to thy venerable icon.

Though Russia is not directly mentioned in this act of consecration, it is clear that the Holy Father had Russia in mind. For in Russia precisely, an *honored place* was ever accorded to the icon of our Lady, and to other holy images.

Our readers know that the icon is a painting, representing our Lord, our Lady, or angels, saints, and prophets. Icons may also picture various scenes from Scripture, the great events of the liturgical year, and episodes in the lives of the saints. Let us now enter more deeply into the meaning of iconography.

It must be recalled that in the Eastern Church there are no statues, since sculpture was considered as a survival of paganism. This is why Christ, the *Bogoroditza,* and the saints were represented in paintings known as icons, i.e., "portraits" in Greek. The oldest of these, an icon of our Lady, is attributed by ancient tradition to St. Luke the Evangelist, who was not only a physician but also a painter.

The icon came to Russia from Byzantium and Russian religious art followed the pattern established by her Mother Church. Without entering into minute technicalities, it can be briefly said that Byzantine painting imitated a very remote and ancient art. It is believed by recent archaeological studies that the primitive icon was inspired by paintings on Egyptian mummies and by the art of Asia Minor. Icon painting flourished between the sixth and the fourteenth centuries. Byzantine painters established a number of fixed rules and created a series of definite religious themes. Our Lord was represented most often as the Divine King, the Pantokrator, seated on His throne. Christ was also sometimes represented hanging on the cross, but these paintings were more rarely done, and the passion of our Lord was less dramatized and less grimly realistic than in Western religious art. The Byzantine painter more often depicted the Glorified Saviour, i.e., the transfigured or the risen Christ. Many icons, called *Deisis,* showed our Lord between St. John the Baptist and the Holy Mother of God. Often they show our Lady with the Infant which she tenderly holds in her arms. Others depict scenes of Mary's life: the presentation to the Temple, the Annunciation, the Nativity, the Assumption, or "Dormition" as it is called in the East; there are admirable *pietas* and *stabat maters*. In the majestic *Deisis,* our Lady is glorified with her Son and stands as our intercessor by His side.

Byzantine art was developed by icon painters of Constantinople, Mount Athos, Crete, and Salonica. It was a great and exalted art despite the fact that there was something rigid about it. Byzantine painters sought to avoid all human, emotional, sensual approach to their subjects. There was something which still had to be revealed in icon painting. This secret of religious art was disclosed by the Russian masters.

Russian icon painters observed the strict rules and disciplines prescribed by the Greeks. Background, vestments, faces, hands and feet, all were rendered by them in certain definite shapes and colors only. So were the landscapes, the skies, the trees, the foliage, and the beasts — the ox, the donkey, and sheep of the Nativity; the dragon defeated by St. George, and his fiery steed. The figures, settings, and accessories in the story of the Redemption could not be abandoned to artistic fancy. They had to tell the story according to the *rule,* the so-called icon-painter's "Canon." The Russian masters followed this canon with great docility and in all humility. But there was something which they could not and would not withhold, even under duress of tradition and discipline. It was a reserved, but very deep emotion, a tenderness, a sacred joy, something, no doubt, gentler and more mellow than the themes which Byzantine sacred art had wanted to express.

The Russian icon is painted on a wooden panel, dimensions varying from several inches to several feet. The paints originally used were tempera, the same as those used by the Italian school of primitives of the quatrocentro. Sometimes gold leaf or powdered gold enhanced the painting, just as in the pictures of Fra Angelico. Later, in the seventeenth and especially in the eighteenth centuries, these paintings on wood panels were covered with embossed gold and silver leaf; the faces, hands, and feet of the original figures only remained uncovered. During that later period, icons were often bedecked with pearls and precious stones. Glittering halos crowned the head of every figure. These precious ornaments added great material value to icons, and were often the work of great craftsmen. But the true value of an icon is not in these ornaments; the icon connoisseur will remove them, for, obviously he is interested in the painting itself.

Two main schools of icon painting developed in Russia during the later middle ages — one in the North, in the city of Novgorod, the other in Central Russia. Each of these schools reflected the various aspects of the Russian character.

The Novgorod icons were painted with a "bold inspiration, even a certain indifference to detail," to quote the scholar W. Ryabushinsky, who specialized in iconography; while the Moscow school "was more elaborate, refined, and of a contemplative strain."[1] The greatest master of the Moscow school is Andrei Rublev (end of the fifteenth century), whose icon of the Holy Trinity is considered as the summit of Russian religious art. Rublev, a monk of a Moscow monastery, can be compared to the great western master, Fra Angelico. Like the Italian artist-monk, Rublev was not only a painter but a contemplative as well. His Trinity expresses an entire theology, clothed in beautiful lines and colors, which have both an aesthetic and a mystic meaning.

Rublev's painting represents the Holy Trinity in the form of three biblical figures — the three angels who visited Abraham and were served a meal under the famous oak, on a spot still shown to pilgrims in the Holy Land. The mystic meal presented by Rublev is obviously the prefiguration of the Eucharistic banquet. The angels symbolize the Father, the Son, and the Holy Ghost; one of them is Christ extending His blessing on the cup, or chalice placed before Him. This composition is of ineffable beauty and grace: each angel with his staff, sitting down as a wanderer on a long journey on earth — and at the same time forming a vision which the contemplative mind alone can reach.

This is how the late art expert A. Avinoff writes about "The Trinity":

> The angels of the Old Testament Trinity, an ancient theme in Christian art, known also as the "Hospitality of Abraham" since the sixth-century mosaics of Ravenna, acquire a novel spirit never

---

[1] W. Ryabushinsky, "Russian Icons and Spirituality," in *The Third Hour*, issue V, 1951.

encountered before and never fully restated since, an aspect of gentle grace and supernatural luminosity. It seems as if an unearthly peace rests upon this image. The figures are balanced in a subtle composition of symmetry with an imperceptible swing, as flowers would look in a field faintly swayed by the breeze. . . . The faces of the three angels are similar to the point of a triple identity, although each countenance conveys something distinctly personal in expression. The whole perspective of the scene is treated with the abstractness and bold independence of a Chinese composition. The eyes of the onlooker are carried to another world, not by means of geometrical recessions of Western draftsmanship but by the path of associational imagery. An interrelationship of the orders of visual images and ideal conceptions is reflected throughout the whole composition. For instance, the shape of the chalice, placed in the center of the table, is repeated by the contour outlined by the robes of the two angels on either side. The phantom form of a cup emerging here adumbrates the chalice of the Last Supper and the Eucharist as though that symbol were lifted into a celestial world above the turbulence and impermanence of things on this earth. Scarcely ever in the history of art has the theme of Trinity been treated with such a fusion of reverent traditionalism, abstractness of vision, delicacy of sentiment, and creative originality.[2]

Rublev's works are very few. There are some frescoes attributed to him in the Cathedral of the Assumption in the Moscow Kremlin one of them representing St. Michael. And there is the famous icon of Our Lady of Vladimir.

Rublev's Trinity at Zagorsk has been transferred to the Tretyakovsky Art Gallery in Moscow, as has also Our Lady of Vladimir.

*　　　*　　　*

There are many kinds of Russian icons; as we have said, some of them are tiny images, others large and impressive compositions. The latter usually form part of the *Iconostasis*, the screen, which separates the altar from the nave in a Russian Orthodox church. Many devout Russians in the olden times, especially the Raskolniky, had private oratories where their most precious icons were kept. But generally speaking, the icon is important in every Russian Christian home. The holy image may be placed alone,

---

[2] A. Avinoff, *The Russian Icon; Its History and Characteristics, Russian Icons,* Collection of George R. Han.

or with several others in a small shrine, the *Kivot,* encased in glass and lined with silk or velvet. Or it may simply be hung in the eastern corner of each room, the so-called *Red corner.* For "red" is synonymous in the old Slavonic language with "beautiful," and is still sometimes used to denote something out of the ordinary, festive, or exceptionally important. Thus for instance the "Red Square" in Moscow, often believed to be a Communist expression, is, as we have seen, a very old name given to the largest and most beautiful square of the tsar's former capital. We can see how much these synonyms have served communist propaganda. The Red Square has become the famous setting of Soviet parades and pageants. As to the "red corners" in the peasants' homes, the godless tried to replace its icons with Lenin's portrait; but this propaganda stunt did not succeed. For every peasant, even if illiterate, knows the difference between an icon and a portrait.

The "red corner" in a peasant's hut was often decorated with immaculate white towels of homespun linen elaborately embroidered at both ends with bright red cotton or silk thread.

Before the icon, a small altar lamp burned day and night. In the rich man's home, the icon was decorated with gold and silver, the altar lamp wrought in filigrane and crystal. In the humble peasant's hut there would be but some uncouth painting, some cheap reprint of the *Orante* or of the *Pantokrator.* The altar lamp was of cheap glass; a primitive wick of hemp was dipped in oil. The glass was red, blue or yellow, like that of western altar lamps; this was the *Lampada,* shedding its pleasant rays in the room, which received from it both spiritual warmth and atmosphere. In the old days, and actually up to the Bolshevik Revolution, a Russian entering his home or visiting a friend would first of all bow low before the icons and make the sign of the cross, before greeting his family or host. The icons symbolized God's presence; they were a constant reminder of the supernatural life, and appealed to morality and to conscience. It is difficult to lie, to cheat, to be brutal in front of an icon. The communists in Russia did all they could to tear away the icons from men's homes, to deprive them of the image of their God, and to stifle the consciences of the people.

There is in Russian a proverbial expression: before committing a foul deed, "carry out the saints," meaning the holy icons. No doubt the Russian people thought of these words as the godless pursued their sacrilegious work. And so the peasant took the icons from his walls and hid them away, as the Pope said in 1943. Soon after the Act of Consecration was proclaimed in Rome, the icons began to reappear in Russia. They were seen in homes of town and village folk, and even on collective farms.

Little by little, the Soviet government realized its mistake. Not only was it expedient to let the people venerate their icons, but some of these paintings were of great value and could be traded for cash. So it came about, that their preservation was encouraged.

A group of Russian scholars and archaeologists seized upon this happy turn of affairs. In their writings and lectures they re-established the true aesthetic and cultural aspect of icon painting. They brought precious specimens to museums and art galleries. And soon the people flocked to see them. For them the "saints" which had been brought back were not simply museum pieces. Reports from the U.S.S.R. tell us that many visitors to the museums instinctively take off their caps before the holy images.

Perhaps this scene is hard to believe for those unacquainted with the immense spiritual force which the icon always represented in the eyes of the Russian people. They saw in it no ordinary painting, but an emanation of the Holy Spirit. According to tradition, the ancient icon painters prayed and fasted for several days before taking up their brushes. The old believers fiercely defended their holy images during times of persecution. The established Church carried icons in procession each time Russia was threatened by some danger — war, famine, pestilence.

Icon painters often formed guilds and corporations, or set their workshops up near monasteries. Many of them were peasants, leading a communal life. One of these rustic artists' communities existed for many years in an area of central Russia, called Polyekha. They painted icons of extraordinary finesse which resembled Persian miniatures. After 1917, owing to Soviet antireligious policy, the Polyekha community could no longer paint icons. But Soviet cultural agencies appreciated the exceptional talents of the *Polyeshane* as these artists call themselves; they were permitted to live in their community and to continue their work, provided they did not paint holy images; so they did miniatures representing fairy tales and historic scenes.

The works of the Polyeshane are valued by connoisseurs and fetch high prices. Several of their beautiful miniatures were shown in the Soviet Pavilion in 1958 in Brussells, and at the 1959 exhibit in New York. They were admired by visitors, but few of them realized that this was not properly speaking Soviet Art, but typical icon-painting techniques.

CHURCH MUSIC AND HYMNOLOGY

One of the most important elements of the Eastern Liturgy is singing. In fact, practically no liturgical service is celebrated in the Eastern rite without the participation of a choir. There are no organs in Eastern churches, so the choir — which may be a male choir or mixed — sings *a cappella*. The singing may also be done by two alternating choral groups known as "antiphonal."

Church music came to Russia from Byzantium; it was brought by Greek monks experienced in this art and mentioned in early Russian chronicles as the *sladkopevtzy*, i.e., "sweet-singing." Without entering into technicalities we shall briefly point out the essential character of this religious music. It is used for the proper — the hymns, canticles, etc., of the feasts and for the ferias, as well as for the various parts of the Mass — the creed, the canon, the *sanctus*. There are also other chants special to the Byzantine liturgy. The choir also makes all the responses of the Mass and of Vespers, Te Deums, and funeral services.

Chants and responses are sung in *eight tones;* every type of chant is sung but on Sundays one of the eight tones only is used for all the chants. These belong to a fixed Cycle, the *Ochtoikh,*[3]

[3] The *Ochtoikh* (*Ochtoechos* in Greek) contains eight series of chants for an entire week. Each series has for every day of the week different liturgical texts which commemorate: on Sunday the Resurrection, on Monday the Angels, on

which presents a strictly ordered traditional pattern. The liturgical chants were written with special signs of ancient Greek origin, called *kryuky* which resembled the *neums,* the notation of Western Gregorian chant. Later the *kryuky* were replaced by signs of modern musical notation.

Such is the basic pattern first taught in Kiev by the Greeks. As Church life began to develop in Russia, this Greek pattern was imitated by native composers. The original Russian music was composed by the monk Rogov, who later became metropolitan of Rostov. This type of church music flourished in the late middle ages and up to the sixteenth century when it began to be replaced by more modern trends. But traditional chants were preserved in monasteries. In religious communities hymns were chanted not only in church, but also in the halls and refectories. Guests of honor were welcomed by hymns sung and often composed for the occasion by the monks. Among the guests, there were, as we have seen, many prominent boyars, and sometimes the tsars, seeking the abbot's advice or blessing. Some of them were great connoisseurs of Russian church music, and themselves even composed religious hymns. Paradoxically enough one of the chants, famous in ancient Russian church music, was written by Tsar Ivan the Terrible. In those days he was still a sincerely devout young prince and wrote this hymn in honor of Peter, Metropolitan of Moscow, canonized by the Russian church.

Tsars, princes, and their retinues attended all liturgical events in cathedrals and abbeys, and would often sing in the choir. Every young Russian nobleman and even the tsar's sons were sent to special schools where they had to learn the art of singing. One of these schools was directed in the sixteenth century by the priest Sylvester, the Tsar's own spiritual adviser.

Peter the Great visited the Solovetzk monastery in the early eighteenth century. At that time he had already manifested his dislike of religion insofar as it interfered with his reforms. He was,

---

Tuesday St. John the Baptist, etc. See Irmgard M. de Vries, "The Epistles, Gospels and Tones of the Byzantine Liturgical Year," in *Eastern Churches Quarterly,* Spring X, 1953.

however, still attached to the ancient traditions to which he had been accustomed in childhood. The records of the Solovetzk monks relate that the tsar attended the services and sang in the choir. From this document we learn that Peter had a tenor voice.

Many Latin-rite Christians have been impressed by the liturgical chants they have heard in Russian churches. The liturgy of St. John Chrysostom sung by famous Russian émigré choirs, like Afonsky, Kedrov, and the choirs of Russian-Orthodox Churches in Paris, has been recorded and is often played in the West. But, like the Icon, the Eastern liturgy has a profounder meaning which needs to be understood: it is not only a remarkable manifestation of liturgical art, it is also a medium through which the Russian people have learned their catechism, their texts from Holy Scripture, and their mystical and moral theology.

As we have seen, the choir gives the responses which represent a considerable part of Byzantine liturgy. Thus for instance, at Mass there are four litanies, i.e. prayers of rogation, said aloud by the priest or by the deacon. To each supplication the choir gives the response "grant us, O Lord," or "Lord, have mercy," the latter corresponding to the "Kyrie Eleison" of the Latin Mass. The congregation of a Russian church follows these supplications not only most devoutly, but *word by word,* for each of them expresses things both simple and sublime. These are prayers for the Church, the ecclesiastical authorities, the clergy, the monks, the benefactors, and pious laity, and others: for the salvation of souls, for the living and the dead, for peace and union, for the fruit of the earth, for travelers on land and sea, for the sick, and for prisoners. The litanies are chanted so that the words are understood. But it is the choir's responses which give them their full meaning. The faithful pray with the priest and with the choir, either repeating the responses or marking each of them with the sign of the cross. This is why the men and women attending such a service may seem to Western eyes perhaps too dramatic, and their prayer stressed in an almost spectacular way. But as the learned Dominican writer C. J. Dumont, points out, the Russians pray most fervently when they are together, when they join in a collective, communal act of worship.[4] Yet, each member of the congregation prays individually too, for each finds his own hopes, fears, or joys expressed in this or that part of the litany. In other words, the Eastern liturgy and especially its religious chants offer great opportunities for participation. People learn how to pray, remember how to pray, because they hear these prayers often and beautifully sung. In fact, most Russians were so well trained in worship that when the godless closed their churches during the revolution, they kept liturgical tradition intact. From Peter the Great to the illiterate, all could and can still learn from the liturgy, not only by attending it, or by following it in a missal (missals in Russia were rarely used) but by *singing* it aloud, or by repeating it in the silence of their hearts.

In order to understand the importance of the spiritual training offered by the Eastern liturgy, a few words must be said about the *proper* which often varies. These variations are numerous, so that there is a great number of chants, reflecting all the feasts of the Byzantine liturgical calendar.

There are the *Stepenny* or graduals, with their psalmodies, including verses from the psalter, and antiphons of the Eight Tones or modes. There are the biblical canticles of Anna, the canticle of Habacuc, the canticle of Isaias, of Jonas, and of the three young men. There are also canticles from the New Testament, referring to the Blessed Virgin. The psalms and canticles, being scriptural, are therefore inspired. To this fundamental framework there were added hymns of later composition which formed a setting of great beauty: these were the hymns of St. John Damascene for the eight above-mentioned tones. There are also the *Prokimenons*, meaning "that which precedes" in Greek, corresponding to the Sunday liturgies and the movable feasts, as well as daily vespers. The *prokimenon* is a scriptural verse preceding the lesson of the day; it is chanted by the lector in one of the eight tones, and is repeated by the choir, which also sings the Alleluia (corresponding to the Latin gradual).

---

4 C. J. Dumont, *Sources Principales et traits caracteristiques de la spiritualite russe*, in *Russie et Chretienté*, No. 1–2, 1949.

Besides the *Stepenny* and the *Prokimenons,* there is a great, many-stanzaed hymn of Easter matins composed by St. John Damascene; there are the hymns of Holy Week (Thursday vespers and Friday's burial of Christ), hymns for wedding and funeral services, hymns of the *molebny* (*Te Deums*), and others.

There is finally another very remarkable set of Eastern Church liturgical chants: these are the *Troparions* and the *Kondakions,* which celebrate in a few verses, sometimes in a few lines, the event marked by a feast: Christmas, Epiphany, the feasts of the Blessed Virgin, Palm Sunday, Easter, Ascension, Pentecost. *Troparions* also refer to the feasts of the Archangels, saints, and martyrs, as presented by the Church calendar.

The *Troparions* and *Kondakions* translated from the Greek into the Slavonic vernacular have become part of Russian popular hymnology. Each feast is described with an extraordinary economy of words. Each *Troparion* is like a picture, like a miniature icon transcribed in a few words and a few notes of music.

Here, for instance, are the Christmas *Troparion* and *Kondakion:*

Troparion

Thy nativity, O Christ our God, has shed upon the world the light of knowledge; through it, those who had been worshipers of stars have learned from a star to worship Thee, O Sun of Justice, and to recognize in Thee the One who rises and who comes from on high. O Lord, glory be to Thee!

Kondakion

Today the Virgin gives birth to the One who surpasses all created essences, and the earth offers a cave to the Inaccessible. The angels sing His glory with the shepherds, and the Wise Men follow the star: for unto us is born an Infant, God in all eternity.[5]

The Eastern liturgy contains a set of hymns dedicated to the Blessed Virgin Mary. These hymns are sung continually throughout the liturgical year at Mass, Vespers, and all the canonical hours (especially observed in monasteries).

These hymns also were translated from the Greek into the Slavonic vernacular, acquiring in the translation a freshness, fullness, and color, which are very striking. One of these hymns,

---

[5] Byzantine Missal.

starting with the words *Dostoyna yest* (worthy art thou) is especially popular in Russia, as described in our chapter on the Blessed
Virgin.

Many early Russian composers have written their own music for
this special category of Marian hymns, known as the *Dostoyniki.*
Like the *Troparions* and *Kondakions,* these hymns are very short
and concise. They can easily reach the faithful, who know them
by heart and often repeat them after the choir.

*   *   *

Russian church-music flowered from the fourteenth to the seventeenth centuries, and these early chants are still considered as
classic liturgical patterns. However, the ancient chants were later
modified or even replaced by a set of new hymns which reflected
something of western church music. Russian travelers abroad heard
the Latin Mass, the organ accompaniment, and the compositions
of Italian masters such as Palestrina. This new experience had
quite considerable influence on the development of Russian liturgical singing in the eighteenth century. The story of a famous
composer of that time, Dmitry Bortnyansky, is worth relating.

Bortnyansky was born in the Ukraine in the first part of the
eighteenth century. The Ukraine is famous for its fine men's
voices and the young Bortnyansky was an excellent tenor. A youth
of moderate means and of obscure parentage, he had a brilliant
career. He went to Petersburg, today Leningrad, in those days the
capital of Russia. There, the boy entered the choir of the Imperial
Court Chapel which picked its singers from among the best.
Bortnyansky also sang a small part in the court opera. He gained
the appreciation of the opera's director, the Italian Galuppi, author
of the famous sonatas for the clavichord, who held a prominent
position as musician of the Russian court. Galuppi was much impressed by young Bortnyansky's talents: when he returned to Italy,
he took Bortnyansky with him. The young Russian court singer
received a scholarship to study music abroad, first under Galuppi
in Venice, then in Rome, Naples, Vienna. Galuppi trained Bortnyansky in every branch of the music composition of his time:
Bortnyansky, still in his teens, composed sonatas, songs, and even

operas, according to western style. One of these operas was produced in Venice. Actually, however, Bortnyansky's vocation was that of a composer of religious music. During his life abroad, which lasted some ten years, he wrote several pieces of liturgical music, but still according to the western pattern. He composed a Mass, in German, apparently under Lutheran influence. When Bortnyansky visited Rome, he became well acquainted with the Latin Catholic Mass. At that time he composed many chants for the Latin Liturgy: a Credo, a Kyrie, an Agnus Dei, and a Salve Regina. Meanwhile, rumors of Bortnyansky's successes had reached the Russian capital. He was recalled and appointed head of the Imperial Court Chapel in which he had sung as a choir boy. From that time on until his death Bortnyansky devoted himself to Russian Eastern Church music. In the West, and especially under Galuppi, Bortnyansky had acquired a perfect technique. The scores he wrote during and after his apprenticeship are preserved in Russian museums, and reveal great craftsmanship. Bortnyansky applied this experience to the composition of Russian liturgical music. The ancient *Kryuki,* or "hook" notation similar to Gregorian *neums,* was replaced by contemporary western signs. For the rest, however, Bortnyansky did not remain in the Western tradition. He turned to his native Russian style for his liturgical chants. His production during those years was enormous. He wrote several hymns for each feast. He composed the so-called Troparions for all the great occasions of the Russian liturgical year: Christmas, the Epiphany, Palm Sunday, Easter, the Assumption; he wrote music for the Lenten penitential psalms and hymns to our Lady, as well as *Glorias* and *Sanctus.* He wrote, besides a Mass of his own, some hundred other liturgical compositions.

Bortnyansky can indeed be considered as the founder of contemporary Russian liturgical music. Moreover, he organized and conducted his choir according to a strict vocal technique. He chose and trained the best voices available.

Despite his great success in his own time, Bortnyansky was later criticized by Russian musicians. He was declared too "Western," too "Italian," as compared to the ancient Moscow liturgical standards.

This, in a way, is true, so that in the nineteenth and our twentieth centuries, Russian liturgical schools sought to revive the ancient art of church singing, especially in monasteries. The best known of the modern composers of Russian Church music are Tchesnokov, and Smolensky whose hymns are sung in Russian churches today. The Old Believers have preserved the ancient liturgical chants dating from Avvakum.

It is worthy of note that most great Russian composers have tried their hand at liturgical music. Tchaikovsky wrote a Mass often sung in our days. Musorgski took his inspiration from old Russian Church music for his opera "Boris Godunov," and Prokofiev adapted ancient chant for the score of "Ivan the Terrible."

The famous singer Feodor Chaliapin was very found of religious chants. He sang the creed from Grechaninov's Mass and chanted the deacon's part in the litany supported by a trained choir. Both these performances were recorded shortly before Chaliapin's death. At his funeral in Paris another Russian singer, who was his friend, sang in the choir at the Russian Cathedral as a tribute to the great artist.

Even today in the U.S.S.R. opera singers often take part in the liturgy, drawing packed audiences, among whom, no doubt there are many atheists. But who knows what the so-called "unbelievers" experience when they attend the liturgy which they may never have heard before, or have forgotten, and which still perhaps speaks to their hearts?

CHAPTER TWELVE

Easter

CHRISTOSS VOSKRESSE . . . "Christ has arisen." These solemn words mark, so to say, the climax of the Eastern Feast of Resurrection, of *Paskha,* as it is still called in Russian, according to the Hebrew tradition. The rejoicing of this *Paskha,* the Feast of Feasts, is not confined to the solemn chants of the Liturgy. The Easter spirit in Russia is like the Christmas spirit in Western lands. It is impossible to ignore it, or to forget about it. Easter, the Luminous Day, as it is called, is celebrated by all Russians. The mystery, the joy, the wonder of our Lord's Resurrection thrills every heart. It is experienced by each devout Russian, as a personal joy, a personal wonder, a mystery in which every man participates. The godless Communists have been obliged to permit Easter services in all Russian churches and cathedrals because of the people's irresistible will to celebrate their Paskha.

The preparation for the great feast is observed, as it should be, a long while before it. Most pious Russians attend the Liturgy during entire Lent, with great fervor and devotion. It is the more solemn, because, as should be remembered, frequent Communion, as practiced in the West, is not usually observed in Eastern Churches not in union with Rome. But every Russian Orthodox is expected, just as Catholics, to go to Confession and Communion at *least* once a year, during Lent and more particularly during Holy Week.[1] Therefore, Lent and Holy Week are really a period

---

[1] In recent years, Communion among the Russian Orthodox is becoming more frequent, but is not a common practice. It is rendered difficult due to the infrequency of masses in most churches, by strict eucharistic fast regulations, and especially because confession is an obligation before every Communion. To go to Communion without the sacrament of penance as practiced in the West for daily or frequent communicants is often considered by Russian Orthodox as not only unusual but almost sacrilegious.

of preparation, of mortification, of intensified prayer and penance. Abstinence and fasting are very strict in the Eastern Church. Not only meat, but butter, milk, cheese, and eggs, are forbidden. Even ordinary sugar is not allowed, because beet sugar is refined with bones. Fish is plentiful in Russia, especially on the banks of the great rivers, and along the Northern and Southern seashores. There are mushrooms, too, in the Russian woods, and they are considered in Russia as a delicacy which can appear on the table of rich and poor alike. Butter is replaced by vegetable oil produced from hemp, flax, or sunflower seed: there are no olives, no peanuts in Russia, so the choice is limited and the taste of the oil quite unattractive. These regulations are not forcefully imposed, but rather suggested. However, the people, especially the peasants, did observe Lent to the minutest detail. And even more: many a Russian peasant and peasant woman practically ate nothing but bread and water and a few potatoes during the entire Lenten period.

Most rigorous is the observance of Holy Week, which starts on Monday: every devout Russian attends services regularly, twice a day from Holy Monday through Holy Saturday. During the week, the priest and deacon are vested in black or purple.

We have already said that frequent Communion is not observed in Russia. For this reason, no doubt, Communion on Thursday or Saturday of Holy Week is a solemn event, something quite essential and decisive in spiritual life. To be worthy of receiving our Lord, the Russian will fast, abstain, sacrifice many small items of comfort, and fervently attend the daily morning and evening services. Each day of Holy Week and at every service the prayer of St. Ephrem is said by the priest, the deacon, and the faithful, accompanied by three genuflections or *metanya*;[2] this prayer is, so to say, the keynote to the entire liturgy of these days of penance:

> O Lord and Master of my life, grant that I may not be infected by the spirit of slothfulness and sadness, of ambition and vain talk.

---

[2] *Metanya* are prostrations which accompany the most solemn moments of the liturgy.

Grant instead to me Thy servant the spirit of purity and humility of patience and charity.

O Lord and King, bestow upon me the grace to behold my sins and not to judge my brother, for blessed art Thou for ever and ever.

At Holy Thursday Vespers, twelve sequences taken from the four Evangelists and describing the Passion, are solemnly chanted, often alternately by several priests.

On Holy Friday, there is the "procession of the entombment," the priest and several members of the congregation carrying around the church the image of our Lord lying in His shroud. Some of these images are masterpieces of ancient icon painting, others are embroidered and spun in velvet or brocade or bedecked with pearls and precious stones. The hymns of Russian Holy Friday are among the most beautiful of the Slavonic Liturgy. Both during the "Twelve Gospels" on Thursday, and during the Friday service, the faithful stand with lighted candles. These services are very long, with many litanies, antiphons, and hymns. In most churches they last about four hours, in monasteries five or six hours. There are no pews or chairs in Eastern Churches: the faithful stand or kneel on the floor. The admirable harmony and severe beauty of these services creates an atmosphere of exalted piety and devotion; so that even people who are not physically strong, and who have fasted strictly, are able to stand for hours in Church; they listen to every litany and every hymn, which they have known by heart since early childhood. There is, for instance, the famous chant about the Good Thief, sung on Holy Thursday during the Twelve Gospels. In the old Slavonic text, he is described not as "the good," but as "the reasonable" robber. The Hymn is sung by a trio, picked from the best voices of the choir.

Not only in every Russian church, but in every Russian home, there is during Holy Week an atmosphere of mourning, of sadness, and sincere contrition. Thus, as has often been said, a Russian child, brought up in a Christian-practicing atmosphere, gets most of his religious education from example; he learns by observing his elders and the other little boys and girls who are his playmates. In the old days, before the Revolution, there was much in wealthy, sophisticated homes which could be learned from the servants; the old nurses, the maids, the footmen and butlers, mostly of peasant origin, who often observed Holy Week much more strictly than their masters. No child, however spoiled, would dare to play and romp under the severe gaze of these household censors. Today, they are no more, but there are still millions of Russians who observe the Holy Week tradition despite antireligious propaganda. They still remember the lessons of their grandmothers who taught them these customs of long ago.

Outside Russia, the Russian émigrés, the refugees, the D.P.'s, cling to these traditions as to something which still links them to their fatherland. In Europe and the U.S.A. Russians have magnificently preserved the spirit of Easter. Churches are filled to capacity as soon as Holy Week begins.

However strict the fast and severe the silence in a Russian home on Good Friday, something is beginning to stir in the household. . . . Despite the long services, the confession, the contrition, a Russian housewife cannot completely neglect her more practical duties: preparations must be made for the Great Feast, and they have to be started in good time. Special food must be served at Easter and each housewife will try to do her best in the culinary field. Fast is to be strictly observed until Easter morning.

The Mass on Holy Saturday is already filled with the theme of the risen Christ. Black or purple vestments are replaced by shining white and gold ones after the Gospel which speaks of the resurrection.

This is usually the Mass at which many Russians receive Holy Communion as in anticipation of the joyful *agape*. They have been to confession the day before and have preserved since then holy silence and recollection. Saturday afternoon is filled with the atmosphere of the approaching feast. According to ancient custom, the food prepared for Easter must be blessed by the priest. It is brought to the nearby parish church and left there until the Easter vigil. Before the communist revolution, this custom was observed all over Russia; after 1917, the godless tried to stop it, but to no avail. According to reports from the U.S.S.R., the streets of Moscow and of other cities are thronged on Holy Saturday with the faithful bringing their Easter foods (*Paskha, Kulich,* and colored eggs) to the cathedrals and churches reopened in the soviet capital. This demonstration of faith irritated communist authorities — but there was nothing they could do to stop it.

As the vigil of the feast draws to its end, a great quiet settles down in Russian towns and villages. Then, a little before midnight the bells begin to peel and the faithful begin to stream to Church — for Easter Matins. Even if it is an early Easter, there is spring in the air; ice is breaking on the rivers, snow is melting in the fields and meadows. If it is a late Easter, the first leaves and buds are out, and even some lilac is in bloom. Spring comes suddenly in Russia, as in all Northern countries, and there is something youthful and vigorous about it which seems to bring to all men the joy of the Resurrection.

This joy of spring in nature symbolizing the joy of heaven, is reflected in the Russian Easter liturgy with extraordinary power. To describe the *ordo,* to enumerate the antiphons and rubrics of the Eastern liturgy, is not enough. We must enter into its spirit, experience it with the people, sing with them the *Christoss-Voskresse,* "Christ has risen," which opens the Easter Matins.

Let us quote from the journals of a Russian Orthodox writer who describes Easter Matins celebrated in 1940 (during the war) in Paris.[3] The ceremony took place in the chapel of the Russian Home for the Poor, founded by a nun, Mother Mary Skobstzov. This was a humble chapel installed in a garage, but it observed the feast according to strict liturgical tradition. Easter Matins start with a procession symbolizing the holy women going to the Tomb and hearing that Christ has risen. From that moment, the joy of Easter fills the church and the heart of each member of the congregation. The priest blesses the faithful, holding in each hand a lighted candelabra, bedecked with roses, while the hymn "Christ is risen" is intoned:

---

[3] Constantine Motchoulsky, "Mother Mary Skobtzov," *The Third Hour,* issue III.

April 28th. Midnight Easter service. Mother Mary has made a white silk vestment for Father Dmitry; it has no ornaments, except the monogram: Jesus Christ — Alpha and Omega, embroidered in red silk on the chasuble. . . . The city is wrapped in darkness, the sirens shrill in the night. The Easter procession, with crosses and banners, moves across the dark court-yard and stops at the gates of the house. Father Dmitry loudly knocks three times. The gates swing open. After the darkness, a dazzling light. A sea of burning candles. In the hall, between two windows, an altar has been set; it is decorated with flowers: white and pink apple-blossoms, white lilac, lilies, narcissus. Youra, wearing a festive white silk acolyte's robe, holds a candle and roses in his hand.

Father Dmitry seems to fleet through the air, his light white vestments resemble a pair of wings. He "rejoiceth" in the Lord. In a ringing, gleeful, triumphant voice, he exclaims: "Christ hath arisen." The crowd steps back to let him pass, the flames of the candle tremble and glitter, a multitude of joyful voices respond: "In truth, He hath risen." Father Dmitry is already at the foot of the altar, where he recites a short litany, then, once more he hastens back to the crowd a dazzling white, winged figure, with crimson roses in his hands. It seems to me that he looks like the angel who pushed back the stone of the tomb. Mother Mary stands near the altar, the flame of the candle lights up her face. Her eyes are full of tears, and yet radiant.

This account is particularly moving, because the liturgy was celebrated in 1941 during the occupation of Paris by the Germans; a few months after the celebration of the Feast of Feasts, Mother Mary was arrested by the Gestapo for harboring Jews. She was deported to the prison camp of Ravensbruck where she died heroically. Her son, the acolyte Youra, also perished.

Wherever Easter Matins are sung in the Russian-Byzantine rite — whether in the little chapel described by Motchoulsky, or in a large cathedral, the same joy, the same almost mystical transfiguration of priest, choir, and people occurs with overpowering force. This atmosphere, as if filled by the breath of the Holy Spirit, is created by the very structure of the midnight liturgy.

The Easter canticle of St. John Damascene, which is sung immediately after the procession vividly describes and reveals in poetic words and colorful allegories the meaning of the Feast of

Feasts. Here are a few verses of this magnificent chant.

> This is the chosen and Holy Day, the one King and Lord of
> Sabbaths, the feast of feasts and the triumph of triumphs: wherein
> let us bless Christ forever more.
> Christ is risen from the dead.
> O come on this auspicious day of the Resurrection, let us partake
> of the fruit of the new vine of divine gladness of the Kingdom of
> Christ, in song magnifying Him as God forever more.
> Christ is risen from the dead.
> Cast thine eyes about thee, O Zion, and behold! for Lo! from
> the west and north from the sea and from the east, as to a light
> by God illuminated, have thy children assembled unto thee, bless-
> ing Christ forevermore.
> O most Holy Trinity, Our God, glory to Thee.

There follows the call to brotherly love, the invitation to love
all, even those who hate us. Joyfully, warmly the voices resound
as St. Damascene's chant tells us:

> The *Paskha* joyful, the *Paskha* of the Lord, the *Paskha* all
> majestic hath shown forth upon us! *The Paskha!* With joy let us
> embrace one another O *Paskha!* Release from sorrow! for today
> from the tomb as from a chamber of repose, hath Christ shone
> forth and hath filled the women with joy, saying: proclaim the
> glad tidings to the Apostles. Glory to the Father, and to the Son
> and to the Holy Spirit, now and ever and forever and ever.
> The Day of Resurrection! Let us be illumined with the solemn
> feast. Let us embrace one another, let us say Brethren! and because
> of the Resurrection forgive all things to those who hate us, and in
> this wise exclaim: Christ is risen from the dead, trampling down
> death by death and to all in the grave bestowing life.[4]

Another beautiful part of the Easter Matins is the reading of the
"Catechetical Address of St. John Chrysostom." In order to grasp
its message, it should be heard as it is given in full. But here are
a few excerpts which are specially loved by the Russian people:

> If any man be devout and loveth God, let him enjoy this fair
> and radiant triumphal feast. If any man be a wise servant, let him
> rejoice and enter into the joy of his Lord. If any have labored long
> in fasting let him now receive his recompense. If any have wrought

---

[4] *Orthodox Service Book.* See Bibliography.

from the first hour, let him today receive his just reward. If any have come at the third hour let him with thankfulness keep the feast. If any have arrived at the sixth hour, let him have no misgivings, because he shall in no wise be deprived therefore. If any have delayed until the ninth hour let him draw near fearing nothing. If any have tarried even until the eleventh hour, let him also be not alarmed at his tardiness, for the Lord, who is jealous of His honor will accept the last even as the first; He giveth rest unto him who cometh at the eleventh hour, even as to him who hath wrought from the first hour. And He showeth mercy upon the last and careth for the first, and to the one He giveth and upon the other He bestoweth gifts and He accepteth the deeds and welcometh the intention, and honoureth the acts and praiseth the offering.

Trustingly, lovingly the faithful listen, for this message seems to address each of them personally. Good or bad, they can participate in the *Agape*. For once, there is room for all, for the great Father of the Church tells us:

Wherefore enter ye all into the joy of the Lord and receive ye your reward, both the first and likewise the second. Ye rich and poor together hold ye high festivals, ye sober and ye heedless honour ye the day. Rejoice today both ye who have fasted and ye who have disregarded the fast. The table is full-laden, feast ye sumptuously. The calf is fatted; let no one go hungry away. Enjoy ye all the feast of faith: receive ye all the riches of loving kindness. Let no one bewail his poverty, for the universal kingdom has been revealed. Let no one weep for his iniquity for the Saviour's death hath set us free.[5]

This call to the Banquet, to the joyful agape, prepares the faithful for the Easter Mass which follows immediately after matins. Here indeed the climax is reached. All the responses are interwoven with the Paschal hymn: again and again we hear the words: "Christ hath arisen," as if priest, deacon, choir, and people can never cease announcing the good tidings. The usual hymns to our Lady are replaced by an Easter Marian chant:

The blessed angel cries out:
Rejoice, immaculate Virgin, rejoice,
And again I say, rejoice,
For thy son hath risen. . . .

[5] *Ibid.*

The Gospel of the Easter Mass is from St. John 1:1, and is usually read by several priests, who concelebrate on that occasion. The verses are read alternately by them in Church Slavonic, Greek, Latin, and in modern tongues: English, French. This is done to symbolize the universal message starting with the words:
"In the beginning was the Word."

The joy of Easter is also symbolized during matins and Mass by all the doors of the iconostasis being left open throughout the entire service. And at this Mass the faithful do not kneel but stand to symbolize the risen Christ.

The faithful receive Communion during the Easter Mass, if they have not done so on Holy Thursday or Saturday. During Matins or immediately after Mass, all embrace each other three times. This is the Kiss of Peace which St. John Chrysostom calls for in his address and which the concelebrating priests exchange at the altar.

The more strict the fasting, the more joyful the "breakfast," the *Rozgovenye* as the Russians call it. Right after the Easter Liturgy is over, the Paschal Feast starts in a Russian home. All relatives, friends, and even chance acquaintances are welcome, for, as Scripture says, on such a night indeed, "The Calf is Plentiful." For long after the Easter Liturgy is over, the spirit of Easter remains with the faithful until Ascension day and Pentecost, until the day which in the Eastern liturgy is called "the giving up of Easter."[6]

This "breakfast," in the true sense of the word, is not the privilege of the rich. Actually, the Easter table is not necessarily expensive, nor does it belong exclusively to the "Gourmets." Everyone in Russia, or outside of Russia, who has remained true to his Russian Orthodox faith, will celebrate the Paschal Feast. A little cottage cheese, a few eggs, will suffice. There is a belief among Russians that however hard up you are, however desperate your situation, there will always be enough for the Rozgovenye.

---

[6] Every great feast of the Russian liturgical calendar has, so to say, an extension, corresponding to the Western Octaves but considerably longer. This extension reflects the liturgy of the feast and ends with the "giving up" of the event which was celebrated.

CHAPTER THIRTEEN

The Monk and the Priest[1]

IN THE novels of Dostoyevsky, who first used the Russian monk as a literary character, we find two memorable portrayals: Bishop Tikhon, in *The Possessed*, patterned after St. Tikhon of Zadonsk, the famous eighteenth-century bishop, who after some years of pastoral work retired again to his cell; and Father Zossima, an old monk of extreme humility, the staretz of Alyosha Karamazov, who talks to the people, to the peasants, the poor and forsaken. "The Russian monk," he reminds his disciple, "has always been on the side of the people."

These words should be recalled by tourists to Russia today. The official government itinerary for cultural exchange visitors comprises not only industrial, agricultural, and scientific centers of the U.S.S.R., but also great religious shrines, like the Monastery of the Caves in Kiev and the Monastery of the Trinity and St. Sergius near Moscow, which has been re-established as a seminary for the training of monks and priests. Tourists visit the workshops of the monasteries, where ancient icons are restored and new ones painted; in Kiev, the tourists attend beautiful liturgical services. They are awed by the caves which were the catacombs of medieval ascetics. In these underground cells and corridors the bones of the early hermits are still preserved, together with their instruments of penance, chains, and hair shirts. Only a few years ago, these relics were ridiculed by the communists and exhibited in antireligious museums.

What is the secret force which restored these relics to their

---

[1] This chapter appeared with a few variations in *Jubilee* (*see* Bibliography).

shrines? It is Russian monasticism. In order to understand it, we must first of all realize that it is a hidden, silent force, not obvious in ordinary Russian life, and yet extremely potent and alive. Its hidden quality is of its very essence. In the words of the late Pope Pius XII, the Eastern monastic tradition is a "desert spirituality, a contemplative spirit which waits upon God in silence and destitution."

This spirit began to flourish in Russia soon after the baptism of Prince Vladimir of Kiev (in 988). Monasticism came to Russia through Byzantium, the monks following the fourth century rule of the great Eastern father, St. Basil the Great. The most zealous guardians of the Basilian tradition (which was later to influence St. Benedict in the west) were the monks of Mount Athos and those of the Studion monastery at Constantinople. But even before Russian monasticism was systematized, there were a number of Russian anchorites living according to the severe desert spirituality of the Egyptian, Syrian, and Palestinian fathers.

Elements of almost superhuman asceticism can be found in the lives of the early monks of the Kiev Caves. Anthony, the *igumen* or abbot of the primitive Caves, closely followed the pattern of his great predecessor, St. Anthony of the Desert. The hermits dug deep into the limestone of the Kiev hills. There was little communication between themselves and still less with the outside world. Anthony's disciple, Theodosius, followed his master into the Caves: praying, fasting, observing strict silence, wearing heavy chains, and suffering many other mortifications. But slowly Eastern monasticism tended more and more to give up the solitude of the hermitage, and to establish cenobitic (community) life.

After Anthony's death, Theodosius considerably mitigated the iron discipline of his predecessor. As *igumen*, he brought his monks out of the Caves, building cells and a church above them. Soon pilgrims began to visit the Monastery in hundreds.

Theodosius, in introducing the Studite rule from Constantinople, came to be considered the father of Russian monasticism. His rule, like that of St. Benedict whom he closely resembles, was founded on the principle of *"Ora et Labora."* Moreover, the *igumen* of the Caves was always concerned with the people outside the monastery walls. The community welcomed the poor, the sick, the widows and orphans. They were always free to enter the monastery gates, which were closed to everyone else. Even the prince of Kiev had to ask for special permission to enter and did not always obtain it. Theodosius and his monks cultivated their land, cut wood, and made collections of alms, begging, as the Russian monk says: "For the sake of Christ." No hoarding of earthly goods was permitted, except for the community's elementary needs: everything in excess of these had to be given to the poor. Theodosius, now a saint of the Orthodox Church, lived before the schism, and so, is a Catholic saint, too; he is commemorated every Sunday at Mass by Russian Catholics of the Eastern rite, as by the Russian Orthodox.

Another great cultural and religious landmark in Russia is the laura or abbey of the Trinity and St. Sergius of Radonezh, near Zagorsk, in the Moscow region. The monks of the original abbey, which was founded in the middle of the fourteenth century, were subjected to less rigorous disciplines than those of the Kiev Caves. However, their saintly *igumen* and founder, Sergius, faithfully observed the essential elements of Theodosius' rule: poverty, humility, silence, work, and prayer. For all of this, St. Sergius played an important part in the history of his time. For it was he who, as we have seen, strengthened the spirit of Dimitry Donskoy and urged him to be reconciled with the other princes, thus making Russia's liberation from the Mongols possible. St. Sergius, it will be remembered, also gave Dimitry his blessing on the eve of the battle of Kulikovo.

Russian history and Russian monasticism have often been linked. The monasteries were the living source of the nation's spiritual life, a source which even the princes could not ignore. In the days when Moscow proudly assumed the name of "the Third Rome," and the tsars tried to turn the Church into a state institution, the monasteries refused to bow before the usurpation of authority. Philip, metropolitan of Moscow, who raised his voice against Tsar Ivan the Terrible and his rule of terror, was a monk and *igumen* of the monastery of Solovetzk.

The Solovetzk monastery, on an island of the White Sea, was one of Russia's most venerated shrines. Its very location attracted pious souls. It was a center of contemplative life and liturgy, in a region where parishes were scarce and isolated. All the inhabitants of the Russian north made pilgrimages to Solovetzk: not only peasants, but many young couples about to be married and industrial workers from St. Petersburg made the pilgrimage. Some of them spent a few days of retreat, offering their services to the various workshops of the community. The monastery, which had about fifty workshops, was entirely self-sufficient: it had carpenters, blacksmiths, leatherworkers, shipbuilders, silversmiths, and jewelers, glass blowers and crystal grinders, bakers, fish smokers, vegetable and fruit canners. There was work for every volunteer; some of them did not go back into the world, but remained in the monastery either as permanent guests or as postulants.

During the bolshevist revolution, part of the monastery was turned into a prison for bishops, priests, and laymen. And so the great North Sea abbey became the scene of indescribable suffering, hardships, and martyrdom for both Russian Orthodox and Catholics, who were interned side by side, condemned to hard labor or death as described in a previous chapter.

Another important northern retreat was Valaamo, on Lake Ladoga, off the Finland shore. Valaamo, one of Russia's most ancient monasteries, is believed to have been founded in the early tenth century, even before Russia's conversion, when the first Greek missionaries arrived. Valaamo, too, was built on an island, and could only be reached by a boat on a thirty-mile voyage, often through perilous fog and storms. Even in good weather the pilgrim had the feeling of a break with the world and the discovery of a new spiritual dimension. Holy obedience was the fundamental rule of Valaamo. Nothing could be undertaken without the *igumen's* permission. Like Solovetzk, Valaamo was self-supporting and had a crew of skilled builders and engineers, skippers and technicians. When the *igumen* gave permission to a monk or visitor, it was said of him that he "announced" or "proclaimed" his decision, not as a master, but rather as a heralding angel. In Valaamo, as in most

Russian abbeys, there were several categories of monks: the *ieromonakhy*, i.e., monks ordained to the priesthood; the *monakhy*, who were professed monks but not priests; the *poslushniky*, or novices and postulants. There was still another category in these monasteries, as in all Oriental communities of strict observance: these were the *shimo-monakhy*, or anchorites, who by special permission of the abbot lived in complete retirement, occupying special dwellings in the woods or underground cells, far from the rest of the community. These hermits were pledged to observe absolute silence, sometimes over a period of years speaking only to their confessors. They were dispensed from manual labor in the monastery, and were brought food from the refectory. They came to Mass or celebrated it in their "caves," according to the *igumen's* decision. They were allowed to receive visitors, but rarely and only by permission.

The food at Valaamo was plentiful and good. No meat was allowed, but there is a great variety of fish in Lake Ladoga, and berries and vegetables grow in the islands. Milk, butter, and eggs were not permitted during Lent; the staple food was buckwheat, millet, fruit, black bread, and vegetable oil. The shimo-monach's diet was more restricted: there was no fish and only certain vegetables and herbs.

Valaamo was one of the last resorts of Russian monasticism. It was still active under Finland's protection after the revolution, but was later closed by the Soviet border authorities. Its monks were dispersed; some of them settled in Finland, others rebuilt a community in Russia.

In the eighteenth and nineteenth centuries, two important spiritual centers were established; both of them were based on traditional monasticism, yet introduced a new spirit. These were the Sarov and Optyna "deserts."

The Sarov monastery became famous because of St. Seraphim, one of Russia's most popular saints.[2] This was first an underground community, living in caves, in the Tambov region. Later, the hermits built cells and a church on the surface.

---

[2] As described in Part One, Chapter Nine.

The other great monastery of the new spirituality was Optyna Pustyn in the Kaluga region, south of Moscow. Its site was the former hideaway of Opta the Highway-man, a sort of Russian Robin Hood, who at the end of his life repented and became a hermit. In the nineteenth and early twentieth centuries, Optyna was an important retreat house, directed by experienced and learned monks. Many Russian intellectuals and writers made these retreats, among them Gogol, Tolstoy, Solovyev, and Dostoyevsky. The community had taken over from Mount Athos the main trends of eastern monasticism, the hesychast method: a constant repetition of the Jesus prayer (Lord Jesus Christ, have mercy on me, a sinner) and spiritual direction administered by the *staretzy,* who demanded absolute obedience from those who came to them for instruction.

Both monks and nuns in Russia were dedicated, like the Benedictines in the west, to the *Opus Dei.* The liturgical office, closely resembling the Benedictine hours, started at midnight and went on throughout the day, with matins and lauds and vespers and compline sung for several hours each, and two or three communal Masses every morning. The entire community was to attend all offices, except the hermits, who read the psalter in their caves both day and night.

Beside the *Opus Dei,* the Russian monk was specially dedicated to the poor, the hungry, and the sick. The nuns of Shamordino, where Tolstoy's sister was a nun, established a public health and welfare center, according to the best techniques of their time. Solovetzk received about fifteen thousand visitors a year, who were sheltered, fed, and clothed by the monks. Even today the abbey of Zagorsk receives not only tourists, but many poor wanderers and pilgrims. They come on foot to worship before the relics of St. Sergius. They also go on foot to the Caves of Kiev, covering hundreds of miles. This is nothing unusual: a pilgrimage in Russia, even in the days of the first railroads, was to be undertaken on foot. And so it goes on, with our modern means of communication.

What has happened to monastic life in Russia under the Soviet rule? We have seen that St. Sergius and the Caves monasteries are open, but that Solovetsk and Valaamo are closed. According to the most recent information, there are some sixty or more religious communities still alive in Russia. For a time, during the antireligious persecutions, many monasteries went underground or were registered as "agricultural communes." Today, these communities are officially recognized. In the Russian north, not far from the ancient city of Pskov, a number of monks from Valaamo have re-established their center in the Petchera monastery and have revived the strict observance of their rule. In Kiev, near the Caves, there are two communities of nuns who make priests' vestments.

Despite forty years of government propaganda, then, Russian monasteries still exist. The visible number is small. But how many hermits still dwell in the woods and caves and dugouts in the immensity of Russia no one can say. No doubt, in the wilderness, or on the shores of distant lakes and seas, the spirit of Russian monasticism still shines under silent skies, just as Alyosha Karamazov saw it on the night of his great initiation.

*   *   *

Beside the monk so vividly portrayed in Russian history as well as in Russian literature, we find the almost "unsung" hero of the Russian Church: the secular priest or representative of the "white clergy."

In the Moscow chronicles secular priests appear but rarely. We have had some glimpse of them in the days of tsar Alexis, when Avvakum and the other zealots of piety wanted a complete moral reform and manifested spiritual vigor and unusual devotion. Unfortunately, as we have seen, the "zealots" were drawn into the turmoil of the *Raskol*, and their great ethical teachings were engulfed in a tidal wave of fanaticism and bitter disputes. But even so, we can see that the white clergy belongs to a different type of spirituality. The secular priest is active in the community; he preaches in the city, leads the people, directs the tsar himself and forms a strong opposition to the hierarchy whenever the latter fails in its duties. This happened in the days of Patriarch

Nikon; it happened again, when the Holy Synod lost control on the eve of the revolution.

Let us now see how the Russian-Orthodox priest is formed and what is his background. Let us first of all remind the reader that the Catholic Church recognizes the validity of Greek or Russian-Orthodox orders. Unlike the Anglicans, the Eastern Churches have retained, even after the schism, Apostolic Succession, which makes all their sacraments valid. Both Russian ordained monks, so-called "black," and secular, "white," clergy are therefore "priests forever, according to the order of Melchisedech."

The main difference between the "white" and the "black" clergy is, obviously, the fact that the Russian-Orthodox secular clergy is married. A priest of the Eastern Church may marry, but only before he has received the deacon's orders. Many deacons of the Eastern Church are not finally ordained to the priesthood, but their role in the liturgy is very important. The deacon actually conducts many parts of this liturgy, including the Litanies. Only if no deacon is available are the Litanies sung by the priest.

The deacons or future priests are married before their final ordination. After this last step they cannot remarry if they are widowers. The deacon and priest-to-be usually wed the daughter of a priest or a young girl raised in devout lay circles. The wife of a Russian priest has a very special vocation — not only as a devoted wife and mother, but also as her husband's helper in the parish and the corporal works of mercy. She is usually addressed as "matushka," i.e., "mother," to distinguish her from the matron and housewife of a layman's home.

The very fact that the Russian secular priest is married excludes him from the higher hierarchy. Bishops, archbishops, metropolitans, and patriarchs of the Eastern Church must be monks and are therefore never recruited from the white clergy. The highest ranks a secular priest can attain are those of *Protoyerei* (Archpriest) or *Mitroforny Yerei*, i.e., one permitted to wear a miter. This rule eliminates the ambition of the secular priest to reach the higher hierarchy. But it in no way minimizes the role of the white clergy in Russia.

One of the most famous representatives of Russian secular priesthood was John Sergeyev, known as Father John of Cronstadt (1829–1908). He was the son of a poor village deacon in the north of Russia and later came to Petersburg as a seminarian. He graduated from the Theological Academy and after his ordination became the rector of a small parish in Cronstadt, the fortified island at the mouth of the river Neva, near Petersburg.

Father John did not belong to the prominent clergy of the capital; he rarely left his little parish; but he became a great influence in his own right as a teacher, spiritual director, adviser of the Tsars, helper of the sick, and even healer. He was very devoted to the sick, and many cures are attributed to his prayers. For Father John of Cronstadt was essentially a man of prayer and taught this method:

> Prayer, he wrote, is the lifting of the mind and heart to God, the daring converse of the creature with the Creator.

But such a "daring converse" is not possible without that which is the center of Christian experience: the Eucharist. John of Cronstadt deeply realized the Eucharistic life and specially promoted it. As we have seen, frequent Communion was not practiced, nor even encouraged, in Russia. Even in Latin countries frequent Communion was spread by St. Pius X only in the early twentieth century. In asserting the central role of the Eucharist, John of Cronstadt was a precursor.

This great representative of the white clergy left a series of writings: the most important is his *"My Life in Christ."*[3] These writings are still used as Russian-Orthodox spiritual readings. Father John of Cronstadt belonged to a relatively peaceful and conservative period of Russian ecclesiastical life. He was greatly respected by two successive Tsars, welcomed by court circles and high-ranking nobility and officialdom. But he was also beloved by the poor. His remarkable contribution to his Church was the reaffirmation of the secular priest's pastoral mission. Others continued his work.

[3] See *A Treasury of Russian Spirituality*.

As the role of the white clergy grew in Russia in the early 1900's there grew also a tension between the secular priest and the black clergy, i.e., the hierarchy.

This tension was due in part to the fact that the bishops and metropolitans belonged to Russian monasticism. Even when occupying the key posts of ecclesiastical life and administration they often retained an aloof and exclusive way of life. In the late nineteenth and early twentieth centuries, the Russian prelate observed a prudent and passive attitude; he was unwilling to deal with immediate problems, social or political. He accepted the authority of the State, the prerogatives of the autocratic Tsar and of a wealthy industrial and rural economy. The hierarchy was well provided for and could live in comfort — even luxury. This was not the white clergy's lot. Secular priests had a modest allowance sparingly granted by the State; they lived very much like the poor workers and peasants to whom they ministered in small towns and villages. And so the priests became aware of social and economic problems. Some of them even joined the radical movements in the name of social justice (a fact usually ignored by communist propaganda because the priests were not communists). During the years preceding the revolution, the social and political consciousness of the white clergy was also manifested in higher ecclesiastical circles. Thus, for instance, there was an open conflict between Archpriest George Shavelsky (chief chaplain of the Russian Army and Navy during World War I) and several members of the higher hierarchy. Father Shavelsky opposed some prelates who favored Rasputin, the false prophet and adventurer, who was exercising such a fatal influence on the Tsar and his family. Father Shavelsky was among those who not only openly condemned Rasputin, but repeatedly admonished the Tsar himself, imploring him to deal drastically with the impostor.[4]

The Chief Chaplain also strove to solve many problems pertaining to the relations between Russian-Orthodox and Catholics in Poland and the Ukraine. Had his advice been followed, many political mistakes inside Russia as well as much bitterness be-

---

[4] *See* Bibliography.

tween Russian-Orthodox and Catholics in the Russian-Polish lands
would have been averted.

These are but a few examples of the role of the white clergy
in Russia. All were not, of course, as inspired as Father John of
Cronstadt or as dynamic as Father George Shavelsky. But the
priest had a great mission to fulfill at all levels of Russian religious life of the twentieth century.

First of all, of course, the secular priests were, in a way, integrated in the everyday life of the Russian people, and of their
leaders: tsar, government, political groups, army and navy, industrial workers and rural populations were all more constantly
in touch with the white clergy than with the monks and *staretzy*
of faraway monasteries. This led the priest to adopt a spirit of
Christian charity, of understanding, and forgiveness, which in
turn permitted a closer contact between church and laity, a
ministering to each man's immediate spiritual needs, regardless
of class, race, social or economic status.

*   *   *

An important aspect of the Russian secular clergy tradition
is the priest's family environment. He is, with his *matushka,* a
link in a long ecclesiastical lineage. For it is usual for a Russian
priest's son to follow in his father's steps. Thus a spiritual and
social group was long ago established. This situation is sometimes
criticized by the Russians themselves — since young men often
entered the priesthood without a special vocation, just because
of heredity. This does not mean, of course, that all priesthood
in the Russian-Orthodox Church is a closed "caste." Both in
Russia and in the emigration, many priests recently ordained come
from various other social strata. One may say that the trend *today*
is against hereditary priesthood.

Even among descendants of ecclesiastical families we do not
find an automatic rule of transmission. Some of these descendants
remained laymen. Dostoyevsky's grandfather, for example, was a
priest, but his father was a doctor. The great religious philosopher,
Vladimir Solovyev, was also the grandson of a priest and his
father was a distinguished layman and historian. Some of the

descendants of priests turned violently against their family tradition, becoming rebels, revolutionaries, atheists. But even so, they somehow retained a certain spiritual "backbone": a strong sense of duty, of a dedicated and ascetic life, of self-denial and service. It has often been pointed out that even the atheist Russian intelligentsia's ideology and behavior show a religious strain. This may be in part attributed to their ecclesiastical origin.

A curious indication of ecclesiastical descent is found in many Russian family names, which originally belonged to priests and were passed on to their lay progeny.

The members of the Russian secular clergy were often given symbolic names: deriving from flowers (tuberosa, rose, symbolic of spiritual fragrance) or from precious stones (diamond, sapphire, amethyst, and other ornaments of God's throne in St. John's Revelation) or names of great liturgical feasts, like the Nativity, the Assumption, the Transfiguration, the Feast of the Archangels, etc. In most Russian symbolic names, some of them Latin (like Benefactov or Benedictov), an ecclesiastical origin can usually be traced. Some militant Russian atheists or materialistic philosophers still bear names reminiscent of a spiritual lineage, long forgotten or rejected. Thus, for instance, the name of a Soviet diplomat Bogomolov, which comes from the compound word "to pray God," is clearly ecclesiastical. It is also the name of a ballerina of the Bolshoy theater.

The fact that the priesthood was generally transmitted from father to son has often been pointed out as having created a special clerical class; young men were trained in the seminaries and later ordained, not because of a true vocation, but because they were children and grandchildren of priests. These criticisms were usually made by anticlerical writers seeking to minimize the Russian Church, though in some cases the objections were valid enough.

Needless to say, however, there were many true and sincere vocations among the descendants of the Russian clergy.

The priest's family, his house, and home life were in themselves preparation for priesthood. For the young boy it was a firsthand religious training and a devotional living experience. Long before the youth entered the seminary and was graduated from the Theological Academy (the highest degree in religious education) he knew many things through oral tradition and the liturgy in action, as celebrated by his father.

The prominent Russian-Orthodox theologian, Father Sergius Bulgakov, is typical of this ecclesiastical background. Father Bulgakov was the son of a small town parish priest. He was raised in humble and even poor surroundings. Yet in his diary Sergius Bulgakov wrote: "I am a Levite in the sixth generation." This means that when the Romanovs ascended the Moscow throne in the early seventeenth century, Father Sergius' ancestors were already celebrating the liturgy.[5]

There is much in the Bulgakov story which is characteristic of Russian hereditary priesthood — its traditional setup, its atmosphere of deep devotion and pastoral zeal, as well as its conflicts and spiritual struggles. As Father Sergius tells us in his diary, he considered his ecclesiastical heritage as a "blessing," as a source of "spiritual wealth," and as a "fundamental moral and liturgical training."[6] However, the young Sergius Bulgakov was a rebel. In the early 1900's he was deeply troubled by the problems of his time. The Church offered no solution to social injustice, to the peasant's bitter lot, to industrial exploitation. So Sergius Bulgakov gave up his preparation for the priesthood, joined the young revolutionaries, became a Marxist. His experience was similar to that of Nicholas Berdyaev, the young nobleman who renounced his privileges, joined the revolutionary movement, was jailed and exiled, first by the Tsarist government, then by the bolsheviks. Both Berdyaev and Bulgakov were soon disappointed in Marx. Both realized that communism denied not only God but all moral values and freedom and the dignity of the human person. Berdyaev, Bulgakov, and a number of other young "rebels" came back to the Church and became famous religious writers. Sergius Bulgakov was ordained a priest in 1918 in Petersburg, which was already under Communist rule. The ceremony was attended

[5] *See* Bibliography.
[6] *Ibid.*

by a group of intimate friends: Berdyaev, the poet Vyacheslav
Ivanov, and Father Paul Florensky, the brilliant philosopher, writer,
and mathematician. Florensky was to die a few years later in
a concentration camp. Berdyaev and Bulgakov were exiled in 1923
and settled in France, where they taught and wrote for many
years. They made immense contributions to religious thought,
theology, and the Christian social revival. Vyacheslav Ivanov also
left Russia and reached Italy in the late twenties. He joined the
Catholic Church and taught in Rome until his death in 1952.

These remarkable men represented the flowering of Russian
religious life on the eve of the revolution and during the tragic
days of Lenin's victory, when both priests and laymen had joined
their efforts to stem the tidal wave. If they did not succeed,
neither can one say that they were defeated. They remained a
dynamic force, because in the very first decades of our century
these priests and laymen had asserted themselves, together with
all progressive elements of Russian society. Some of them were
elected members of the Duma (the short-lived Russian parliament,
1906–1917); others served as army chaplains, and were killed
in battle, unarmed; they were professors, social workers; some
became prominent writers and preachers. When the antireligious
persecutions started, many of these priests, whose names have
never been listed, died as martyrs or went underground awaiting
better days. After persecution ceased, the priest reappeared in the
U.S.S.R., resumed the celebration of the liturgy openly, rebuilt
and reconsecrated parish churches, and officiated in collective
farms where he assumed the humblest task of a rural worker.
Soviet papers bitterly complain of the "infiltration" of the Kolkhoze
by ecclesiastics. There are many vocations to the priesthood today
in Soviet Russia, and seminaries receive a considerable number
of applications. There are some 200 students in the St. Sergius
Seminary at Zagorsk.

At the height of the bolshevik fight against religion, many
priests left Russia and established parishes in Europe, America,
Asia, Australia — wherever the wave of refugees settled in their
exodus. They built many churches, some of them large, others

quite small: mere chapels with a few icons, set up in garages by a few volunteers.

A number of young men became priests in exile; Father Alexander Yelchaninov and a few others were prominent in Russian-Orthodox religious circles, either in their apostolic work, or in the intellectual field, or both. Father George Florovsky, professor at Harvard University, is considered as the Russian-Orthodox Church's greatest theologian. Father Vassily Zenkovsky is the author of a major work on the history of Russian religious thought. Father Alexander Schmemann, the youngest of the group is an excellent teacher, brilliant speaker in Russian, French, and English, a historian and a professor of St. Vladimir Russian Seminary in New York City. During his student days in Paris, he was in Father Yelchaninov's class and was formed by this remarkable educator.

Born in 1881, the son of a layman, Alexander Yelchaninov was graduated from the school of Philology and History of Petersburg (today Leningrad) University. In the early twentieth century he lived and worked in Petersburg and Moscow, was close to the most dynamic circles of the intelligentsia, met Berdyaev, Florensky, Ivanov, and joined the "Christian Brotherhood of Struggle," a radical group, but not Marxist. Later, he became headmaster in a high school. His vocation was clarified step by step. Came the Bolshevik revolution and we find Alexander Yelchaninov a refugee in France, a priest and the rector of a Russian-Orthodox parish in Nice. He was a married man, the father of two children, and therefore secular. Later he became an outstanding educator of Russian-Orthodox youth in exile. He worked on the Riviera, and later in Paris, where he exercised a profound spiritual influence. He was a leader of the "Russian Student Movement," which sought to revitalize the religious life of the Russian youth in exile. His *Diary* retains the notes he made at that time for his personal record. He did not plan to publish them himself, and the *Diary* was brought out, after his death in 1934, by his widow, Mrs. Tatyana Yelchaninov. Father Alexander spent the

last years of his life entirely dedicated to his mission. From his
diary as well as from the testimony of his close friends and
followers, we know that Yelchaninov had his own method of
spiritual guidance. The late Professor Fedotov described this
method as follows:[7]

> Far from the spirit of proselytism, and with a distaste for the
> use of force whatsoever, he (Yelchaninov) simply opened to those
> under his guidance the way of self-examination.

And Yelchaninov himself, as Fedotov points out, was a "master
of the technique of self-examination." He demanded from his
penitents true contrition preceded by a careful preparation for
the sacrament of penance. In his "Letters to Young Men" (not
as yet published in English translation) Father Yelchaninov wrote:

> As far as confession is concerned, do not postpone it. A weak
> faith and doubts are no obstacles. By all means go to confession,
> admitting your weak faith and doubts, as your sinful frailties. And
> this is what they actually are. A full faith belongs only to those
> who are just and strong in spirit. How can we — impure and weak
> — equal their faith? If we had this faith we would be saints and
> would not need the help which the Church offers us.[8]

Such was Father Yelchaninov's method: "he was not," writes
Fedotov, "a struggler or a mystic but a serene and kind coun-
selor, meek, but interiorly austere, a stranger to any kind of
opportunism."[9]

Once more referring to his "Letters to Young Men," we find
a few essential rules for spiritual guidance. Father Alexander was
constantly concerned with the daily problems of life; he preached
on marriage, death, fasting, Lent, the New Year. He spoke to
communicants, to boy scouts, young girls, old women. His appeal
to souls was due to the fact that he combined austerity, strict
morals, and loving obedience to the Church with a deep knowl-

---

[7] Introduction to fragments of A. Yelchaninov's Diary, English Translation.
A Treasury of Russian Spirituality, Sheed and Ward, 1948. "Spiritual directions,"
Jubilee, October, 1959.
[8] *Ibid.*
[9] *Ibid.*

edge of psychology and even psychiatry. He had the gift of distinguishing the true spiritual life from imagination and fantasies. He was a mediator, always ready to forgive and comfort his children. And, those who followed his rule also attained a change of heart. He writes:

> You must keep yourself in spiritual purity and clarity so that your light illuminates the path of others . . . look for this light in yourself and others — maintain and cultivate in yourself and others every spark of good and light and do not believe in darkness; close your eyes upon them for they are but phantoms.[10]

From his spiritual children, Father Yelchaninov demanded a serious attitude to life; he reminded them that the sacrament of penance is not mere "social talk" about oneself and others, but a true account of one's sins. It is not enough to say "I have not killed, murdered, nor committed adultery." The penitent should also say how many times he failed in Christian charity. Father Yelchaninov points out that people who have no religious practice do not always know how to start a confession. The priest should help them, pray with them and for them, open for them the way of penance, which should not be an automatic, mechanical act. In his "Letters to Young People," Yelchaninov insists a great deal on daily prayer and spiritual reading: at least a few minutes of prayer and gospel reading are recommended to beginners. Further readings are mentioned in his "Letters" — the Fathers of the Church, especially St. Ephrem the Syrian, Abba Dorotheus, Simeon the New Theologian, as well as Russian spiritual teachers, including Father John of Cronstadt. Yelchaninov also recommended Catholic spiritual writings: St. Francis of Assisi, and St. Therese (the Little Flower). The Curé d'Ars is also mentioned in Yelchaninov's writings, an evidence that Russian-Orthodox priests today are drawing from the fount of our common Christian heritage: the heritage of Scripture, tradition, and the saints. And there was also in Father Yelchaninov's experience the way of the cross. He died prematurely in 1934, exhausted by his works of

---

10 *Ibid.*

mercy, prayer, devotion, in a world where even in his days security meant nothing. But he could write on the eve of his death:

The cult of the cross, the infamous instrument of execution, has recruited for Christianity men with the uttermost interior freedom.

CHAPTER FOURTEEN

The Pilgrim's Way[1]

"BY THE grace of God I am a Christian man, by my actions a great sinner, and by calling a homeless wanderer who roams from place to place. My worldly goods are a knapsack with some dried bread in it on my back, and in my breast pocket a Bible. And that is all." Thus begins an extraordinary account of the life of a pilgrim, a wanderer-in-Christ who perhaps without ever intending to do so, has done a great deal to bring the soul of Eastern Christianity to light in the Western world. By his own confession he was neither a professional man of letters, nor a journalist; neither a preacher, nor, as far as we know, a saint. The fact is we know very little of this man except what he has chosen to tell us of himself. His name is lost, his manuscript unsigned; we do not know whether he wrote his own story, or told it to someone else who wrote it down. All we can gather from written evidence is that this man lived a hundred years ago: a peasant of Central Russian origin; that he was crippled in one arm from childhood (due to the malice of an older brother), and that, at about the age of twenty, he started on his spiritual journey.

His story, "The Candid Narrative of a Pilgrim to his Spiritual Father," was discovered in manuscript at the Greek monastic community of Mount Athos by a Russian abbot on visit from his monastery at Kazan, on the Volga. The abbot copied the manuscript, and from his copy the book was published in Kazan in 1884; almost immediately it caused a stir in Russian religious circles

---

[1] This chapter was published with a few variations in *Jubilee*.

198

and was later published in translation in both England and America.[2]

He was an obscure peasant, living in the tyrannical era of Tsar Nicholas I, traveling on foot through stretches of an enormous land. His journeyings took him widely through Russia and into Siberia. At the end of his account he is planning to go on a further journey — this time to Jerusalem in company with another pilgrim. He carries a knapsack containing two books and a few crusts of bread, and in his hand a rosary. In the immensity of the steppes he is like a speck of dust, yet he is strengthened by a formidable grace; the power of *unceasing* prayer.

He tells us that he was born in Orel, a fertile "black-earth" region south of Moscow. His parents died when he was still a child, and he and his older brother were adopted by his grandparents, an innkeeper and his wife who, though not rich, were sufficiently well off to keep the children from privation. The innkeeper was a very pious man who read from the Bible every day — the same Bible which the pilgrim was at last to carry with him on his travels. The older brother was wild, and even as an adolescent took to drink. The younger boy, however, stayed at home and was taught to read and write, a rare enough privilege in nineteenth-century Russia. Grandfather, grandmother, and the young grandson attended church in the village with devout regularity; at home they prayed together. The boy would read aloud from the psalms, the *Miserere* in particular, while both grandparents knelt down and bowed their heads to the floor in frequent prostration. (This very exacting form of physical penance is seldom practiced in the Church today except by monks or nuns of certain eastern communities, or by rare individual members of the laity.)

The boy was seventeen when his grandmother died; shortly afterward, his grandfather made a match for him with a "worthy and sensible girl." A year or two later, when his grandfather died, the young man was persecuted by his older brother, whose hatred drove him to set fire to the house. Escaping from this calamity

---

[2] *See* Bibliography.

only with their lives and the family Bible, the young couple built a hut, and worked as landless peasants. They never abandoned their religious life, reading the family Bible which had been saved from the flames, fasting, praying, and making a thousand prostrations every evening. This penitential exercise, the pilgrim relates, did not weary them; on the contrary, they enjoyed it. But after two years of this sort of life they were struck once again by adversity: the peasant's young wife was suddenly taken ill with a virulent fever and died. Now he was entirely alone; saddened even by the sight of his hut, he sold it and gave his belongings to the poor. Whatever else he might do in life, he was determined to make a pilgrimage to Kiev, and there to pray for guidance. His crippled arm proved to be of some help to him at this moment: it allowed him to register officially as an invalid and entitled him to a passport, a very valuable document in the days of Nicholas I when a man, particularly a wanderer, traveling from village to village without one was liable to arrest, imprisonment, or even to exile in Siberia. Special passports were issued to the sick and disabled but these were subject to investigation if the bearer's behavior appeared to be in any way extraordinary. Our peasant was now free to leave his native village and with the Bible in his knapsack, to start on his pilgrimage.

Russian pilgrims, according to a very old custom, always attempt to visit Kiev where the bones of St. Theodosius are enshrined along with those of many other early monks and hermits at the Monastery of the Caves. (The Soviet government has within recent years reopened these reliquaries to present-day pilgrims.) Our pilgrim, in making straight for Kiev, was following tradition. Later he visited other cities renowned for shrines and miraculous icons. But still he was not satisfied: he sought for something more, for something deeper. He hardly could have stated what it was until one Sunday at Mass in a village church he was struck by a sentence from St. Paul's Epistle to the Thessalonians: "Pray without ceasing." "It was this text more than any other," he tells us, "which forced itself upon my mind, and I began to think how it was possible to pray without ceasing."

The pilgrim now had a definite goal: he set out to find a man who could teach him how to engage in ceaseless prayer.

In the year which followed he was to walk many hundred miles, before finally discovering a *staretz,* a monk particularly gifted as a director, who taught him the method of devotion he had long desired: the Prayer of Jesus.

"The continuous interior Prayer of Jesus," the *staretz* told him, "is a constant, uninterrupted calling upon the divine Name of Jesus with the lips, in the spirit, in the heart; while forming a mental picture of His constant presence and imploring His grace, during every occupation, at all times, in all places, even during sleep. The appeal is couched in these terms, 'Lord Jesus Christ, have mercy on me.' "

After this brief instruction followed by an assurance that the prayer would lead to spiritual progress and bring with it many consolations, the *staretz* gave the pilgrim the *Philocalia,* a famous anthology of spiritual writings by medieval Greek fathers on the way of continuous prayer. The pilgrim was puzzled by the unqualified esteem in which this book was held by his adviser. "Is it, then, more sublime and holy than the Bible?" he was led to ask.

"No, it is not that," answered the *staretz,* "but it contains clear explanations of what the Bible holds in secret. . . ."

Now the pilgrim continued his way, carrying in his knapsack the Bible and the *Philocalia.* At last he had truly entered upon a life of constant prayer.

What does this Prayer of Jesus actually involve? . . . It is a devout entreaty addressed to the Lord: an efficacious means of grace profoundly anchored in the spiritual life through constant repetition. As prescribed by the *staretz,* this spiritual exercise, as we have seen, was already common in Russian monastic practice in the fifteenth century — at the time of St. Nilus of Sorsk.

It is interesting to note that controlled respiration was suggested as an accompaniment to the Prayer of Jesus. In Hesychast teaching, as expounded by St. Nilus and his masters at Mount Athos, the Prayer of Jesus had to perform a special operation: "to make

the intelligence descend into the heart" — in other words, to con-
centrate entirely on prayer and prayer alone. "Breathing is the
natural way to the heart," the Hesychast fathers taught. Therefore, "having gathered in your intellect . . . impell it, joined to
the inhaled air, to descend into the heart and remain there." The
idea that deep breathing, quietude, and concentration dispose the
mind to prayer, may, as some writers have suggested, show the
influence of the Indian *guru* on Russian mysticism. It is quite
true that Yoga teaches breathing exercises and their control — inhaled, retained, or expelled breath — but in spite of superficial
resemblances, the Hesychast method can scarcely have been de-
rived from Hinduism. As a French writer, J. A. Cuttat,[3] has
pointed out in a work on Hesychasm, the Prayer of Jesus stems
from the Desert Fathers, the Greek Patristic teachings, and "the
summit of Byzantine spirituality."

Rightly instructed in a sound discipline, the pilgrim escapes
the dangers of spiritual egotism to which a myopic adherence to
his "method" might otherwise have led. Selfishness and its at-
tendant loneliness are hardly permitted to the pilgrim, who is
constantly on the move and always praying. In his wanderings,
he meets people of every description, many of whom, beggars,
soldiers, businessmen, and peasants, join him from time to time;
he begs and receives from them all; he gives his help wherever
he can. He is constantly threatened with danger, is robbed of his
two precious books (which he later retrieves), is attacked by a
wolf (which he scourges with his rosary and miraculously fright-
ens away). Renouncing all selfish desire and giving himself up
to Jesus Christ through prayer, the wanderer becomes a part of
the world and its suffering.

The pilgrim's narrative is unusual because of its straightforward
documentation of one man's profound religious experience; however, there always have been wanderers-in-Christ in Russia; they
are typical of the native scene. To the peasants in isolated, winter-
locked villages, the pilgrim is a familiar figure, filled with graces
which he freely bestows on all those whom he encounters in his

---

[3] J. A. Cuttat, *La Rencontre des Religions*. See Bibliography.

journey. With his gospel, an icon, and bread crusts in his knapsack, he carries a word of peace, sped on his way with a blessing:
"May the all-loving Grace of God shed its light on your path, and
go with you, as the Angel Raphael went with Tobias!"

Before the Revolution, Russian pilgrims not only walked for
hundreds of miles to visit native shrines and miraculous icons.
They saved enough money to get transportation to the Holy
Land or were taken over free of cost by religious organizations.
The Holy Land is a place every Russian-Orthodox wants to visit
before he dies. There are still today several Russian monasteries
in Jerusalem; one of them belongs to the see of an émigré prelate.
The remains of grand duchess Elizabeth, a sister of the tsarina,
who was also murdered by the bolsheviks, were brought to this
monastery. Among the nuns there is a member of the Imperial
family. Another monastery is under the jurisdiction of the Patriarch of Moscow and according to old tradition maintains "a zone
of Russian influence" in the Holy Land.

In our days, pilgrims from Russia rarely get as far as Jerusalem. But they continue to roam throughout Russia, covering
hundreds of miles to pray at Zagorsk in the Abbey of the Holy
Trinity, where the relics of St. Sergius are enshrined. Tourists
who visit Zagorsk all report having seen these pilgrims fervently
praying at the shrine or resting on the steps of the Church. Pilgrims also visit the great abbey of the Caves at Kiev, where the
"candid wanderer" prayed a hundred years ago.

The wanderer-in-Christ is frequently encountered in Russian
literature: Tolstoy has described one of them — Grisha, the saintly
fool who bound chains under his peasant shirt. Tolstoy had seen
him as a boy in his parents' home and later, remembering him,
he wrote: "Oh, Grisha, great Christian: your faith was so strong
that you felt the nearness of God; your love was so great that
the words flowed of themselves from your lips . . ." Again, in
War and Peace we read of pilgrims and beggars welcomed on
the great estates as Christ's own messengers and "God's folk."

Another pilgrim, or at least a penitent, figures in *The En-
chanted Wanderer* by Nicolai Lyeskov, a less-known master of

Russian prose who often wrote of religious life. Lyeskov's story is the fictitious autobiography of one of these men who was always on the move throughout Russia's immensity. Filled with remorse because he has carelessly caused the death of a man, he becomes a wanderer, but not a completely exemplary one. A final episode in his career leads him to commit another crime, and we see him at last seeking expiation in the monastic life.

A penitent wanderer is also featured in a poem by N. Nekrasov, poet and political writer, who first discovered the young Dostoyevsky. In his poem, entitled *Vlas,* Nekrasov tells of a pilgrim much like Lyeskov's whose conscience is burdened with several crimes as he sets out in search of salvation: a haunted-looking, white-haired old man in a ragged coat, a copper icon hung about his neck, he roams from city to city collecting alms.

Many pilgrims, renouncing their own goods, collected alms as Vlas did for churches and monasteries. In turn, the religious houses were prepared to shelter these pilgrims, seeing Christ in each. For this reason the monks did not question them closely as to who they were, where they came from, what sins were yet behind them, or what temptations had pursued them. The secrets of the pilgrim's heart remained hidden from all but his *staretz.*

An entire chapter of Dostoyevsky's *Diary of a Writer* is devoted to Nekrasov's Vlas, with the comment that the pilgrim's way of reparation seems to him typically Russian: simple and yet paradoxical. Saint and sinner meet on this same road in their search for God: "I am still of the opinion," writes Dostoyevsky, "that theirs will be the last word — I mean, these other Vlases, the repenting and the nonrepenting: they will show us the new path, and the new solution to all the difficulties which now seem so insoluble."

*   *   *

Russians have always had a great admiration for pilgrims. As we have seen, they have conceived St. Nicholas as not only visiting, but wandering through their native country. The great Russian poet, Fedor Tyutchev, whose works are not only perfections of style and beauty, but also have a metaphysical content, has represented Christ, not triumphant or transfigured but as the "Man of Sorrows," laden with the burden of the cross, roaming Russia in the form of a servant, blessing the poor villages — the land of "long suffering."

In an essay devoted to the mystical and theological interpretation of the way of the pilgrim, the Russian religious writer L. Zander tells us that visiting of ancient shrines is a revival of past events, it is "an experience of a past reality, a victory over time." And Mr. Zander goes on to say:

> The metaphysical structure of the pilgrimage resembles that of the Eucharist. Its essence is the *anamnesis*. The sacred past becomes the present *hic et nunc*. In the celebration of Holy Mass we become the contemporaries of the apostles; we truly participate in the feast of love, we eat the same bread, we drink the same wine as the one that Christ gave to his disciples. In pilgrimage we enter with Christ into Jerusalem, we are present at His passion on Calvary and at his burial in the Sepulcre. . . . In Rome we share the sufferings of the apostles in the Mamertine prison, and of the martyrs in the Coliseum . . . at Subiaco we pray with Saint Benedict in the *Sacro Speco* . . . we land with St. Columba on the Island of Iona . . . we see the light that came to the Russian people in Kiev.
>
> If the media of pilgrimage — journeying on foot — means for us a victory over space, it is a victory over time which is given us when we reach the goal.[4]

And so with Zander's profoundly ecumenical words we pause on our own pilgrimage through ten centuries of the history and life of the Russian Church. But we feel that this is not Journey's End, for Russia's monks and priests and beggars will continue to roam for a long time along the roads of their native land and perhaps along the roads of other lands: after Kiev, there will be Rome; after Moscow and the Holy land, there will be St. Benedict's desert. On these wanderings in the footsteps of Christ and of His saints, Russia will meet her Western brothers, and they will embrace each other in joy as the Eastern liturgy invites them. This then will be the goal, a universal goal of union of all in Christ, who carried His cross for all.

---

[4] L. Zander, *Le Pelerinage, see* Bibliography.

Bibliography

Attwater, Donald, *The Dissident Eastern Churches* (Milwaukee: Bruce, 1937).

Avvakum, Archpriest, *Life*, (H. Iswolsky, Tr.), in *A Treasury of Russian Spirituality* (*see* Fedotov).

Baumgarten (N. de), "Aux origines de la Russie" in *Or. Christ. Analecta*, fasc. 119, 1939.

Bulgakov, Protoyerey Serguey, *Avtobiographicheskye Zametky* (Paris: Y.M.C.A. Press, 1946).

Butler, A., *Lives of the Saints*, rev. ed. (New York: Kenedy, 1956).

Carpini, Plano, *Travels, Liber Tartarorum*.

Chetverikov, S., *Optyna Pustyn* (Paris: Y.M.C.A. Press, 1926).

Congar, Yves, O.P., *After Nine Hundred Years* (New York: Fordham Univ. Press, 1959).

Cross, H. C., *Medieval Russian Churches* (Cambridge, Mass.: Medieval Academy, 1949).

Cuttat, J. A., *La Rencontre des Religions. Avec une Étude Sur la Spiritualité de l'Orient Chretien* (Paris: Aubier, 1957).

Dobbie-Bateman, A. F., translation of *"St. Seraphim of Sarov"* and *"The Conversation of St. Seraphim with Nicholas Motovilov"* (London: The Society for Promoting Christian Knowledge).

Dostoyevsky, F., *A Writer's Diary* (New York: Chas. Scribner's Sons).

——— *The Brothers Karamazov*, Garnett, Constance, tr. (New York: Modern Library).

Dvornik, F., *The Idea of Apostolicity in Byzantium and The Legend of the Apostle Andrew* (Cambridge, Mass.: Harvard Univ. Press, 1958).

——— *Les Slaves, Byzance et Rome au IX siecle* (Paris: Champion, 1926).

——— "Patriarch Photius in the Tradition of the Western Church," *Third Hour*, issue III, 1947.

——— *The Photian Schism, History and Legend* (England: Cambridge Univ. Press, 1948).

Fedotov, G. P., *The Russian Religious Mind* (Cambridge, Mass.: Harvard Univ. Press, 1946).

Svyatye Drevnei Russi (Paris: Y.M.C.A. Press, 1931).

A Treasury of Russian Spirituality (New York: Sheed and Ward, 1948) (Edited by G. P. Fedotov).

Findeisen, L., *Istoria Russkoy Musiky* (Moscow: Gosisdat, 1948).

Florovski, G., *Puti Russkago Bogosloviya* (Paris, 1937).

Gagarin, J., S.J., *La Russie sera-t-elle catholique?* (Paris: C. Douniol, 1856).

Golubinsky, E., Y. Y. *Istoria Russkoi Tzerkvi I–II* (Moskva Universitetskaya Tipographia, 1901–1911).

Gordillo, S.J., Rev. Mauria, *The Devotion of the Russian People to Mary* (New York: Russian Center, Fordham University, 1959).

Gorodetzky, Nadejdo, *The Humiliated Christ in Modern Russian Thought* (London: Society for Promoting Christian Knowledge, 1938).

Gratieux, A., *A. S. Khomiakov et le Mouvement Slavophile* (Paris, 1939).

Il'in, *Sviatoi Serafim* (Paris: Y.M.C.A. Press, 1925).

Iswolsky, Helene, *Soul of Russia* (New York and London: Sheed and Ward, 1943–1944).

Khomyakov, A. S., *Sochinenya* (Tchekhov Publishing House).

Klyuchevsky, V. O., *Kurs Russkoi Istorii*, 5 vols. (Moscow: Gosisdat, 1923).

Kondakov, N. P., *The Russian Icon*, I–IV (plates) (Prague, 1928–1933).

Miliukov, P., *Outlines of Russian Culture* (Philadelphia: Univ. of Pennsylvania Press, 1942).

Mirsky, D. S., *A History of Russian Literature* (New York: Knopf, 1949).

Nestor, St., *Life of St. Theodosius.* H. Iswolsky tr. in *A Treasury of Russian Spirituality* (see Fedotov).

Nilus, Sorsky, St., *The Tradition of the Disciples, The Monastic Rule, St. Nilus' Last Will*, H. Iswolsky tr. in *A Treasury of Russian Spirituality* (see Fedotov).

Pascal, P., *Avvakum et les Debuts du Raskol: La Crise Religieuse au XVII siecle en Russie* (Paris: l'Institut Francais de Leningrad, H. Champion, 1938).

Philokalia, writings, tr. from the Russian text of *Dobrotolubiye* by E. Kadloubovsky and G. E. H. Palmer (London: Faber and Faber, Ltd., 1953).

Pierling, Paul, S.J., *"La Russie et le Saint Siege,"* in *Etudes Diplomatiques* (Paris: Plon-Nourrit, 1896–1901).

Pilgrim, The, N. Tumanova tr. in *A Treasury of Russian Spirituality* (see Fedotov).

Platonov, S., *Smutnoie Vremia* (Leningrad: Izdanie Vremia, 1923); (Prague, 1924).

Povyest Vremennykh Lyet (I–II), podgotovka teksta, D. S. Likhacheva (Moscow: Academy of Sciences, 1950).

Pravda o Religiu iv Rossi (Moskovskaya (Partriakhya, 1942).

Pravoslavny Tzerkovny Kalendar Na 1949 (Moskovskaya Partriakhya).

Pushkin, A. S., *Poems, Prose and Plays* (New York: Modern Library).

——— *Boris Godunov,* tr. Alfred Hayes (New York: E. P. Dutton & Co., Inc.)

Raya, Reverend Joseph, of the Patriarchal Clergy and Baron Jose de Vinck, *Byzantine Missal.*

Rozanov, V., *Fallen Leaves* (London: The Mandrake Press, 1929).

Schmemann, Protoyerey Alexander, *Istorichesky Putj Pravoslavia* (New York: Tchekov Publishing House, 1954).

Scolardi, Paulin-Guard, *Krizhanitch, messenger of Christian Unity, father of Panslavism, in the service of Rome and Moscow in the Seventeenth century* (Paris: Picard, 1951).

Service Book of the Holy Orthodox Catholic Apostolic Church, E. Hapgood, tr. (Y.M.C.A. Association Press, 1922).

Shavelsky (Protopresvyter), *Vospominanya.* Chekhov editions (in Russian).

Solovyev, V., *Complete Works,* 1901, St. Petersburg.
Russia and the Universal Church, tr. Geoffrey Bless (London, 1948).

Taube, Michel de, *Rome et la Russie avant l'invasion des Tatares,* Editions Russie et Chretiente, Ed. du Cerf (Paris, 1947).

Timasheff, N. S., *Religion in Soviet Russia* (Sheed and Ward, 1942).

Tolstoy, D., *Rimsky Katolitzism v Rossii* (St. Petersburg, 1876).

Tolstoy, L., *Childhood, Boyhood and Youth in Complete Works* (Oxford Univ. Press).

Tschizewskij, Dmitrij, *Das heilige Russland.* Russische Geistesgeschichte. I. 10–17 Jahrhundert. *Rowohlt's Deutsche Enzyklopedie.* 1959. Hamburg. S. 170.

Tykhon, St. of Zadonsk, *Biography and Letters,* H. Iswolsky tr. in *A Treasury of Russian Spirituality* (see Fedotov).

Tyszkiewicz, S.J., and Dom Th. Belpaire, O.S.B., *Ascetes Russes* (Namur: Les Editions du soleie Levant, 1957).

Vernadsky, G., *The Origins of Russia* (London: Oxford Univ. Press, 1959).

—— *Ancient Russia* (London: Oxford Univ. Press, 1959).

Vernadsky, G., and M. Karpovich, *History of Russia,* Vol. III (New Haven, Conn.: Yale Univ. Press, 1947).

Zander, Leon, *Le pelerinage,* Editions de Chevetogne, Extrait de 1054–1954: *L'Eglise et les Eglises.*

Zenkovsky, S. A.

Reprint from *The Russian Revue.*

—— *The Ideological World of the Denisov Brothers.*

Zenkovsky, V. V., *A History of Russian Philosophy* (New York: 1953).

Zernov, N., *St. Sergius, Builder of Russia* (London: Society for the Promotion of Christian Knowledge, 1937; New York: Macmillan, 1939).

PERIODICALS

Blackfriars.

Eastern Churches Quarterly, The, St. Augustine's Abbey, Ramsgate, England.

Greek Orthodox Theological Review, The, 1959.

Informations, catholiques internationales.

Irenikon, Revue Trimestrielle, Prieure Bénédictin d'Amay, Chevetogne, Beligique or Duckett, 140, The Strand, London, England.

Russie et Chretiente, Revue Trimestrielle Centre d'Études. Istina, Paris, France, 25 Bvrd. d'Auteuie.

Vestnik Russkogo Studentcheskogo Dvizhenya, Paris.

Zhurnal Moskovskoy Patriarkiy, Moskovsky Patriarkhat. Moscow, 1949.

Index